Making Connections Matter

Compiled by the

University of Wyoming
English 1010 Reader Committee

1 2 3 4 5 6 7 8 9 0 SCI SCI 17 16 15 14

ISBN-13: 978-1-259-40332-3
ISBN-10: 1-259-40332-7

Learning Solutions Consultant: Angela Stone
Project Manager: Lynn Lyons

Contents

Preface

If you are to get the most out of your education, learning requires your active participation, at UW and beyond. This participation asks you to be engaged and creative as you prepare for a world where the majority of today's kindergarteners will have jobs that do not yet exist and where most of today's college students will have between 10 and 14 jobs by the time they are 38 years old. How well are you prepared to thrive in such a world? English 1010 can help you answer that question with confidence as you develop and strengthen skills needed to thrive in that world.

Our 1010 reader, *Making Connections Matter*, is a text that can help you to develop these skills and get involved in the issues you find most important. Whether crafting new ideas or encouraging new actions, your involvement will be stronger if you can establish connections across a variety of issues—safety, health, environment, religious beliefs, political choices, and many others. This may all seem abstract, but actually this sort of connective thinking—of linking ideas and possibilities that seem unrelated—is part of our everyday lives. For example, just a few years ago, who would have imagined a thought that a phone would also play music, function as a camera, and keep people textually connected?

As UW's first required composition course, English 1010 fosters your engagement and teaches connective thinking, thus helping you make the transition from high school to college. According to UW students and national reports, this transition requires that you read a greater variety of texts, write more complex arguments, and integrate a wider range of resources than you generally did in high school. Based on these expectations, we have designed this reader and potential writing sequences to prepare you for the academic work UW requires. In particular, English 1010 will prepare you to write expository essays that show your ability to **make meaning** (not just accept what others say), and to participate in conversations relevant to this course and beyond. We break this broad goal into three smaller goals:

1. Read and thoughtfully respond to extended, complex expository writings from a range of disciplines.
2. Understand foundational academic writing tasks, such as rhetorical strategies, summaries, analyses, and synthesis.
3. Develop your own argument, supported with credible evidence.

READING THE WORLD

All of you read a variety of texts every day: text messages, internet news, social media posts, etc. And yet, you may not be familiar with the types of readings assigned in college. English 1010 focuses on complex readings from a range of disciplines—the authors in this reader are religious scholars, economists, environmentalists, sociologists, technology specialists, cultural critics, even comic writers. Written for public audiences, these readings have appeared in some of the most important and bestselling books in recent years, such as *Freakonomics* and *Alone Together,* and in widely circulating print outlets such as *The Atlantic* and *The New Yorker*.

As you will notice, these readings do not come in units, because opportunities and problems in life do not come bundled in tidy units. Instead, these interdisciplinary readings can be combined in all sorts of ways, thus encouraging you to draw upon a wide range of conceptual connections as you come up with original arguments. Despite their diversity, all of these readings can help you refine your perspective on pressing issues of our modern lives: What is the meaning of "community" in today's globalized world? How is technology changing our relationships with friends, co-workers, and civic organizations? What is the impact of the United States' changing demographics, whether, as our readings explore, due to the exodus from rural America or from the end of White America? What is the influence of government surveillance, neuro-enhancing drugs, or even marketing on our identities?

Answering these questions requires you to understand the underlying concepts and perspectives that define these issues. For example, to imagine how best to diversify Wyoming's job market (a possible 1010 research topic), we should turn not only to people from business and mining, but also to those from the non-profit, health care, and agricultural sectors as well as those from policy studies, law, medicine, and technology fields. Developing sophisticated strategies for reading (e.g., annotating, building concept maps) can help you understand the contexts informing these readings and, therefore, can help you draw upon the readings' diverse perspectives to support your own arguments.

UNDERSTANDING ACADEMIC WRITING

As a reader and writer in the 21st Century, you'll need to be a thoughtful and active participant in the world around you. Though the class will focus on traditional academic writing, you'll also develop new ways to understand the wide variety of digital, oral, and written messages that define communication in today's world. You may explore comic books, *TEDTalks*, multimedia new articles, or TV ads in order to broaden your understanding of the ways that authors, speakers, and composers shape your response to their messages. And, in turn, you'll become more adept at using these persuasive strategies in your own writing and communication as well.

Additionally, to be an effective academic writer, you'll need to be able to summarize, analyze, and synthesize complicated readings. You'll need these core skills in future assignments that may ask you to report an article's main and supporting ideas (a summary), identify and explain key pieces of a writer's argument (analysis), or compare a reading to other documents you've read for class (synthesis), a practice we often call putting sources "in conversation."

The skills you learn in English 1010 will transfer to nearly all of the academic writing that you'll do, no matter what you ultimately choose as your major. In fields as diverse as art (where you may be asked to critique a painting) and engineering (where you may be asked to evaluate the effectiveness of a lab report against some hypothesis), the basic tasks of summary, analysis, and synthesis will guide your writing. English 1010 provides you with extensive practice with these building blocks and presents you with readings that can serve as models for your own writing.

ENGAGING IN ACADEMIC ARGUMENT (OR MAKING MEANING IN TODAY'S COMPLEX AND CHANGING WORLD)

After reading complicated texts, analyzing their ideas and structures, and making connections among those texts, you will develop your own argument. Unlike some popular definitions of "argument," which may bring to mind images of people screaming at each other in a parking lot, academic argument is defined by a clear set of expectations that will help you develop more sophisticated ways of engaging with the world around you. Such engagement encourages you to know what you believe, support that position with good evidence, and develop compelling structures that can persuade others to share your perspective.

As these expectations make clear, academic argument does not merely regurgitate what others have said, does not claim that something is good or bad, does not force other texts to support some pre-determined idea, and does not merely comment on or critique others' ideas. Instead, argument, as practiced in English 1010, gives you the chance to forward your own ideas about an issue, make the issue relevant to others, and implement a range of strategies to create effective change within your society.

Ultimately, English 1010 asks you both to investigate issues that will have an impact on you—and those around you—for the rest of your lives and to build the skills that can help you influence the conversations and actions that inform these issues. To accomplish these goals, English 1010 teaches the reading, writing, and thinking skills that can help you actively and innovatively to participate in the world. The experiences you will have in English 1010 provide not only a foundation for academic writing but also the opportunity for you to develop a mindset that can allow you to become an effective communicator in a variety of settings throughout your academic career and beyond.

Mary P. Sheridan
Rick Fisher
Joyce Stewart
English Department
University of Wyoming
May 2014

Special thanks to:
English 1010 Reader Committee: Pam Galbreath, Jason Kirkmeyer, April Heaney, Val Pexton, and Michael Knievel

Harvey Cox (1929–   ), an influential Protestant theologian who has explored the relationship between secular urban culture and Christianity, was born on May 19 in Phoenixville, Pennsylvania. He received an A.B. with honors in 1951 from the University of Pennsylvania, a B.D. cum laude in 1955 from Yale University, and a Ph.D. from Harvard University in 1963. An ordained American Baptist minister who has been criticized for his political bent, Cox has taught or worked at Oberlin College, American Baptist Home Mission Society, Andover Newton Theological School, and Harvard Divinity School, and also served as a U.S. Merchant Marine.

Cox has sought to emphasize the need to "do theology," to apply Christian principles to contemporary life. In the late 1960s, Cox deemphasized his optimistic view of technological society in an attempt to revitalize the symbols and rituals of Christianity. He has come to advocate a "playful" attitude toward religion. After exploring various Eastern religions, Cox analyzed their dangers and benefits, finally championing the Judeo-Christian tradition, which he said "can still answer the human yearning for friendship, authentic experience, and even for trustworthy authority."

His many writings include *The Secular City: Secularization and Urbanization in Theological Perspective* (1965; rev. 1966); *God's Revolution and Man's Responsibility* (1965); *On Not Leaving It to the Snake* (essays, 1967); and *The Feast of Fools: A Theological Essay on Festivity and Fantasy* (1969). He has also contributed to *Technology and Culture in Perspective* (1967) and has edited or co-edited other volumes.

∞∞∞∞

Understanding Islam

Harvey Cox

Odious Western images of Muhammad and of Islam have a long and embarrassingly   1
honorable lineage. Dante places the prophet in that circle of hell reserved for those stained by the sin he calls *seminator di scandalo e di scisma*. As a schismatic, Muhammad's fitting punishment is to be eternally chopped in half from his chin to his anus, spilling entrails and excrement at the door of Satan's stronghold. His loyal disciple Ali, whose sins of division were presumably on a lesser scale, is sliced only "from forelock to chin." There is scandal, too. A few lines later, Dante has Muhammad send a warning to a contemporary priest whose sect was said to advocate the community of goods and who was also suspected of having a mistress. The admonition cautions the errant padre that the same fate awaits him if he does not quickly mend his ways. Already in Dante's classic portrait, we find the image of the Moslem linked with revolting violence, distorted doctrine, a dangerous economic idea, and the tantalizing hint of illicit sensuality.

Nothing much has changed in the 600 years since. Even the current wave of   2
interest in Eastern spirituality among many American Christians has not done much
to improve the popular estimate of Islam. It is fashionable now in the West to find
something of value in Buddhism or Hinduism, to peruse the *Sutras* or the *Bhagavad
Gita*, to attend a lecture by Swami Muktananda or the Dalai Lama, even to try a
little yoga or meditation. But Americans in general and Christians in particular seem
unable to find much to admire in Islam. As G. H. Hansen observes, with only a mod-
icum of hyperbole, in his book *Militant Islam*, the mental picture most Westerners
hold of this faith of 750 million people is one of " . . . strange bearded men with burning eyes, hieratic figures in robes and turbans, blood dripping from the amputated
hands and from the striped backs of malefactors, and piles of stones barely conceal-
ing the battered bodies of adulterous couples." Lecherous, truculent, irrational, cruel,
conniving, excitable, dreaming about lascivious heavens while hypocritically enforc-
ing oppressive legal codes: the stereotype of the Moslem is only partially softened
by a Kahlil Gibran who puts it into sentimental doggerel or a Rudolph Valentino
who does it with zest and good humor.

There is, of course, one important exception to the West's rejection of the reli-   3
gious value of Islam. This exception's most visible representatives have been
Muhammad Ali and the late Malcolm X. Most Americans who seem genuinely drawn
to the call of the minaret are blacks. But given the racial myopia that continues to
affect almost all American cultural perceptions, this exception has probably deepened the distrust most white Christians feel toward Islam. The dominant image
was summed up brilliantly in a Boston newspaper's cartoon showing a Moslem seat-
ed in prayer. Over his head the balloon contained one word: "Hate!"

This captious caricaturing of Moslems and Arabs is not confined to the popu-   4
lar mentality. In his *Orientalism*, Edward Said describes a study published in 1975
of Arabs in American textbooks that demonstrates how prejudices continue to be
spread through respectable sources. One textbook, for example, sums up Islam in the
following manner:

> The Moslem religion, called Islam, began in the seventh century. It was started by a   5
> wealthy businessman of Arabia, called Muhammad. He claimed that he was a prophet.
> He found followers among the other Arabs. He told them they were picked to rule the
> world.

This passage is, unfortunately, not a typical. Although phrased with some degree   6
of restraint, it coheres all too well with the popular medieval picture of Muhammad
as a sly trickster or the current comic-book depictions of the sated, power-mad Arab.
Moreover, Dante's unflattering portrait of the prophet was rooted in traditions that

existed long before his time. These primal shadowgraphs have notoriously long half-lives, and they continue to darken our capacity to understand Islam to this day.

Allah works in mysterious ways. Through the stubborn geopolitics of oil, 7 Westerners are being forced, like it or not, to learn more about Islam than they ever thought they would. Inevitably this reappraisal has begun to include a rethinking of the relationship between Islam and Christianity. In the fall of 1979, the World Council of Churches sponsored a conference on the subject in Kenya, and Christian scholars with direct experience of Islam were invited from all over the world. The results were mixed since, ironically, theologians from countries where Islam is a small minority seemed much more eager to enter into dialogue with their Moslem counterparts than did those from countries where Christians form a small minority in an Islamic world. Still, the recent upsurge of Islamic visibility will surely increase enrollments in courses on Islam wherever they are offered, and sales of books on the subject are up.

All such activities are welcome. But what about the shadowgraphs? Conferences 8 and courses will help only if their participants become aware of the deep-lying, nearly archetypal images that subvert the whole enterprise from the outset. Along with study and analysis, a kind of cultural archaeology or even a collective psychoanalysis may be necessary if we are to leave Dante's Inferno behind and live in peace with our Moslem neighbors on the planet Earth. The question is, How can Westerners, and Christians in particular, begin to cut through the maze of distorting mirrors and prepare the ground for some genuine encounter with Moslems?

The first thing we probably need to recognize is that the principal source of 9 the acrimony underlying the Christian-Moslem relationship is a historical equivalent of sibling rivalry. Christians somehow hate to admit that in many ways their faith stands closer to Islam than to any other world religion. Indeed, that may be the reason Muhammad was viewed for centuries in the West as a charlatan and an imposter. The truth is, theologically speaking at least, both faiths are the offspring of an earlier revelation through the Law and the Prophets to the people of Israel. Both honor the Virgin Mary and Jesus of Nazareth. Both received an enormous early impetus from an apostle—Paul for Christianity and Muhammad for Islam—who translated a particularistic vision into a universal faith. The word "Allah" (used in the core formula of Islam: "There is no God but Allah and Muhammad is his prophet") is not an exclusively Moslem term at all. It is merely the Arabic word for God, and is used by Arabic Christians when they refer to the God of Christian faith.

There is nothing terribly surprising about these similarities since Muhammad, 10 whose preaching mission did not begin until he reached forty, was subjected to considerable influence from Christianity during his formative years and may have come close—according to some scholars—to becoming an Abyssinian Christian. As Arend van Leeuwen points out in his thoughtful treatment of Islam in *Christianity in World History*, "The truth is that when Islam was still in the initial stages of its development, there was nothing likely to prevent the new movement from being accepted as a peculiar version of Arabian Christianity." Maybe the traditional Christian uneasiness with Islam is that it seems just a little *too* similar. We sense the same aversion we might feel toward a twin brother who looks more like us than we want him to and whose habits remind us of some of the things we like least in ourselves.

The metaphor of a brother, or perhaps a cousin, is entirely germane. Muhammad considered himself to be in a direct line with the great biblical prophets and with Jesus. The title he preferred for himself was *alnabi al-ummi*, the "prophet of the nations" (or of the "gentiles"). He believed he was living proof that the God who had called and used previous prophets such as Abraham and Job, neither of whom was Jewish, could do the same thing again. Later on, Moslem theologians liked to trace the genealogy of Muhammad back to Hagar, the bondwoman spouse of Abraham. The Old Testament story says that Hagar's giving birth to Ishmael stirred up such jealousy between her and Sarah, Abraham's first wife and the mother of Isaac, that Sarah persuaded Abraham to banish the bondwoman and her child into the desert. There Hagar gave up hope and left the child under a shrub to die. But God heard the child's weeping, created a well of water in the desert to save them both, and promised Hagar that from her son also, as from Issac, He would "create a great nation." According to the symbolism of this old saga, the Jews and the Arabs (and by extension all Moslems) are the common offspring of Abraham (called "Ibrahim" in Arabic). This makes Christians and Moslems cousins, at least by legendary lineage.

The similarity between Christians and Moslems does not stop with religious genealogy. The actual elements of the Koran's message—faith, fasting, alms, prayer, and pilgrimage—all have Christian analogues. Despite its firm refusal to recognize any divine being except God (which is the basis for its rejection of Christ's divinity), Islam appears sometimes to be a pastiche of elements from disparate forms of Christianity molded into a potent unity. Take the Calvinist emphasis on faith in an omnipotent deity, the pietistic cultivation of daily personal prayer, the medieval teaching on charity, the folk-Catholic fascination with pilgrimage, and the monastic practice of fasting, and you have all the essential ingredients of Islam. All, that is, except the confluence of forces which, through the personality of Muhammad and the movement he set off, joined these elements in the white heat of history and fused them into a coherent faith of compelling attractiveness.

Like Paul, who said his apostleship was to both Jews and gentiles, Muhammad believed his mission was twofold. He felt called by God to bring the law and the Gospel to the heretofore neglected peoples of Arabia. But he also felt he had a mission *to* those very peoples—Christians and Jews (whom he called "peoples of the book")— *from* whom the original message of salvation had come. In one important respect, therefore, Muhammad's mission was different from St. Paul's. Since Muhammad carried on his preaching in the early decades of the seventh century, he not only had to deal with a Judaism he considered corrupted (as Paul had too); he also had to face an even more corrupted form of Christianity. Fortunately for St. Paul, since the Christian movement was only a decade or so old when he lived, he had to cope only with a few legalizers and gnostics. The infant Church had not yet tasted the corruption that comes, perhaps inevitably, from power and longevity. From a certain Christian perspective, Muhammad was as much a reformer as an apostle. A prophet of the gentiles, he also saw himself as a purifier of the faith of all the "peoples of the book," Christians and Jews, calling them away from the ornate and decadent versions of the faith they had fallen into and back to its simple essence, at least as he understood it. There is always something of this urge to simplify, to return *ad fontes,* in any reformer. And Muhammad was no exception.

No one should minimize the fact that in any genuine conversation between   14 Christians and Moslems certain real differences in theology and practice will have to be faced, what scholars often call "rival truth claims." But such conflicting assertions can be properly understood only against the fleshand-blood history that has somehow made them rivals. Religious teachings do not inhabit a realm apart. They mean what they do to people because of the coloration given to them by long historical experience. Therefore a previous question has to be asked. It is this: If Christianity and Islam share such common roots and, despite real differences, some striking similarities, why have they grown so bitter toward each other over the centuries? Why did the average white American feel less sympathetic to Islam than to any other world religion even *before* our current flap with the ayatollahs?

The explanation for this hostility is not a pretty story. Its major lineaments   15 can be indicated with the names of three figures who symbolize its most critical stages. The first is Alexander the Great, whose career corresponds to what might be called the prehistory of Christianity. The second is Constantine the Great, who exemplifies its early period. The third is Pope Urban II, who expresses its classical phase, one of the most formative in the Christian-Moslem interaction.

Christopher Dawson, the late Roman Catholic cultural historian, once remarked   16 that "Muhammad is the Orient's answer to Alexander the Great." At first this sounds like one of those wonderfully sweeping but highly improbable aphorisms. Muhammad, after all, lived and preached a full thousand years after Alexander. The prodigious Macedonian disciple of Aristotle conquered everything between Greece and northern India before he was thirty-three and spread the culture and values of Hellenism wherever his soldiers trod. But a thousand years is not a long time when one is dealing with cultural domination and the backlash it ultimately elicits. This is what Dawson had in mind.

Alexander did more than conquer everything before him. Unlike previous con- 17
querors, who sought mainly booty and tribute, he wanted to convert his colonized peoples into Hellenists. Alexander's conquest mixed military, political, and religious power. It was obviously going to require a comparable fusion of elements to throw off his conquest. After a thousand years that response finally came. It was Islam.

As Albert Memmi writes in his classic book *The Colonizer and the Colonized*, 18
" . . . the colonized can wait a long time to live. But, regardless of how soon or how violently the colonized rejects his situation, he will one day begin to overthrow his unlivable existence with the whole force of his oppressed personality. . . . He attempts to . . . reconquer all the dimensions which the colonization tore away from him." When the Islamic response to Roman-Hellenistic domination exploded in the early seventh century, the entire world was stunned by its vitality. In retrospect, howev-er, we can understand its religious ideology in large measure as a reverse mirror image of what it was overthrowing. Take its rejection of the divinity of Christ, for example. Alexander had allowed himself to be viewed as a divine being, a god-emperor, and this ideology persisted through centuries of European culture in one form or anoth-er. The Koran's strenuous insistence that there was only one God, and its rejection of all semidivine beings, must be seen at least in part as a rejection of the political use of Christology to sacralize various forms of human rule.

The Moslem rejection of the divinity of Christ is not just simpleminded monothe- 19
istic stubbornness. It began as "political theology." For the Arabians, living on what were then the outskirts of the Eastern Empire, it marked a rejection not only of the non-Semitic categories in which the doctrine of Christ's divinity were elaborated in the Church councils (the "being of one substance with the Father") but also of the political hierarchy the doctrine helped to sanctify, especially in the Byzantine environment. When the Pantocrator Christ began to sacralize an empire in which the Arabians were the underdogs, their refusal of the doctrine made perfect sense. Alexander the Great had created the cultural imperium for which Christianity even-tually supplied the sacred ideology. The Islamic revolt against this system was a revolt not against the Gospel as they understood it but against what Christianity had come to be. Islam's implacable insistence on one God not only freed thousands of people from their fear of the evil jinns and united the feuding tribes of Arabia (and later a vast part of the known world); it also served as a counter ideology to the political function that Christian trinitarianism was beginning to serve. No "rival truth claim" debate between Christians and Moslems can begin until this history is recognized.

Islam began as a liberation theology, but, like Christianity, which had a com- 20
parable beginning, it could not resist the wiles of wordly power. As in the case of most

successful liberation movements. Islam incorporated many of the cultural and political characteristics of its enemies. Though Muhammad was hounded out of Mecca by its local power elites, one hundred years after his death a glittering capital for the new Islamic empire was founded at Baghdad, the "Constantinople of Islam." Moslems became imperialists themselves, although in most instances they allowed Christians and Jews to practice their faiths. Forced conversions were rare. Above all, Moslems became the supreme masters and cultivators of the very Greek wisdom that had been imposed on them by Alexander. They became devout disciples of the same Aristotle whose zealous pupil had set out to spread his master's learning in their lands a millennium before. It was the Arabs, after all, who brought Aristotle back to the West and eventually to the cluttered desk of Thomas Aquinas. At its height, Islamic culture vastly outshone that of the Christian West, which most Moslems more or less accurately regarded as a barren outpost. But at the same time, the original liberating impulse of Islam had begun to run out. Today, paradoxically, this very spoiling by success may provide a needed bridge between Christians and Moslems, since Christians have experienced the same sad, familiar story in their own history.

Muhammad's judgment on the Christianity of his day is one of the great ironies   21
of history. This Christianity, which began in the life of a Palestinian Jew who was executed because he was viewed as a threat to the Roman Empire and to the Hellenistically inclined rulers of his colonized nation, was seen a few centuries later by Muhammad, the prophet of another down-trodden nation, as the religious sanction for his own people's domination. What is remarkable about Muhammad is not that he rejected current theories about the divinity of Christ but that he did *not* reject Jesus himself. Rather he tried, from his own vantage point, to bypass the caricature of the Gospel which imperial Christianity had elaborated and to reclaim the faith of a people much like his own who had once looked to Allah for justice and mercy.

Jesus, then, is another vital link between the two faiths. To this day, Jesus holds   22
a central place in Islamic teaching and is sometimes even depicted as a kind of supreme exemplar of what is meant by "submission to God" (the meaning of the word "Islam"). In popular Islamic belief, Jesus often occupies an even more important position. Thus many Moslems believe that when the long awaited "Twelfth Iman," whose name is *al-Mahdi*, finally appears to usher in the reign of justice on earth (*not* in the sky, incidentally), he will either be accompanied by Jesus or will turn out to be the same one whose "coming in Glory" the Christian creeds confess. Obviously there is much to discuss here between these two "Jesus traditions," if the ground can be cleared of spiteful stereotypes and the sibling rivalry can be held at bay.

Both Christianity and Islam began as visions of captive peoples who yearned for   23
deliverance and caught a glimpse of hope in the promise of God. The two can understand each other only when both begin to acknowledge these common roots, step

out of the long shadow of Alexander the Great, and try to learn from each other what has gone so terribly wrong over the years of their common history.

Constantine the Great, Roman emperor from 313 to 337 A.D. represents the historical turning point that eventually created the second great obstacle between Christians and Moslems. The Christian movement began not only as a message of hope to a colonized nation but also as the faith of the poor and the brokenhearted. But three centuries later, when Emperor Constantine beheld the cross shining across the sun and later claimed to have won the imperial throne with the help of Jesus Christ, all that changed. Although St. Paul could write to one of his fledgling congregations that there were "not many wise, not many powerful" in their midst, and the common name for Jesus' followers in those earliest days was simply "the poor," Constantine's well-timed and canny conversion totally altered all that for good. It is impossible to understand Muhammad's view of Christianity unless one remembers that he was basing it not on the Gospel accounts but on his observation of how the Church was actually functioning in his world. By their fruits ye shall know them. 24

Muhammad claimed to be one of the poor, at least when he started, and he never tired of reminding his followers that he was only an illiterate camel driver. He saw his humble origins not as a disgrace but as a wondrous proof that God could raise up from the very stones children unto Abraham. The *al-ummi* with whom Muhammad identified himself has a double sense. The word means not only the "gentiles," or "people without the Law," but also the unlettered, something close to the *am-ha-aretz*, the poor "people of the land" with whom Jesus sided against the learned scribes and Pharisees. The historian H. G. Reisman says that Muhammad was "a leader of the masses against the privileged minorities of wealth and sophistication." This may also explain in part the popular Islamic belief, baffling to many Christians, that every child is a "born Moslem." With growing up and education comes sophistication and corruption. In the Koran, similar to an idea St. Paul defends in the first chapter of his Epistle to the Romans, every person has an inborn, natural awareness of God. We all start out pious but are misled by a fallen civilization and perfidious religions. It is the task of preaching to call us back to what we were, or were intended to be, in the first place. 25

The Koranic vision of a simple faith by which the poor and the unlettered can withstand manipulation at the hands of the powerful and the better educated makes Christians uncomfortable today, and understandably. It is painfully reminiscent of the "Blessed are the poor" with which Jesus began the Sermon on the Mount and the subsequent "Woe to you rich" with which he made sure he was not misunderstood. The Church has never completely lost its recognition of this aspect of its history. It surfaces repeatedly in such places as Simone Weil's lifeshaking discovery that 26

Christianity is essentially a faith of the poor, or in the Latin American bishops declaring that the Church's special responsibility is to stand with the jobless and landless. Nor has Islam, despite prodigiously rich oil sheikhs, ever completely lost this central core of its tradition either. Each faith will find it easier to appreciate the other when this special role of the *al-ummi* becomes the major rather than the minor theme of its message. In this respect, Christianity probably has more recovering to do than Islam has.

Pope Urban II, who occupied the throne of Peter from 1088 to 1099, is the third great actor in the tragedy of Christianity's cumulative falling-out with Islam. He was an energetic reformer who became Pope during a period of divisiveness in the Church; his main challenge was to bring it into some semblance of unity. Like many other rulers before him, religious and secular, Urban hit upon a surefire unifying idea. Realizing that nothing unites like an external foe, and inspired by requests from the beleaguered Christians of the East, he preached a holy war against the infidels who were even then holding the Holy Sepulchre and promised the fullest spiritual benefit to those who would take up the cross. Christians and other Americans who criticize the concept of the jihad, or holy war, and decry the taking of hostages and conversion at sword's point are right, of course. But it does not require much reading in this not-so-glorious chapter in Western Christian history to see that Moslems were neither the first nor the only guilty parties in this department. In fact, there is at least one prominent school of historical scholarship that sees the first Moslem expansion not as a jihad but as a large-scale migration similar to the one that had brought the Germanic tribes into the Roman Empire from the other direction. The concept of holy war can be found in more than one Old Testament verse. It did not originate with Islam. To many Arabs it must have seemed the only sensible response to the not entirely pacifist manner in which the Christian empire dealt with its recalcitrant provinces and with those forms of Christianity, such as Nestorianism, that the bishops deemed unacceptable.

Like all wars, holy or unholy, the Crusades produced their quota of atrocity stories on both sides. They also produced countless incidents of generosity and unexpected interfaith respect. The mutual admiration that developed between Richard I of England and the theologically articulate Saladin, celebrated in legend, seems to have had a factual basis. Still, it was the Crusaders and not the Saracens who boasted that when they first took Jerusalem the blood of the infidels, including wives and children, flowed through the streets as deep as the horses' stirrups. Such memories do not die easily, and it is important to recall that although Westerners would sometimes like to reduce the "wars of the cross" to tales of chivalry and late-night movie fare, for many Moslems the Crusades—Christian jihads—remain the most graphic expression of what the cross means. All the more amazing, then, that even the Ayatollah Khomeini, talking to a group of visiting American clergy on Christmas Day, 1979, could ask why, as those who worship the wounded Jesus, Americans were so incapable of understanding a wounded people such as his own. Apparently some feeling for the real meaning of the cross has survived in Islam, despite the Crusades.

If it took Muhammad a thousand years to respond to Alexander the Great, 29 perhaps it should come as no surprise that it has taken the Islamic peoples another 900 years to respond to Pope Urban II, Peter the Hermit, and the hordes of idealists, adventurers, and thugs who in successive waves burned and pillaged their way across Europe toward the Holy Land for nearly 400 years. True, some historians hold that the Crusades might never have occurred had it not been for the previous threat of militant Islam to the West. Still, once the Crusades began, they acquired a lethal momentum of their own. Christian armies started by burning the nearest ghetto, and when their attempts to seize the Holy Sepulchre did not fully succeed, turned their cross-bedecked banners toward the pagan Baltic peoples and the Albigenses of southern France. It is an ugly history. But until the sorry story of Crusade versus jihad is faced frankly and then replaced by a more generous and conciliatory attitude, the hatred and suspicion between Christians and their Moslem cousins can only escalate.

No discussion of the relations of Moslems and Christians can proceed very far 30 without raising the parallel question of the equally long and similarly vexed interaction of Moslems and Jews. The Jewish historian S. D. Goitein is the leading scholar in the study of what he calls the "symbiosis" between Jews and Arabs. Now at the Institute for Advanced Study in Princeton, after having taught at the Hebrew University of Jerusalem, Goitein has spent a lifetime probing Moslem religious literature, the medieval Geniza (documents written in Hebrew characters but in the Arabic language), and the fascinating histories of the so-called Oriental Jewish communities—those of the Arab and Moslem worlds. His *From the Land of Sheba* is an anthology of Yemenite literature. It would be hard to find a more reliable guide to this intricate area.

Goitein believes that Islam is actually far closer to Judaism than to Christianity 31 in its core ideas. In taking this position, he joins a debate that has been going on for years (the other side contending that the similarity with Christianity is more important). Goitein bases his case on the obvious fact that both Islam and Judaism are religions of the Holy Law, and that Moslem law is in many respects similar to the Jewish Halakah, which he calls its "older sister." Both therefore differ, at least in this respect, from Christianity, which, with its emphasis on grace, has always harbored a certain suspicion of religious law (even though Christian theologians have managed to spin out yards of it over the years).

Goitein's "sister" image of the bond between Islam and Judaism should not be   32
surprising when one bears in mind the saying, attributed to Muhammad, "You will
follow the traditions of those who preceded you span by span and cubit by cubit—so
closely that you will go after them even if they creep into the hole of a lizard." This
colorful advice takes on even more significance in light of the fact that there were
large Jewish settlements in the city of al-Medina, the birthplace of the first Moslem
community, and that the biographers of the prophet almost all agree that these communities, far from being an obstacle to the spread of Islam, were in fact wondrous evidence of Allah's merciful and providential preparation of the people for a monotheistic
faith. As with Christianity, the early years of Islam seem in retrospect to have promised mostly fraternal—or in this case sororial—congeniality with Judaism. But again,
the roiling history of Jewish and Islamic peoples has often turned familial ties into
tribal vendettas. Must it always be so?

In his informative book *Jews and Arabs: Their Contacts Through the Ages*, Goitein   33
does what only a seasoned scholar ever dares to do. He compresses eons of history
into one volume, risks a few well-grounded generalizations, and even hazards some
guesses about the future. He divides the millennialong give-and-take between these
two peoples into four periods. The first, corresponding perhaps to the Alexandrian
age of the Christian-Islam story, begins before historical memory and reaches up to
the sixth century A.D. and the appearance of Islam. During this early period, a critically formative one for the Jews since it saw the compilation of both the Bible and
the Talmud. Goitein believes Jews and Arabs had quite similar social patterns and
religious practices. He firmly rejects any notion of a common Semitic race, however, as a modern idea concocted from the misapplication of a term invented by a
German scholar in 1781 to denote a group of related languages, not· "races," or even
peoples. The distinction is an important one. There are several examples of peoples who for a variety of historical reasons now speak a language spoken by other peoples with whom they have no ethnic consanguinity at all. Black Americans are a case
in point. Likewise, Jews and Moslem Arabs are related, according to Goitein, but
by history and tradition, not by race.

The period from, roughly, 500 A.D. to 1300 A.D. is Goitein's second one. He   34
describes it as one of "creative symbiosis," in which early Islam developed in a largely Jewish environment. Although he agrees that Christian influences, coming especially from monastic groups, played some role in this primal period, he believes that
Judaism was even more important, so much so that he is willing to say—with some
reservations—that Islam appears to be "an Arab recast of Israel's religion." But the
influence was not one-way, and the impact of Islam and the Arabic language on Jewish
thought and the Hebrew language was, he adds, at least as considerable. Goitein also

reminds his readers that although Jews experienced some legal disqualifications under Moslem rule, they always fared better than they did under Christian dominance.

Goitein's third period begins in about 1300, when the previously high-riding   35
Arabs began to "fade out" of world history at the same time that the Oriental Jews began to fade out of Jewish history. During this phase, which lasted until about 1900, the Arab nations fell to various conquerors until the entire Arab world had become a colony of the modern West. Meanwhile Jewish religious and intellectual life flourished in Europe, while Jews living in the beleaguered Moslem world, though they nurtured a rich internal culture, shared the suffering and obscurity of their Moslem neighbors.

The present period in Goitein's scheme begins in about 1900 with the coinci-   36
dental revival of Jewish and Arab cultural and national identities, both influenced by the growing nationalism of nineteenth-century Europe. Since Zionism was an almost exclusively European (and American) movement, however, it was perceived by Arabs and other Moslems more as a new Western intrusion into the East, a pattern going back at least to the Crusades, than as something essentially Jewish, at least at the beginning. But shortly after the founding of the State of Israel, Israelis had to cope with a kind of mirror image of this "intrusion" as Jewish immigrants from Arab countries, the "forgotten Jews" of the previous period, streamed into Israel, making it less "European" with every passing day. The paradox of this apparent double intrusion was illustrated recently when an Oriental Jewish scholar living in Israel complained to a visitor about all the remarks he heard from his European colleagues lamenting the "Levantizing" of Israel. "How," he asked, "can you 'Levantize' something that is already the Levant?" His comment underscores Goitein's thoughtful prophecy that since the future of Jewish-Moslem relations has everything to do with the relations between Israel and its Arab neighbors, Israel's internal policy toward its Oriental Jews and its Arab citizens will be of decisive importance. Whether or not this turns out to be true, remembering the roller-coaster history of Jewish-Moslem relations helps one not to become too depressed about the steep decline these relations have taken in recent decades. There have been downs before, and ups, and it is not impossible that the tiny minority of Arab-Israeli citizens who are also Christians might eventually be able to play a conciliatory role. Likewise, though it seems farfetched today, the global Jewish community, with centuries of experience in the Christian and the Moslem worlds, might someday provide an essential bridge between these two faith traditions, both in some ways its offspring. In any case, whatever happens to facilitate the conversation that must go on among Christians, Jews, and Moslems is bound to benefit all three.

Jews may help, but in the final analysis, given the role our religions play in both   37
our cultures, no real rapport between the Arabs and the West seems possible unless

Christians and Moslems make a more serious effort to understand each other. Curiously, after being warned for years that our greatest enemies in the world were godless and atheistic, Americans are now faced with a challenge that emanates from profoundly religious sources. Although Islam has never accepted the dichotomy between religion and the civil polity that has arisen in the West, there can be little doubt that the present Islamic renaissance is not a deviation but an authentic expression of the elements that were there at its origin. So we are now told that, instead of atheists, we are dealing with "fanatics," or "Moslem fundamentalists." This language is not very helpful either.

Sometime soon a real conversation must begin. Perhaps the moment has come 38 to set aside Dante, Urban II, and the rest; to remember instead the two children of Father Abraham, from both of whom God promised to make great nations; to recall that Jesus also cast his lot with the wounded and wronged of his time; to stop caricaturing the faith of Arabia's apostle; and to try to help both Christians and Moslems to recover what is common to them in a world that is just too small for any more wars, especially holy ones.

Patrick J. Carr, from Drogheda, Ireland, is an Associate Professor of Sociology at Rutgers University. He received his Ph.D. in sociology from the University of Chicago in 1998. His interests include communities and crime, and young people. In addition to teaching, Carr is also a co-Principal Investigator for the MacArthur Foundation's "The Heartland Study," a five-site national study that focuses on teenagers transitioning to adulthood. Carr's most recent book, co-authored with his wife, Maria Kefalas, is *Hollowing Out the Middle: The Rural Brain Drain and What It Means to America* (2009). His other works include *Clean Streets: Controlling Crime, Maintaining Order, and Building Community Activism* (2005), as well as numerous articles in the *American Journal of Sociology and the International Reviews of Victimology.*

Maria Kefalas is an Associate Professor of Sociology at St. Joseph's University, Philadelphia. Kefalas was awarded her Ph.D. from the University of Chicago. Her works include *Working Class Heroes* (2003), *Promises I Can Keep: Why Poor Women Put Motherhood Before Marriage* (2005), and co-author of *Hollowing Out the Middle: The Rural Brain Drain and What It Means to America* (2009). In addition to her books, Kefalas's work has appeared in the *New York Times*, the *Washington Post*, *Time* magazine and on NPR. Kefalas is also an Associate Member of the MacArthur Foundation's "Network on Transitions to Adulthood."

The Heartland and the Rural Youth Exodus

Patrick J. Carr and Maria Kefalas

> For generations in our national life, progress was the preserve of cities. . . . Inventions, standards of services, and social styles and trends lagged in their adoption in rural areas. The countryside was a time machine in which urbanites could see the living past, and feel nostalgic or superior, as the sight inclined them.
>
> —Calvin Beale

In a fast-paced and uncertain world, it is comforting to believe in small-town America's idyllic possibilities. The trouble is that few people ever seem to penetrate much deeper than the bucolic ideal. A closer and more clear-eyed examination reveals that our country is in the throes of a most painful and unpredictable transition. In what has become an all-too-familiar story, rural states such as North Dakota and West Virginia share an unsettling problem: too many young people in their twenties and thirties are leaving. Rural counties in Kansas and Georgia report the highest rates of population loss nationally, and this hemorrhaging of people, specifically the younger generation, is hollowing out many of the nation's small towns and rural communities. The rural youth exodus is not a new phenomenon; young people have always left small towns for big cities and bright opportunities. But as the new century's first decade ends, the loss of such a huge share of them could spell the end of small-town America.

Headlines from both the *New York Times* and *Los Angeles Times* blame rural out-migration on "regional competition" from "warmer climates and hipper scenes." This explanation suggests that the flight of young adults is a natural occurrence, an inevitable consequence of progress, and that there is little reason to worry. However, with time and taken altogether, these individual choices have devastating consequences for the communities left behind. Scattered throughout the nation, thousands of towns find themselves twenty, ten, or even five years away from extinction because there are too few taxpayers, consumers, and workers to keep going. For many locales, the final death knell sounds when there are no longer enough children to keep the doors of the area school open.

Economists warn that shifts in population among professional-class elites have contributed to uneven economic growth nationally. During the 1990s, the rise of Richard Florida's "creative class"[1]—educated and entrepreneurial cultural consumers and producers—and the infusions of human capital they brought with them injected cities such as Austin and Phoenix with a potent booster shot. "Left behind are those regional losers—the laggard, blue-collar red states"[2] that find themselves fighting to keep their communities and counties viable as the destructive social forces of graying populations and depopulation take their toll. During the past half-century, Iowa, North Dakota, and West Virginia ranked dead last—forty-eighth, forty-ninth, and fiftieth, respectively—among all the states for population growth.[3] This accompanying map shows the more than seven hundred rural counties that have lost 10 percent or more of their populations since 1980. The greatest outflow is on the plains, from North Dakota through Texas.

The decisions that young people on the edge of adulthood make about whether to stay or leave home have profound implications for the future of rural America. The fact is that the birth of a child cannot replace what small towns lose every time a young adult moves away. Because twenty-somethings are the ones leaving the countryside in such dramatic numbers, we might expect the stark realities of the economy and the more effervescent nature of being young to rank among the more obvious reasons for their concentration in metropolitan areas. No one would deny that finding work in today's countryside means facing a triple threat: a failing farm- and factory-based economy, rising unemployment, and shrinking wages and benefits. Contrary to conventional thinking about the "problem with young people today" who are bored with life in the countryside,

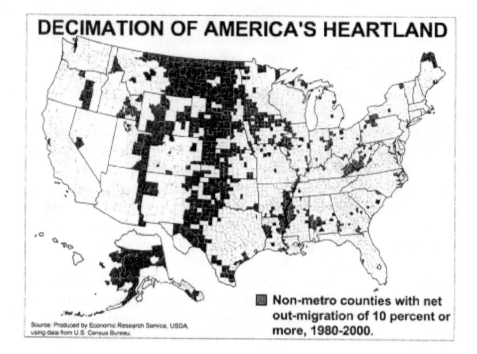

DECIMATION OF AMERICA'S HEARTLAND

■ **Non-metro counties with net out-migration of 10 percent or more, 1980-2000.**

Source: Produced by Economic Research Service, USDA, using data from U.S. Census Bureau.

the majority of young people who are leaving aren't motivated by the possibility of trading in flannel shirts and pickup trucks for Diesel jeans and club scenes. Leaving small-town life requires a plan and a willingness to cut oneself off from a world that is familiar and predictable. There are some young people who can't wait to break free, but far more choose the ties and obligations of home, where things just seem to get harder. They fear that the outside world will expect them to change too much of who and what they are.

The problem of rapidly aging demographics in nonmetropolitan[4] counties, a majority of which now have fewer residents under age eighteen than they did a decade ago and more deaths than births, is not our sole concern.[5] Another, perhaps more pressing problem is that the young people moving away include the most highly educated.[6] In a twenty-first-century world, acquiring human capital through education and training brings with it the promise of socioeconomic and geographic mobility, and so the flight of the countryside's young people is also a brain drain. Back in 1940, when just 5 percent of Americans possessed a college education, degreed teachers, physicians, and business owners were scattered across small towns and cities fairly evenly.[7] By 1970, five years after President Lyndon B. Johnson signed the Higher Education Act[8] into law, thus creating a

5

massive, federally funded financial-aid system and dramatically expanding access to higher education for Americans from all walks of life, "only five percentage points separated the most highly educated regions in the United States from the least highly educated regions."[9] Three decades later, in 2000, "the regional educational gap" had more than *doubled* to 13 percentage points.[10] In New England, the most highly educated region of the United States, one-third of the adult residents possess bachelor's degrees, while in the southern section of the nation—in Alabama, Mississippi, Tennessee, and Kentucky—fewer than one in five adults could make the same claim.[11]

Although the brain-drain phenomenon does not afflict only the country-side—upstate New York and Philadelphia lose more educated people than they gain—the picture "is particularly bleak for rural America,"[12] where, in any given year, more than 6 percent of America's nonmetropolitan bachelor's degree–holders migrate to a metropolitan area.[13] One of the clearest symptoms of this problem is the fact that it is now a struggle to find replacements for retiring small-town doctors, business owners, and teachers in much of the countryside.[14] The youth exodus is a zero-sum phenomenon: it benefits the destination cities and hurts the regions that migrants flee. For every thriving metropolis now, there are dozens of agroindustrial brain-drain areas where economic growth has stalled. Experts believe these regions are in so much trouble largely because too few of their most-likely-to-succeed types with college credentials and upwardly mobile aspirations remain, and too many of the local kids with vocational certificates and the most diminished economic prospects do.[15]

6

AN OLD WAY OF LIFE COMES TO AN END

Throughout the twentieth century, generations of young people coming of age in the countryside depended on family farms or local plants for their livelihood. As the seismic shifts in agriculture and manufacturing made firms and farms outsource and automate, rural regions witnessed a collapsing demand for labor.[16] With fewer opportunities for work that paid a decent wage, more young people found it necessary to abandon this old way of life. Despite the emptying out of the Heartland and the myriad forces conspiring against rural areas' backbone industries, the nation's belief in the insulated vibrancy of small towns appears oddly unshaken. Yet look beyond the postcard-perfect barns standing empty and unused: they are the rural equivalent of the inner city's shuttered factories and crumbling smokestacks.[17] Although the fact that there are fewer farms in Iowa today is common knowledge, the extent of the financial and demographic devastation in agriculture is less well known: just 2 percent of Americans operate farms now, for example, and 42 percent of Midwestern farms earn less than

7

$20,000 a year.[18] By the end of the twentieth century, independent farmers became "more like modern-day sharecroppers," and "the Jeffersonian ideal of pastoral life" was subsumed by "the corporate, agribusiness model of mega-farms."[19] The fundamental paradox of the family farm's demise—which kept the rest of us from seeing how bad things had become—was that the single greatest cause of the rural crisis was, more than anything else, progress.[20] Improvements in crop science and innovations in farm management boosted output while reducing the need for farmers themselves.[21] In the end, "the intrusion of technology"[22] into the countryside would become one of the single most important reasons for depopulation.

During the 1970s and '80s, when agriculture started going corporate and the credit crisis drove so many off their land, farmers looking for a new way to support themselves believed they had gotten a reprieve with the arrival of new manufacturing jobs. Grateful ex-farmers ignored how these companies and their competitors had fled cities and other towns in search of cheap labor and land. The farmers, who lost everything in places such as Iowa and Minnesota, just wanted to rebuild their lives and raise their kids. In the countryside, there was a long history of using nonfarm work to make up for lost incomes during those years with disappointing harvests, and many thought that building Deere tractors or Maytag washers would be the answer to their prayers. But just as they settled into work on an assembly line, they would hear rumors of layoffs or of relocation to another state—or maybe even to China or Mexico—where the local politicians promised the bosses even sweeter sweetheart deals. Harvard University sociologist William Julius Wilson famously chronicled how the very same processes of deindustrialization, unemployment, global market shifts, and the flight of the middle class gave rise to hyper-ghettoes and fueled the decline of cities.[23] As millions[24] of factory jobs left the countryside, the identical global market transformations behind the urban crisis gave rise to a rural one.

And just as in the inner cities, those left behind in shattered small towns have felt the consequences of this demographic shift in a host of social problems, among them rising rates of poverty. Of the twenty-five poorest counties in the nation, five are in Nebraska, and four are in Texas and South Dakota. Nebraska's Loup County has a per capita personal income of $6,404.[25] Nonmarital child-bearing is on the rise in Iowa, where one in four first births is to an unmarried woman. And in Oklahoma, which has the dubious distinction of having the highest divorce rate in the nation, welfare dependency and poverty among women and children have overwhelmed state officials.[26] In addition, the rate of serious crime in Kansas and Nebraska in 2002, the peak of the methamphetamine epidemic, was as much as 50 percent higher than in the state of New York.

In 2004, the Iowa Division of Narcotics Enforcement reported fifteen hundred meth-lab busts in the state, which was the second-highest number of any state in the nation, behind only Missouri. According to recent data from the U.S. Drug Enforcement Administration, that ranking has improved with the dramatic decline in meth labs. Still, in 2006, Iowa recorded the sixth-highest number of meth-lab incidents in the United States as a whole.[27]

When one economic phase ends and another begins, the negative effects are never felt equally by everyone, and this was no less true in the Heartland. At the moment that manufacturing declined and agriculture got supersized, other societal changes opened up opportunities for those ready to take advantage of them—specifically, greater access to higher education, particularly among women. What the new economy's winners grasped was that the hunger for highly skilled labor would mean college credentials were no longer a luxury but a necessity for those serious about assuring their place in the middle class. Young people have always left small towns to attend college, but by the early 1990s there were more opportunities and more compelling reasons to do so than ever before.

Even as getting a college degree became increasingly possible for greater numbers of high school graduates, it was the children of the middle and upper middle classes, not surprisingly, who were following this path in far greater numbers. And because the drive to leave had long been connected to earning a degree, in less than a generation the Heartland's most valuable export was no longer its crops or hogs but its educated young people.[28] As the highly skilled, highly educated, and highly paid congregated in superstar cities such as San Francisco and Boston, their counterparts of more modest means, educations, and resources were left behind in depopulating rural areas from the Great Plains to the Mississippi Delta.[29] These class-structured migration patterns reinforce a level of uneven development not seen since the Civil War.[30]

Given the scope of these changes and the fact that one in five Americans lives in nonmetropolitan areas, what is most surprising is that more attention has not been paid to the future of small towns. "The same politicians who decried the moral, economic, and social decline of cities," notes the writer Timothy Egan, "have been largely silent about the rural downturn."[31] One can speculate that since rural communities are sparsely populated, their problems are more often hidden from view. Perhaps the rural crisis has developed so slowly that the symptoms of decline have been easier to ignore; the rural downturn seeped rather than swept through the region.[32] But it is also quite possible that the main reason is denial; no one wants to admit that the small town's *Music Man* image is nothing more than cockeyed nostalgia.

Though demographers provide us with meticulously tabulated reports about 13
how much the countryside has changed, the truth is that we know precious little about what's behind depopulation and what really motivates the young people driving out-migration. What we do know is that their decisions have
undeniable consequences for huge sections of the nation. Talk to the experts,
and there are two schools of thought about why young people leave small towns.
Economists blame a shortage of jobs, while sociologists and geographers contend
that there is a shortage of things to do.[33] What both explanations gloss over is
why and how the young people leaving look so markedly different from the ones
who don't.

Spend time in the middle of the nation, in one of the thousands of small 14
towns where the hollowing-out process has taken hold, and you see a growing
chasm between the people leaving and the ones who remain. Fueling the out-
migration trends is a regional filtering system pushing some young people to stay
and others to go. Leaving, or not, does not result only from young people's individual preferences; instead, it is a reflection of their resources, particularly the
messages they receive from their social networks. Simply put, leaving is something that young people must be pushed, prodded, and cultivated to do, whereas
staying just sort of happens. Given that young people are now rural America's
most precious declining resource, it seems that the best way to preserve the
nation's small towns will be to create new sorts of conservation efforts to invest
more efficiently in these young people, whose futures—as parents, workers,
homeowners, voters, and taxpayers—will be so critical to the countryside's
survival.

LIVING IN ELLIS, IOWA

We moved to Iowa to try to understand the hollowing-out story. The state of 15
Iowa provides a useful bellwether case: only West Virginia loses a larger percentage of its college graduates to out-migration, and because of this loss of young
adults Iowa is aging more quickly than the rest of the nation. During the 1980s,
the farm crisis dramatically reshaped agriculture in the state, long considered the
buckle of the nation's Corn Belt.[34] Now, only seven other states are more
dependent than Iowa on manufacturing in terms of gross domestic product.[35] In
just three years, from 2000 to 2003, Iowa lost thirty thousand manufacturing
jobs, more than 10 percent of the state's total. During the next five years, work
crept back into the region, but the new jobs were inferior to the old ones, offering fewer benefits and lower wages. Some companies shifted operations overseas,
while others, lured away by other regions' tax breaks, just crossed state lines. But
in the one-plant towns where people depend on jobs at Maytag or Winnebago,

persistent unemployment and shuttered businesses are the first signs that things will get worse before they get better.

On a more symbolic level, Iowa embodies a distinctive "middleness," a reas-   16
suring typicality in the national self-perception.[36] Everyone from presidential hopefuls to rock-star activists[37] visits the state when they want to take the nation's pulse on an issue. After all, Iowa is the Heartland, the place where the "real" and supposedly more authentic[38] Americans reside.

We chose, for our research, a town we call "Ellis," in the northeastern cor-   17
ner of the state, because it is typical of the many towns that are finding it diffi- cult to survive, and its travails could be those of any of the thousands of depopulating rural communities stretching from western Pennsylvania to the Texas Panhandle. Ellis, with its population of 2,014, is not quite large enough to merit a streetlight, but there is a bank, two gas stations, and a family-run grocery store. Like most Iowa towns, regardless of their size, Ellis has two Lutheran churches (the conservative Missouri Synod and more liberal Reformed), and a Catholic, Methodist, and Evangelical church.

As Iowa towns go, Ellis is not noteworthy for its historical significance or its   18
scenic beauty. With grain elevators, a John Deere dealership, and farms perched on the town's outskirts, Ellis has the "look and feel of a farming community with its roots deep in the land."[39] One must remember, though, that Iowa's farm com- munities are not exactly what they seem, since few people still depend solely on the land for their livelihood.[40] Indeed, the most conspicuous aspects of the town's landscape may be the very things that are missing: malls, subdivisions, traffic, and young people. In this day and age, when so many people live in com- munities that look identical, Ellis is fifteen miles away from the nearest McDonald's, forty miles away from the closest Wal-Mart, and, while we lived there, nearly eighty miles from a Starbucks. And the town's graying population means that the median age is forty-four, nearly a decade older than the nation as a whole. Ellis's aging demographics are common throughout the rural Midwest, where the average median age in nonmetropolitan counties now approaches thirty-nine: in fact, nearly 40 percent of the Midwest's nonmetropolitan counties have median ages older than forty years, whereas less than 1 percent of the Midwest metropolitan counties do.[41]

The young people who came of age in Ellis in the late 1980s and early 1990s   19
made their transition to adulthood at a critical juncture for rural America. During the three decades of their lives so far, one in three of Iowa's farms disap- peared, the percentage of Americans with college degrees increased by one-third, and the Heartland states of Iowa, Kansas, Nebraska, and the Dakotas lost hun- dreds of thousands of factory jobs. During the 1980s, when they attended grade

school, the credit crisis pushed family farmers over the cliff. By the time they were in high school, in the early 1990s, the high-tech economy was coming to prominence: their decisions to stay, leave, or return would help seal the fate of the entire region.

In 2002, we moved our family to Ellis[42] and crisscrossed the nation—from California to Florida and New Mexico to Massachusetts[43]—during a span of eighteen months to speak with young people who had attended Ellis High School.[44] This was not the first time we had joined a community to write a book about a place and its people, but our preferred modus operandi is to fade into the background as much as possible. You might assume that two college professors hanging out on corners talking with teen mothers and drug dealers in Philadelphia's Badlands might stand out, but in Philly, most passersby assumed we were caseworkers or cops, frequent visitors to the city's toughest and most troubled neighborhoods. But the minute we arrived in Ellis, we came to be known as the folks renting Libby Duncan's house, and our presence garnered far more attention than we expected or might have liked. Most people made no effort to mask their polite, yet intense, curiosity about what the professors from back East were doing there. Soon after we moved to town, our arrival was heralded in a story in the *Ellis Gazette*. The newspaper's owner, editor-in-chief, primary reporter, and occasional photographer requested an interview with us. Assuming that the piece would be hidden away behind the graduation notices and the want ads, we agreed. A few days later, the front-page lead story, with an above-the-fold headline, announced that the town had been selected to be part of a "national study." Not long afterward, a television reporter from Cedar Rapids and a newspaper columnist from Waterloo called. They wanted to do their own stories on the Heartland Project, us, and what we were studying about Ellis. On both those occasions, we declined, as we had learned our lesson.

We were not celebrities, but it was as though the circus had come to town, and we were one of the main acts. Neither of us is from Iowa, and, though we had lived in Chicago for years, we had only driven through towns like Ellis on our way to someplace else. In places like Ellis, where people stay put for generations, there is a constant accounting of arrivals and departures. Outsiders get tagged and classified through their connections, no matter how attenuated, to the long-term inhabitants. For instance, the owner of one of Ellis's businesses, though he has been in town for more than a decade, is still known as the fellow who moved into Dr. Stillworth's house. For us, our tie was through Dennis and Laura Daugherty. Mentioning them did not always help open doors, but often it did ease suspicions. Pat had met the family when their middle daughter, Kelly, studied in Ireland a decade earlier. We realized quickly that the Daugherty fam-

20

21

ily name almost always granted us safe passage. The first time we tried by phone to set up a meeting with a local minister, he did everything to avoid us except hang up on us. The moment we mentioned that Dennis and Laura had suggested we call, his cool politeness thawed into warm enthusiasm. "Why didn't you say so in the first place?" he would ask later.

This wariness about new people and the desire to maintain the routines of small-town life reflect that one of the greatest pleasures of such an existence is being surrounded by people you know, people who share similar expectations about what constitutes a good life. Uneasiness can rapidly give way to fear when residents are faced with losing the small-town ambience in such communities as Ellis, where people greet each other on the street. It's hardly surprising that breaking the rules, no matter how insignificantly, brings a swift and firm response. Maria was slightly anxious on her first night in Ellis alone and left the front stoop light on. Concerned, a neighbor called our landlord, Bess Swenson, the daughter of the home's owner. Bess had taken over caring for the house since her eighty-two-year-old mother had suffered a stroke the previous year and been confined to a nursing home. At around 9 p.m., Bess appeared at our door, noting that the neighbors had called, worried to see the light left on. Maria apologized, assuring her that despite this apparent carelessness, we were good tenants and neighbors.

Unfortunately, we failed to measure up to the Ellis standards of conduct again when we didn't mow the lawn after the grass had grown too long. To be honest, we thought the lawn looked fine and didn't want to waste gas. This time, our neighbor stopped in himself. First, he explained, our lawn was not as neat and tidy as the neighbors'. Next, he wanted to know if we knew how to use a lawn mower, and, if the answer was no—and something about our conduct made him suspect strongly it might be—he suggested that, for a small fee, one of his boys could cut the grass. Because Pat, a lifelong urbanite, had never even used a motorized lawn mower, Maria assured our neighbor that she would manage the job herself that weekend. If we changed our minds, he said, "My boys could do it, no problem." From then on, we took care of the grass every week. No one ever mentioned the matter again, but the first time Maria mowed the yard, she noticed our neighbor observing her from the side door next to his garage.

These sorts of interactions helped us experience some of the unique features of life in a small, isolated, and homogenous area. To be sure, Ellis is not the easiest place to be if you are a foreigner, gay, not Christian, not white, and obviously rich or poor. There is a certain tolerance for something new, but this often is a long way from being welcoming or embracing. There can be little question that openness increasingly will be an issue for many small towns, as immigration and

the arrival of different people may offer the renewal and regeneration that will
stave off extinction.

It is ironic that in Iowa, one of the whitest states in the nation,[45] where the   25
distinctions between Lutheran and Catholic, German and Swedish, still hold
large sway, strangers represent the best chance for the future and, simultaneously,
the end of an old way of life. For people in Ellis, seeing the lone African
American engineer who works at one of the town's plants, being treated by the
South Asian doctor at the hospital, or doing business with the Jewish lawyer over
in Dubuque are events that are often noted with the detached, scientific tone
one might use to discuss the sighting of a rare flower or butterfly.

We were somewhat of a rarity ourselves, and Pat's being Irish, with spiky   26
hair, round glasses, and a fondness for T-shirts that showcased bands such as The
Pixies and The Smiths, did not make him stand out nearly as much as Maria.
Back home, people who knew about Maria's background, her Greek father and
West Indian mom, found the unusual pairing interesting in a cocktail-party conversation kind of way, while in Ellis, it caused a minor sensation. After one young
woman finished her interview with us, she informed Maria that she "was as dark
as she sounded on the phone." Another time, a local pastor came calling one
night. After some talk about where we lived in Philadelphia and the state of our
vegetable garden out back, the conversation turned, and he wondered, in a tone
that sounded as if he was talking about the amount of rain this month, "Maria,
now, I hear you're Hispanic." More than one person told us they had heard Maria
was Polynesian. Maria started to preempt these questions by figuring out ways to
work into the conversation that her last name was Greek. With the recent
release of the film *My Big Fat Greek Wedding*, we had a useful, if over-the-top,
popular-culture reference point.

Sometimes the interactions felt less benign and more unsettling. At mass   27
one Sunday, when the priest called on the congregation to greet one another
with "Peace be with you," we stood in silence as no one turned to shake our
hands or acknowledge us in any way. Then there was the time Maria was walking home from town alone, wearing a white blouse, sandals, and a colorful cot-
ton skirt. As she made her way off Main Street, a truck, replete with shotgun
rack, slowed down. The two passengers, young men in their twenties who
appeared to be heading home from work, gawked for ten very long seconds as she
walked by. The truck's occupants never took their eyes off her; neither Maria, nor
they, uttered a word. It was almost as though they were trying to figure out what
new species had found its way to their town.

Such encounters offered a window into the struggles that lie ahead and   28
reflected a controversy bubbling just below the surface throughout the rural

Midwest. Back in 2000, then-governor Tom Vilsack initiated a public campaign to make his state "the new Ellis Island." It is no exaggeration to say that immigration in Iowa and much of the rural Midwest is not like anything witnessed before in New York, Chicago, or Boston.[46] "Outside of the cities, the Midwest is mostly 'the Old World transplanted to the New World,' a social system based on everyone acting and looking like everyone else."[47] Given the distinctive sensibilities of small Midwestern towns in Nebraska, Minnesota, Kansas, or Iowa, local life is built on the publicly uniform and fairly unanimous respect for law and on the comfort that comes from being surrounded by people who understand the rules of local life instinctively because they are the direct descendants of the people who created these standards. Small-town people rejoice in the fact that if you get in trouble, your neighbors will close ranks and reach out with aid. This was something we observed firsthand when a young mother in Ellis was paralyzed in a car accident the summer we lived there. As the medical bills started to pile up, the Rotary Club, churches, and neighbors coordinated collections and sponsored an all-you-can-eat waffle breakfast: the line out of the VFW Hall stretched down two blocks.

For now, the majority of Iowa's towns have no immigrants. People in places like Ellis have an accurate sense that when newcomers, namely immigrants, do arrive, their numbers will overtake these emptying-out towns with such breakneck speed that there hardly will be time for the people there to catch their breath.[48] In a single decade, Iowa towns such as Ottumwa, Postville, and Storm Lake transformed from homogenous populations to places where one in three residents was Hispanic, the vast majority of whom were not naturalized citizens.[49] And so, one of the reliable features of life here in Iowa, the thing that keeps so many close—that sense of comfort and familiarity—could disappear in a blink of an eye.

Outsiders who hear locals express worries about immigration might conclude that these anxieties reflect ignorance and prejudice. We believe that these anxieties reflect fears of changes looming on the horizon; small-town dwellers are frightened of losing what they know, and anxious that the things they hold dear will disappear and that no one but them will even care. Others have written about what happens when places such as Hazelton, Pennsylvania, and Denison and Postville, Iowa, face the onslaught of new arrivals—immigrants, "mostly Hispanic, largely dark-skinned, about half in the country illegally, without valid documents"—whose customs, language, and color mark them as alien and different.[50] Our book is different. We tell the story of a community with its arms outstretched, fumbling around in the dark, simply trying not to fall down.

Through the voices of young people, we chronicle the *real* story of small-   31
town America. We take you into the lives of the young Iowans we met as they
figured out whether to stay or go—what would be for many of them the most
important decision of their lives. Yet it wasn't a decision made in an instant.
Despite the romantic notions of the small-town kid eager to reinvent her- or
himself, we find that leaving or staying is a gradual process that unfolds over a
span of years, and we found scores of former and current Iowans who offered
revealing insights into how they had come to take the paths they did. Those who
left—Leavers—were distinctive in how much they valued their encounters with
diversity and learning about a world "where not everyone is Lutheran." A self-
styled "recovering Iowan" reflected on the pull for leaving small-town life in a
New York Times letter to the editor: "I left Iowa after high school eight years ago
in order to learn from a broader diversity of people and experiences than Iowa
could offer. I cherished my Iowa roots but I needed to see the world."[51] But spend
time with the people we dubbed Stayers and Returners, and it seems they take
the opposite view. Of course, the outside world is exciting, but why would you
want to trade in the known and understood for something that feels so uncertain? Underneath the Stayers' rah-rah boosterism for small-town life, one also
detects a subtle feeling of rejection, an ambivalence toward places where life is
strange and unpredictable.

The possible paths these young Iowans might take capture the dilemma of a   32
twenty-first-century world in which people's life chances are defined so dramatically by their access to the education and skills necessary for the new economy.
We talked with college graduates of the University of Iowa who have a six-in-ten
chance of moving out of state once they complete a degree; the high school graduates who told us that they're lucky to earn $15 an hour building ambulances and
assembling microprocessors; and the high school dropouts putting eggs in cartons, slaughtering hogs at the meat-processing plants, or walking the rows of corn
during the harvest alongside undocumented workers. There were those who had
served in the military, including several who were preparing to go overseas as part
of Operation Enduring Freedom. And, of course, there were the lives that had
taken unexpected turns: divorce, time in jail, drug abuse, and unplanned pregnancy and parenthood.

Against the backdrop of demographic shifts and rural out-migration there is   33
a compelling story about the young people whose lives will determine the rural
Heartland's fate. In the pages that follow, we will see how the crucial moment in
these young Iowans' coming-of-age biographies would be when they decide to
follow the paths that will make them Leavers, Stayers, or Returners. But the
young people who follow one path or another are not randomly dotted across the

landscape. Teachers, parents, and other influential adults cherry-pick the young people destined to leave and ignore the ones most likely to stay or return. Civic leaders may lament the rural youth exodus and the accompanying brain drain, but they fail to see how their own actions have helped create the problem. No one can deny that rural areas have less and less to offer their young people economically. Yet it hardly makes sense to expend time and energy on the cadre most likely to succeed and leave while neglecting the needs of the kids with fewer options and resources, the kids most likely to stay.

THE ACHIEVERS

One in five Ellis High graduates finds his or her way to West Point or the   34 University of Iowa. This is no surprise, since Iowa students earn some of the nation's highest SAT and ACT scores. If you could travel back in time to their high school years, it seems that the young people who leave were the teachers' pets or, at the very least, the teachers' pet projects. The young people destined to be Achievers are the Ellis equivalent of a homegrown aristocracy. Kids whom the adults had written off because they would never amount to enough to get out of Liberty County[52] got letters home and detention for missed classes or assignments, while the Achievers consistently escaped such punishments. Most, but not all, of the kids who attended universities were like Sonya Eden,[53] a journalism major now working at a museum in Philadelphia whose mother and father attended college themselves. But other kids came from families in which college would not be a likely destination without direct encouragement from assorted interested adults outside the family. Being one of the students whom the teachers and staff treated differently had the power to change a young person's future: their talents and ability made them recipients of their teachers' and neighbors' attention. Those kids were placed on a different trajectory because the entire town was behind them, cheering for them to make it and supporting them in concrete ways. These young people had the sense that the town's inhabitants instilled all their hopes, best wishes, and expectations in their futures. One of the abiding truths of small-town life is that people want to say they knew the local kid before he or she made it big.

The good news for those among the chosen few is that the school could   35 operate as a meritocracy where talent and drive were identified and rewarded. Yet since fewer than half of the Achievers will live in Iowa after earning their degree, the whole system suffers from an undeniable inefficiency. Paying so much attention to the Achievers drains Ellis's resources, as it serves young people who are least likely to give anything back to the town.

THE STAYERS

In an era in which so many twenty-somethings suffer from "failure to launch"   36
syndrome, Stayers' most unique characteristic may be how quickly they start
looking and acting like adults. They transition to adulthood and families, jobs,
and grown-up lives far more quickly than their peers who out-migrate. A relatively cheap cost of living makes it easier for young people to afford the accoutrements of adulthood. The other key to avoiding the pitfalls of extended
adolescence is that Stayers do not attend college. Twenty-somethings coming of
age in small towns can still find jobs in blue-collar occupations such as factory
work, auto repair, and construction. The conundrum is that many of these jobs
are particularly prone to stagnating wages, disappearing benefits, and downsiz-
ing.[54] And within a decade of leaving high school, nearly one-fifth of the young
people we studied who were Stayers had stopped their education and had never
lived anywhere but Ellis or Liberty County. Forgoing college for a job at the plant
or as a truck driver is, over the long haul, a precarious place to be economically.

A machine operator living in Ellis complains about the struggles facing old-   37
fashioned workers who find themselves trapped in a newfangled economy. The
tragedy is that, in time, Stayers come to realize that not having a college degree
hurts them as they face a future of downward mobility and grave uncertainty.
Stayers are the most visible vestige of the hollowing-out problem. They are also
a group that is ignored in the policy discussions about how to save the rural
Heartland. There is no question that Ellis's Stayers are grappling with a lan-
guishing economy, a dying small town, and a fading way of life. However, the
only policies pursued at the local and state levels are aimed at attracting back the
educated leavers, which ignores both the untapped resource of the people who
stayed and the part that adults played in pushing a select group of kids to leave
in the first place.

THE SEEKERS

"Some people ain't made for small-town living," observes Doc Gibbons in   38
Thornton Wilder's classic *Our Town*, and, indeed, the Seekers devote their childhood and teenage years to plotting their escapes. Whereas the Achievers leave
because everyone expects them to, for the Seekers, fleeing their small town is
something they feel compelled to do. Garrison Keillor, that famous observer of
smalltown life, writes, "Leaving home is a kind of forgiveness. . . . You can start
over." It is, in the truest sense, "a sort of redemption."[55] For the Seekers the most
common pathway out of Iowa is via military service. Of a graduating class of forty
students, Ellis High School records show that at least 10 percent of every class
enlists annually. That percentage of young people joining the armed forces has

stayed the same, and even increased, since the wars in Iraq and Afghanistan began.

Those headed to the military were never destined for college—not because they don't want a degree, but because their parents can't afford it. Neither the best nor the worst students, they are also not the most affluent or the poorest. Talk with their teachers, advisers, and coaches and you learn they are the solid kids: not the captain of the football team, but maybe the second-string player who served the team faithfully every season. They may lack the grades and money to attend the University of Iowa, but they have no desire to settle into married life with their high school sweetheart or get a dead-end job. And, in old age, when they reflect on their lives, they don't want to regret missed opportunities: not seeing the rest of the country or the world, never taking a plane to an exotic destination, never seeing the ocean.

THE RETURNERS: HIGH-FLYERS AND BOOMERANGS

When people manage to pay attention to the rural youth exodus, they focus on a select group of Returners we call the High-Flyers—those twenty-somethings who return to small towns armed with college degrees and entrepreneurial ambitions. These are the men and women whom Iowa's boosters long to bring back home. But when you hear the stories of how these journeys ended—that is, where they started, back home in Ellis—it is hard to imagine how the state can lure many Iowans back to the countryside with the promise of venture capital and bike paths. A very select sort of kid, on track to be the quintessential, college-bound, ambitious Achiever, uses the college years to figure out that big-city life is not what he or she wants or needs and, ultimately, opts to reverse course. Surrounded by valedictorians, captains of the lacrosse team, and suburbanites who took calculus in high school and spent their summers in Europe, Returners abandon the Achiever trajectory. They describe college as a time when they could not find their footing and became increasingly disillusioned with a world that had seemed so appealing when it was just a daydream.

Even though they maintained their grades and earned a degree, college seemed to test their suitability for the outside world, and being away from home took an emotional and psychic toll. Although the high-achieving Leavers and Seekers value their encounters with diversity and come to see small towns as limited and closed, Returners say that the same sorts of experiences—being surrounded by strangers and living a fast-paced life—frustrated them. They found what lay beyond Ellis unwelcoming and disorienting and, given the choice, prioritize the familiar over the possibility of something else.

Although the High-Flyers are the ones to whom politicians market the state,   42
our time in Ellis revealed that most of the Iowans coming home are the
Boomerangs: young people who have far more in common with the Stayers than
the Achievers. The Boomerangs' numbers include former enlisted men and
women who move back to Iowa after leaving the armed forces and the mostly
female graduates of community colleges. For the typical Boomerangs attending
community college, leaving Ellis was only to be a temporary situation from the
outset. While their friends at the University of Iowa were choosing a major, celebrating the fact that they no longer needed fake IDs, and pledging fraternities
and sororities, Boomerangs, who tend to be young women, graduated from their
two-year programs in accounting or nursing and acquired husbands, full-time
jobs, and mortgages—in short, they eagerly embarked upon genuinely grown-up
lives. Boomerangs are in a rush to start a "real life"; they will tell you they have
little interest in backpacking through Europe or renting a tiny apartment with a
roommate and waitressing until they find their dream career. They have chosen
the safe and familiar, and, like young people of another time, they have no desire
to delay pursuing the more traditional goals of early adulthood: marriage and
family.

Ultimately, the most important lessons the Stayers, Leavers, and Returners can   43
teach us is that small towns play an unwitting part in their own decline.
Teachers, parents, and neighbors feel obligated to push and prod the talented
kids to succeed, yet, when their best and brightest follow their advice, the investment the community has made in them becomes a boon for someplace else,
while the remaining young people are neither afforded the same attention nor
groomed for success of any kind. Whether this is willful neglect or a rational
deployment of resources, the result is the same: small towns such as Ellis have
become trapped by their self-fulfilling prophecies. Perhaps the optimistic
Heartland mythology—farmers always believe that the next season will be
better—is one reason that people in towns like Ellis don't advertise how difficult
things have become.

The national debates about failing communities and economic downturns   44
make it sound as if only cities are vulnerable. Politicians shout *over* the rural crisis in the culture wars: either there's the rhetoric about the "real" and patriotic
small-town America[56] or a blaming-the-victim discussion ensues about bitter,
close-minded, and racist rural America.[57]

In the words of former U.S. Rep. Robin Hayes of North Carolina, "The real   45
Americans . . . work and accomplish and achieve and believe in God." And,

indeed, the grand illusion of the mythic rural America gets perpetuated easily.[58] On drives through the countryside and small towns, visitors fail to see that the abandoned barns and quiet Main Streets are symptoms of a decaying way of life in just the same way that burned-out buildings and forgotten urban neighborhoods are monuments to the city's moral and economic decline. The typical imagery of the countryside that adorns coins and stamps embodies all that is right with America—versus the inner city, which symbolizes all that is wrong. They would have us believe, writes the *Wall Street Journal's* Thomas Frank, that "the country is divided into a land of the soulful, hard-working producers and a land of the paper-pushing parasites; a plain-spoken heartland and the sinister big cities."[59] In the big city, it is true, young men sling dime bags on corners in front of vacant buildings, whereas in the rural Heartland, dealers cook meth using salvaged cars and illegally purchased cough syrup at abandoned barns. In the public's imagination, teen mothers exist only in the ghetto, and yet young mothers of the countryside share many of the characteristics of their vilified urban counterparts. Both types of family end up on welfare. Rural young mothers differ only in the order in which they do things; they will wed their children's fathers and then become single mothers *after* a divorce.[60] In each place, there is no shortage of guns: it is just that in the inner city, those guns are illegal, while in small towns shotguns get displayed in the backs of trucks or in polished oak cabinets not far from the family china.

In the end, young people from the countryside (just like the ones in the city) who have talent and earn scholarships get air-lifted out to fulfill their potential someplace else. Back home, those with the fewest options and resources face trying to compete in an economy in which the rules keep getting changed in the middle of the game. The young people who are in-between, the Returners, might come home after the outside world fails to live up to its promise and bet their futures on their hometown holding on just a little bit longer. Others, desperate to free themselves from what they see as the limitations of a small-town existence, volunteer to fight for America, just because heading to war offers something more than getting trapped in the countryside.

    In sum, the *real* America of the Heartland hangs in the balance because of massive global market transformations, and the agriculture and manufacturing sectors' compulsive efforts to eliminate human workers, deskill their jobs, and replace them with technology; and because crime is on the rise, along with drug use; poverty is spreading—and communities and families are coming apart at the seams. Maybe the most useful insight comes from Richard Russo, the Pulitzer Prize–winning author who believes that any story of small-town America is, at its core, the story of the people who stay and the ones who go. Even for young people who leave, there is always a "ghost version" of yourself who can be found "sitting at the bar . . . watching those long-neck bottles of beer line up sweating in front of you." And, for those who stay, small-town life has become a place "where people are hanging on to home and hanging onto pride, and hanging on by a thread."[61]

ENDNOTES

1. Richard Florida, *The Rise of the Creative Class*.
2. Richard Florida, "Creative Class War: How the GOP's Anti-Elitism Could Ruin America's Economy." http://creativeclass.com/rfcgdb/articles/Creative_Class_War.pdf.
3. United States Bureau of the Census, quoted in Matt Weiland and Sean Wilsey, eds., *State by State: A Panoramic Portrait of America*, 536.
4. In the nation, 2,052 nonmetropolitan counties occupy 97 percent of U.S. land area and are home to about one-fifth (almost 44.5 million people) of the U.S. population. The Office of Management and Budget defines metro areas as (1) central counties with one or more urbanized areas, and (2) outlying counties that are economically tied to the core counties as measured by work commuting. Nonmetro counties are outside the boundaries of metro areas and are further subdivided into two types: micropolitan areas, which are centered on urban clusters of ten thousand or more persons, and all remaining "noncore" counties. Overall, in 2000, 17 percent of the national population lived in nonmetro counties, and 21 percent lived in rural areas. For the first time, a slight majority of rural people now live in metro areas ("Measuring Rurality?" USDA Briefing Room, www.ers.usda.gov/Briefing/Rurality/WhatIsRural/).
5. Willis Goudy, "Population Change in the Midwest Lags: Nonmetro Population Growth Lags Metro Increase."
6. There is a huge body of literature on the links between human-capital acquisition and geographic mobility and rural out-migration. For instance, see Thurston Domina, "What Clean Break? Education and Migration Patterns, 1989–2004," 378. Also see Daniel T. Lichter, Diane K. McLaughlin, and Gretchen T. Cornwell, "Migration and the Loss of Human Resources in Rural America," 235–56.
7. Thurston Domina, "Brain Drain and Brain Gain: Rising Educational Segregation in the United States, 1940–2000," 387.
8. The Higher Education Act of 1965 (or the HSA) was enacted on November 8, 1965, as part of President Lyndon Johnson's Great Society

domestic agenda. The law was intended "to strengthen the educational resources of our colleges and universities and to provide financial assistance for students in postsecondary and higher education." It increased federal money given to universities, created scholarships, gave low-interest loans for students, and established a National Teachers Corps. The "financial assistance for students" is covered in Title IV of the HSA.

 9. Domina, "Brain Drain," 387.

10. Ibid., 395.

11. Ibid.

12. Thurston Domina, "The Geography of Educational Segregation." www.insidehighered.com/views/2007/01/19/domina.

13. Domina, "Brain Drain," 395.

14. Domina, "Geography."

15. In his 1920 masterpiece *Main Street*, Sinclair Lewis offers this description of the rural youth exodus: "With . . . small-town life . . . there are hundreds of thousands . . . who are not content. The more intelligent young people . . . flee to the cities and . . . stay there, seldom returning even for holidays. The reason . . . is an unimaginatively standardized background, a sluggishness of speech and manners, a rigid ruling of the spirit by the desire to appear respectable. It is contentment . . . the contentment of the quiet dead, who are scornful of the living for their restless walking" (257–58).

16. For an explanation of changes in agriculture, see Allan Barkema and Mark Drabenstott, "Consolidation and Change in Heartland Agriculture." See also Richard Rathge and Paula Highman, "Population Change in the Great Plains: A History of Prolonged Decline."

17. Monica Davey, "Vanishing Barns Signal a Changing Iowa," A1. www.nytimes.com/2008/09/07/us/07iowa.html.

18. Kathryn M. Dudley, *Debt and Dispossession: Farm Loss in America's Heartland* (Chicago and London: University of Chicago Press, 2000), 5. See also F. Larry Leistritz and Katherine Meyer, "Farm Crisis in the Midwest: Trends and Implications."

19. Thomas Frank, *What's the Matter with Kansas? How Conservatives Won the Heart of America*, 156.

20. Dudley, *Debt and Dispossession*, 5.

21. Economic Research Service, U.S. Department of Agriculture, *Understanding Rural America*, 5.

22. Dudley, *Debt and Dispossession*, 5.

23. William Julius Wilson, *The Truly Disadvantaged: The Inner City, the Underclass, and Public Policy*.

24. It is difficult to offer a precise number for the loss of jobs in the manufacturing sector. Very often employers do not simply eliminate a position; they reduce the hours and benefits, making it easier to let workers go without having to cover the costs of terminating full-time workers.

25. Cited in Timothy Egan, "Pastoral Poverty: The Seeds of Decline." Data from the United States Department of Commerce. Also note that nonmetropolitan counties have the highest poverty rates, and that of the 386 counties categorized as "persistent poverty" counties, 340 are nonmetropolitan counties (USDA, "Rural Income").

26. Though rates of nonmarital childbearing in states such as Iowa still lag behind the national average, they are increasing.

27. See Gary W. Kendell, "Methamphetamine Abuse in Iowa: A Report to the Legislature." www.iowa.gov/odcp/docs/2007_Meth_Report_2_1-07.pdf. In yet another disturbing parallel to the inner city, the countryside's abundance of abandoned barns, easy access to fertilizer and ammonia (key ingredients for meth production), and growing supply of disconnected and disengaged young people offered a perfect storm of conditions for the growth of a rural drug trade; see Egan, "Pastoral Poverty."

28. This line is based on (but is not a direct quote from) Dale Maharidge's book *Denison, Iowa: Searching for the Soul of America through the Secrets of a Midwest Town*, 88. We have read similar lines about young people being Iowa's biggest export in Richard Longworth's *Caught in the Middle* and Stephen Bloom's *Postville*. The president of Saint Joseph's University, Father Timothy Lannon, SJ, a Harvard-educated Jesuit priest who was born, raised, and attended college in Iowa, said to Maria in 2002, "Iowa's greatest problem is that it exports all its young people." So we must credit all of them for this evocative line.

29. Florida, Richard, "The Rise of the Creative Class: Why Cities without Gays and Rock Bands Are Losing the Economic Development Race." www.washingtonmonthly.com/features/2001/0205.florida.html.

30. Florida, "Creative Class War." http://creativeclass.com/rfcgdb/articles/Creative_Clas5_ War.pdt

31. Egan, "Pastoral Poverty," B10.

32. Ibid.

33. For some of the most influential "creative cities" explanations of the concentration of educated, culturally sophisticated elites in metropolitan areas, see Heather Rogers, "Literary Amenities and Cultural Scenes: Assessing the Differential Impact of Quality and Spatial Concentration" ; Terry N. Clark,

"Urban Amenities: Lakes, Opera, and Juice Bars: Do They Drive Development?"; and Florida, *Rise of the Creative Class*.

34. Calvin Beale defines the Corn Belt and Great Plains this way: "If there is an idealized type of the agrarian and small-town image in America, it surely belongs to the Corn Belt and the Great Plains—the land of the Homestead Act, frugal, hard-working farmers, Garland's *Son of the Middle Border*, Rolvaag's *Giants in the Earth*, Lewis's *Main Street*, Inge's *Picnic*, Wilson's *Music Man*, and Grant Wood's *American Gothic*. A land of struggle—not always rewarded—and even occasional strife, but without the degrading legacy of slavery, sharecropping, grinding poverty, and soil depletion that has overlaid the rural South" (*A Taste of the Country: A Collection of Calvin Beale's Writings*, 65).

35. A recession in Iowa means manufacturing jobs most likely will get hammered. During the 1980s, when a national recession deepened into a farm crisis in Iowa and elsewhere in the Midwest, Iowa lost 43,100 factory jobs; 62 percent of all nonfarm positions were cut, state data show. And it was nearly as brutal two decades later, when the recession of 2001 wiped out nearly 32,000 factory jobs. Iowa has lost 2,400 factory jobs through September 2008, and more job losses are coming. Lennox Industries in Marshalltown, Whirlpool Corp. in Amana, and Rockwell Collins in Cedar Rapids announced an additional 1,000 cuts in October 2008. See Donnelle Eller, "How Will the Recession Hurt Iowa's Financial Sector?" www.desmoinesregister.com/article/20081116/BUSINESS/811160327/1029/BUSINESS.

36. William Schmidt, "Ups and Downs Aside, Iowa Has Middleness," A5.

37. In December 2002, when the Irish rock star Bono wanted to garner public support for his work on AIDS in Africa, he organized a bus tour of African performers to do shows throughout the Midwest, including Iowa. During the summer of that year, when we lived in Ellis, Bono also visited a Davenport, Iowa, truck stop to learn what "real" Americans think about the global AIDS crisis.

38. The notion of a "real" or more authentic America is an increasingly controversial claim that harkens back to the red- and blue-state culture wars. We use the term self-consciously to point out how the notion of an authentic America distracts us from the region's more serious concerns.

39. Osha Gray Davidson, *Broken Heartland: The Rise of America's Rural Ghetto*, 1.

40. Ibid.

41. Goudy, "Population Change."

42. Getting to Ellis, Iowa, from Philadelphia requires a flight into Chicago, then crop duster–style air travel to the tiny Waterloo Airport, then an hour's drive. When we traveled, the other air passengers were contractors working for John Deere, National Guard and Army reservists coming home from deployments and trainings, and, on one occasion, the body of an Iowan returning home for burial. The alternative route also took us to Chicago, then a connecting flight to Cedar Rapids, and a two-hour trip by car. When we moved to Ellis for the summer, we packed up our Nissan Altima (one of the only Japanese-made vehicles we ever saw in Liberty County) and settled into a rented, furnished two-bedroom house; our daughter, Camille, then two years old, christened our new residence the "summer house."

43. We interviewed people in fifteen states.

44. The research focused on two cohort sets of young people who had entered the high school as freshmen and would have graduated in 1990, 1991, or 1992 and 1995, 1996, and 1997. We assembled lists of the freshmen classes for these cohorts and, omitting foreign-exchange students and students who started at Ellis but who graduated elsewhere, we distributed a short survey to almost 350 young adults. More than 80 percent completed the survey—some by telephone, some by mail—and from this group we completed in-depth interviews with 104 from February 2002 through March 2003. An extended discussion of the research design and detailed data from the survey and in-depth interviews are available at http://www.hollowingoutthemiddle.com.

45. According to the U.S. Census Bureau, 94.4 percent of the population in Iowa is white, making it the sixth whitest state (U.S. Census, 2009).

46. Richard Longworth, *Caught in the Middle*, 103.

47. Ibid.

48. Ibid.

49. Ibid.

50. Ibid.

51. Dean Krishna, "Try to Imagine the Iowa of My Dreams."

52. Liberty County is a made-up name for the county Ellis is in.

53. All of the names used in this book are pseudonyms.

54. One of the earliest documentations of the relationship between class and social reproduction in school appears in Robert and Helen Lynd's classic 1920s study *Middletown: A Study in Modern American Culture*. They write about the influence of a family's financial status on the educational outcomes of children, in many ways anticipating Annette Lareau's contemporary work on natural growth and concerted cultivation, *Unequal Childhoods: Class, Race, and Family Life*.

55. Garrison Keillor in his collection of essays titled *Leaving Home*, xiv.

56. In the piece "Palin's 'Pro-America Areas' Remark: Extended Version," the *Washington Post's* Juliet Eilperin writes about the extended versions of Governor Palin's comments about the pro-America parts of the country and their contrast with Washington, D.C. (see http://voices.washingtonpost.com /44/2008/10/17/palin_clarifies_her_pro-americ.html). Like Barack Obama (see next note), Palin would later apologize for her comments. Palin explained she never intended to suggest that specific parts of the country are less patriotic or less American. "If that's the way it has come across, I apologize," she told CNN's Drew Griffin. (From Lyndsey Layton, "PalinApologizesfor'RealAmerica' Comments," http://www.washington post.com/wp-dyn/content/article/2008/10/21/AR2008102102449.html).

57. In April of 2008, presidential candidate Barack Obama told a crowd of supporters in San Francisco, "You go into some of these small towns in Pennsylvania, and like a lot of small towns in the Midwest, the jobs have been gone now for twenty-five years, and nothing's replaced them. And they fell through the Clinton administration, and the Bush administration, and each successive administration has said that somehow these communities are gonna regenerate, and they have not. And it's not surprising then they get bitter, they cling to guns or religion or antipathy to people who aren't like them or anti-immigrant sentiment or anti-trade sentiment as a way to explain their frustrations." The full quotation, which was spoken during a fundraiser in San Francisco, was first reported on the *Huffington Post* on April 11, 2008. In an October 15, 2008, *New York Times Magazine* cover story titled "Working for the Working-Class Vote," Senator Obama said that his greatest regret of the campaign, "my biggest bone headed move," had been this comment. "How it was interpreted in the press was Obama talking to a bunch of wine-sipping San Francisco liberals with an anthropological view toward white working-class voters. And I was actually making the reverse point, clumsily, which is that these voters have a right to be frustrated because they've been ignored. And because Democrats haven't met them halfway on cultural issues, we've not been able to communicate to them effectively an economic agenda that would help broaden our coalition."

58. Layton, "Palin Apologizes."

59. See Thomas Frank, "Joe the Plumber and GOP Authenticity." http:// online.wsj.com/article/SB122463199532056477.html?mod=rss_The_ Tilting_Yard.

60. The Bristol Palin pregnancy and the announcement of her engagement, at age 17, brought into stark reality how rural teens might respond differently to early pregnancy. Though the details of Palin's situation are not widely known, the fact that the couple became engaged and presented themselves as a soon-to-be married couple matches the behaviors we saw in rural Iowa, where shotgun marriages have not gone out of style.

61. From an NPR interview with Richard Russo for *Morning Edition*, "Richard Russo's Small-Town America," October 1, 2007.

Hua Hsu is an Assistant Professor of English at Vassar College. Hsu completed his Ph.D. in the History of American Civilization at Harvard University. His areas of expertise include trans-Pacific literary history, cultural studies and *art criticism*. In addition to teaching, Hsu is a contributor to the *New Yorker, Atlantic Monthly, Wired* and *Slate*. Hsu is also on the editorial board of the *New Literary History of America*, the latest edition of the anthology was published in 2009.

The End of White America?

Hua Hsu

"Civilization's going to pieces," he remarks. He is in polite company, gathered   1
with friends around a bottle of wine in the late-afternoon sun, chatting and gossiping. "I've gotten to be a terrible pessimist about things. Have you read *The Rise of the Colored Empires* by this man Goddard?" They hadn't. "Well, it's a fine book, and everybody ought to read it. The idea is if we don't look out the white race will be—will be utterly submerged. It's all scientific stuff; it's been proved."

He is Tom Buchanan, a character in F. Scott Fitzgerald's *The Great Gatsby,*   2
a book that nearly everyone who passes through the American education system is compelled to read at least once. Although *Gatsby* doesn't gloss as a book on racial anxiety—it's too busy exploring a different set of anxieties entirely—Buchanan was hardly alone in feeling besieged. The book by "this man Goddard" had a real-world analogue: Lothrop Stoddard's *The Rising Tide of Color Against White World-Supremacy*, published in 1920, five years before *Gatsby*. Nine decades later, Stoddard's polemic remains oddly engrossing. He refers to World War I as the "White Civil War" and laments the "cycle of ruin" that may result if the "white world" continues its infighting. The book features a series of foldout maps depicting the distribution of "color" throughout the world and warns, "Colored migration is a universal peril, menacing every part of the white world."

As briefs for racial supremacy go, *The Rising Tide of Color* is eerily serene. Its   3
tone is scholarly and gentlemanly, its hatred rationalized and, in Buchanan's

term, "scientific." And the book was hardly a fringe phenomenon. It was published by Scribner, also Fitzgerald's publisher, and Stoddard, who received a doctorate in history from Harvard, was a member of many professional academic associations. It was precisely the kind of book that a 1920s man of Buchanan's profile—wealthy, Ivy League–educated, at once pretentious and intellectually insecure—might have been expected to bring up in casual conversation.

As white men of comfort and privilege living in an age of limited social   4
mobility, of course, Stoddard and the Buchanans in his audience had nothing literal to fear. Their sense of dread hovered somewhere above the concerns of everyday life. It was linked less to any immediate danger to their class's political and cultural power than to the perceived fraying of the fixed, monolithic identity of whiteness that sewed together the fortunes of the fair-skinned.

From the hysteria over Eastern European immigration to the vibrant cultural   5
miscegenation of the Harlem Renaissance, it is easy to see how this imagined worldwide white kinship might have seemed imperiled in the 1920s. There's no better example of the era's insecurities than the 1923 Supreme Court case *United States v. Bhagat Singh Thind*, in which an Indian American veteran of World War I sought to become a naturalized citizen by proving that he was Caucasian. The Court considered new anthropological studies that expanded the definition of the Caucasian race to include Indians, and the justices even agreed that traces of "Aryan blood" coursed through Thind's body. But these technicalities availed him little. The Court determined that Thind was not white "in accordance with the understanding of the common man" and therefore could be excluded from the "statutory category" of whiteness. Put another way: Thind was white, in that he was Caucasian and even Aryan. But he was not *white* in the way Stoddard or Buchanan were white.

The '20s debate over the definition of whiteness—a legal category? a com-   6
monsense understanding? a worldwide civilization?—took place in a society gripped by an acute sense of racial paranoia, and it is easy to regard these episodes as evidence of how far we have come. But consider that these anxieties surfaced when whiteness was synonymous with the American mainstream, when threats to its status were largely imaginary. What happens once this is no longer the case—when the fears of Lothrop Stoddard and Tom Buchanan are realized, and white people actually become an American minority?

Whether you describe it as the dawning of a post-racial age or just the end   7
of white America, we're approaching a profound demographic tipping point. According to an August 2008 report by the U.S. Census Bureau, those groups currently categorized as racial minorities—blacks and Hispanics, East Asians and South Asians—will account for a majority of the U.S. population by the year

2042. Among Americans under the age of 18, this shift is projected to take place in 2023, which means that every child born in the United States from here on out will belong to the first post-white generation.

Obviously, steadily ascending rates of interracial marriage complicate this picture, pointing toward what Michael Lind has described as the "beiging" of America. And it's possible that "beige Americans" will self-identify as "white" in sufficient numbers to push the tipping point further into the future than the Census Bureau projects. But even if they do, whiteness will be a label adopted out of convenience and even indifference, rather than aspiration and necessity. For an earlier generation of minorities and immigrants, to be recognized as a "white American," whether you were an Italian or a Pole or a Hungarian, was to enter the mainstream of American life; to be recognized as something else, as the *Thind* case suggests, was to be permanently excluded. As Bill Imada, head of the IW Group, a prominent Asian American communications and marketing company, puts it: "I think in the 1920s, 1930s, and 1940s, [for] anyone who immigrated, the aspiration was to blend in and be as American as possible so that white America wouldn't be intimidated by them. They wanted to imitate white America as much as possible: learn English, go to church, go to the same schools."

Today, the picture is far more complex. To take the most obvious example, whiteness is no longer a precondition for entry into the highest levels of public office. The son of Indian immigrants doesn't have to become "white" in order to be elected governor of Louisiana. A half-Kenyan, half-Kansan politician can self-identify as black and be elected president of the United States.

As a purely demographic matter, then, the "white America" that Lothrop Stoddard believed in so fervently may cease to exist in 2040, 2050, or 2060, or later still. But where the culture is concerned, it's already all but finished. Instead of the long-standing model of assimilation toward a common center, the culture is being remade in the image of white America's multiethnic, multicolored heirs.

For some, the disappearance of this centrifugal core heralds a future rich with promise. In 1998, President Bill Clinton, in a now-famous address to students at Portland State University, remarked:

Today, largely because of immigration, there is no majority race in Hawaii or Houston or New York City. Within five years, there will be no majority race in our largest state, California. In a little more than 50 years, there will be no majority race in the United States. No other nation in history has gone through demographic change of this magnitude in so short a time . . . [These immigrants] are energizing our culture and broadening our vision of the world. They are renewing our most basic values and reminding us all of what it truly means to be American. Not everyone was so enthused. Clinton's remarks caught the atten-

8

9

10

11

12

tion of another anxious Buchanan—Pat Buchanan, the conservative thinker. Revisiting the president's speech in his 2001 book, *The Death of the West*, Buchanan wrote: "Mr. Clinton assured us that it will be a better America when we are all minorities and realize true 'diversity.' Well, those students [at Portland State] are going to find out, for they will spend their golden years in a Third World America."

Today, the arrival of what Buchanan derided as "Third World America" is   13
all but inevitable. What will the new mainstream of America look like, and what ideas or values might it rally around? What will it mean to be white after "whiteness" no longer defines the mainstream? Will anyone mourn the end of white America? Will anyone try to preserve it?

Another moment from *The Great Gatsby*: as Fitzgerald's narrator and Gatsby   14
drive across the Queensboro Bridge into Manhattan, a car passes them, and Nick Carraway notices that it is a limousine "driven by a white chauffeur, in which sat three modish negroes, two bucks and a girl." The novelty of this topsy-turvy arrangement inspires Carraway to laugh aloud and think to himself, "Anything can happen now that we've slid over this bridge, anything at all . . ." For a contemporary embodiment of the upheaval that this scene portended, consider Sean Combs, a hip-hop mogul and one of the most famous African Americans on the planet. Combs grew up during hip-hop's late-1970s rise, and he belongs to the first generation that could safely make a living working in the industry—as a plucky young promoter and record-label intern in the late 1980s and early 1990s, and as a fashion designer, artist, and music executive worth hundreds of millions of dollars a brief decade later.

In the late 1990s, Combs made a fascinating gesture toward New York's high   15
society. He announced his arrival into the circles of the rich and powerful not by crashing their parties, but by inviting them into his own spectacularly over-the-top world. Combs began to stage elaborate annual parties in the Hamptons, not far from where Fitzgerald's novel takes place. These "white parties"—attendees are required to wear white—quickly became legendary for their opulence (in 2004, Combs showcased a 1776 copy of the Declaration of Independence) as well as for the cultures-colliding quality of Hamptons elites paying their respects to someone so comfortably nouveau riche. Prospective business partners angled to get close to him and praised him as a guru of the lucrative "urban" market, while grateful partygoers hailed him as a modern-day Gatsby.

"Have I read *The Great Gatsby*?" Combs said to a London newspaper in   16
2001. "I am the Great Gatsby."

Yet whereas Gatsby felt pressure to hide his status as an arriviste, Combs cel-   17
ebrated his position as an outsider-insider—someone who appropriates elements
of the culture he seeks to join without attempting to assimilate outright. In a
sense, Combs was imitating the old WASP establishment; in another sense, he
was subtly provoking it, by over-enunciating its formality and never letting his
guests forget that there was something slightly off about his presence. There's a
silent power to throwing parties where the best-dressed man in the room is also
the one whose public profile once consisted primarily of dancing in the background of Biggie Smalls videos. ("No one would ever expect a young black man
to be coming to a party with the Declaration of Independence, but I got it, and
it's coming with me," Combs joked at his 2004 party, as he made the rounds with
the document, promising not to spill champagne on it.)

In this regard, Combs is both a product and a hero of the new cultural main-   18
stream, which prizes diversity above all else, and whose ultimate goal is some
vague notion of racial transcendence, rather than subversion or assimilation.
Although Combs's vision is far from representative—not many hip-hop stars
vacation in St. Tropez with a parasol-toting manservant shading their every
step—his industry lies at the heart of this new mainstream. Over the past
30 years, few changes in American culture have been as significant as the rise of
hip-hop. The genre has radically reshaped the way we listen to and consume
music, first by opposing the pop mainstream and then by becoming it. From its
constant sampling of past styles and eras—old records, fashions, slang, anything—to its mythologization of the self-made black antihero, hip-hop is more
than a musical genre: it's a philosophy, a political statement, a way of approaching and remaking culture. It's a lingua franca not just among kids in America, but
also among young people worldwide. And its economic impact extends beyond
the music industry, to fashion, advertising, and film. (Consider the producer
Russell Simmons—the ur-Combs and a music, fashion, and television mogul—
or the rapper 50 Cent, who has parlayed his rags-to-riches story line into
extracurricular successes that include a clothing line; book, video-game, and film
deals; and a startlingly lucrative partnership with the makers of Vitamin Water.)

But hip-hop's deepest impact is symbolic. During popular music's rise in the   19
20th century, white artists and producers consistently "mainstreamed" African
American innovations. Hip-hop's ascension has been different. Eminem
notwithstanding, hip-hop never suffered through anything like an Elvis Presley
moment, in which a white artist made a musical form safe for white America.
This is no dig at Elvis—the constrictive racial logic of the 1950s demanded the
erasure of rock and roll's black roots, and if it hadn't been him, it would have

been someone else. But hip-hop—the sound of the post- civil-rights, post-soul generation—found a global audience on its own terms.

Today, hip-hop's colonization of the global imagination, from fashion run-   20
ways in Europe to dance competitions in Asia, is Disney-esque. This transformation has bred an unprecedented cultural confidence in its black originators.
Whiteness is no longer a threat, or an ideal: it's kitsch to be appropriated,
whether with gestures like Combs's "white parties" or the trickle-down epidemic
of collared shirts and cuff links currently afflicting rappers. And an expansive
multiculturalism is replacing the us-against-the-world bunker mentality that lent
a thrilling edge to hip-hop's mid-1990s rise.

Peter Rosenberg, a self-proclaimed "nerdy Jewish kid" and radio personality   21
on New York's Hot 97 FM—and a living example of how hip-hop has created
new identities for its listeners that don't fall neatly along lines of black and
white—shares another example: "I interviewed [the St. Louis rapper] Nelly this
morning, and he said it's now very cool and *in* to have multicultural friends. Like
you're not really considered hip or 'you've made it' if you're rolling with all the
same people."

Just as Tiger Woods forever changed the country-club culture of golf, and   22
Will Smith confounded stereotypes about the ideal Hollywood leading man, hip-
hop's rise is helping redefine the American mainstream, which no longer aspires
toward a single iconic image of style or class. Successful network-television shows
like *Lost, Heroes,* and *Grey's Anatomy* feature wildly diverse casts, and an entire
genre of half-hour comedy, from *The Colbert Report* to *The Office,* seems dedicated to having fun with the persona of the clueless white male. The youth market is following the same pattern: consider the Cheetah Girls, a multicultural,
multiplatinum, multiplatform trio of teenyboppers who recently starred in their
third movie, or Dora the Explorer, the precocious bilingual 7-year-old Latina
adventurer who is arguably the most successful animated character on children's
television today. In a recent address to the Association of Hispanic Advertising
Agencies, Brown Johnson, the Nickelodeon executive who has overseen Dora's
rise, explained the importance of creating a character who does not conform to
"the white, middle-class mold." When Johnson pointed out that Dora's wares
were outselling Barbie's in France, the crowd hooted in delight.

Pop culture today rallies around an ethic of multicultural inclusion that   23
seems to value every identity—except whiteness. "It's become harder for the
blond-haired, blue-eyed commercial actor," remarks Rochelle Newman-
Carrasco, of the Hispanic marketing firm Enlace. "You read casting notices, and
they like to cast people with brown hair because they could be Hispanic. The
language of casting notices is pretty shocking because it's so specific: 'Brown

hair, brown eyes, could look Hispanic.' Or, as one notice put it: 'Ethnically ambiguous.'"

"I think white people feel like they're under siege right now—like it's not okay to be white right now, especially if you're a white male," laughs Bill Imada, of the IW Group. Imada and Newman-Carrasco are part of a movement within advertising, marketing, and communications firms to reimagine the profile of the typical American consumer. (Tellingly, every person I spoke with from these industries knew the Census Bureau's projections by heart.) 24

"There's a lot of fear and a lot of resentment," Newman-Carrasco observes, describing the flak she caught after writing an article for a trade publication on the need for more-diverse hiring practices. "I got a response from a friend—he's, like, a 60-something white male, and he's been involved with multicultural recruiting," she recalls. "And he said, 'I really feel like the hunted. It's a hard time to be a white man in America right now, because I feel like I'm being lumped in with all white males in America, and I've tried to do stuff, but it's a tough time.'" 25

"I always tell the white men in the room, 'We need you,'" Imada says. "We cannot talk about diversity and inclusion and engagement without you at the table. It's okay to be white! 26

"But people are stressed out about it. 'We used to be in control! We're losing control!'" 27

If they're right—if white America is indeed "losing control," and if the future will belong to people who can successfully navigate a post-racial, multicultural landscape—then it's no surprise that many white Americans are eager to divest themselves of their whiteness entirely. 28

For some, this renunciation can take a radical form. In 1994, a young graffiti artist and activist named William "Upski" Wimsatt, the son of a university professor, published *Bomb the Suburbs*, the spiritual heir to Norman Mailer's celebratory 1957 essay, "The White Negro." Wimsatt was deeply committed to hip-hop's transformative powers, going so far as to embrace the status of the lowly "wigger," a pejorative term popularized in the early 1990s to describe white kids who steep themselves in black culture. Wimsatt viewed the wigger's immersion in two cultures as an engine for change. "If channeled in the right way," he wrote, "the wigger can go a long way toward repairing the sickness of race in America." 29

Wimsatt's painfully earnest attempts to put his own relationship with whiteness under the microscope coincided with the emergence of an academic discipline known as "whiteness studies." In colleges and universities across the country, scholars began examining the history of "whiteness" and unpacking its contradictions. Why, for example, had the Irish and the Italians fallen beyond 30 the pale at different moments in our history? Were Jewish Americans *white*? And, as the historian Matthew Frye Jacobson asked, "Why is it that in the United States, a white woman can have black children but a black woman cannot have white children?"

Much like Wimsatt, the whiteness-studies academics—figures such as   31
Jacobson, David Roediger, Eric Lott, and Noel Ignatiev—were attempting to come to terms with their own relationships with whiteness, in its past and present forms. In the early 1990s, Ignatiev, a former labor activist and the author of *How the Irish Became White*, set out to "abolish" the idea of the white race by starting the New Abolitionist Movement and founding a journal titled *Race Traitor*. "There is nothing positive about white identity," he wrote in 1998. "As James Baldwin said, 'As long as you think you're white, there's no hope for you.'"

Although most white Americans haven't read *Bomb the Suburbs* or *Race*   32
Traitor, this view of whiteness as something to be interrogated, if not shrugged off completely, has migrated to less academic spheres. The perspective of the whiteness-studies academics is commonplace now, even if the language used to express it is different.

"I get it: as a straight white male, I'm the worst thing on Earth," Christian   33
Lander says. Lander is a Canadian-born, Los Angeles–based satirist who in January 2008 started a blog called Stuff White People Like (stuffwhitepeople ike.com), which pokes fun at the manners and mores of a specific species of young, hip, upwardly mobile whites. (He has written more than 100 entries about whites' passion for things like bottled water, "the idea of soccer," and "being the only white person around.") At its best, Lander's site—which formed the basis for a recently published book of the same name (reviewed in the October 2008 *Atlantic*)—is a cunningly precise distillation of the identity crisis plaguing well-meaning, well-off white kids in a post-white world.

"Like, I'm aware of all the horrible crimes that my demographic has   34
done in the world," Lander says. "And there's a bunch of white people who are desperate—*desperate*—to say, 'You know what? My skin's white, but I'm not one of the white people who's destroying the world.'"

For Lander, whiteness has become a vacuum. The "white identity" he limns   35
on his blog is predicated on the quest for authenticity—usually other people's authenticity. "As a white person, you're just desperate to find something else to grab onto. You're jealous! Pretty much every white person I grew up with wished they'd grown up in, you know, an ethnic home that gave them a second language. White culture is *Family Ties* and Led Zeppelin and Guns N' Roses—like, this is white culture. This is all we have."

Lander's "white people" are products of a very specific historical moment,   36
raised by well-meaning Baby Boomers to reject the old ideal of white American
gentility and to embrace diversity and fluidity instead. ("It's strange that we are
the kids of Baby Boomers, right? How the hell do you rebel against that? Like,
your parents will march against the World Trade Organization next to you.
They'll have bigger white dreadlocks than you. What do you do?") But his light-
hearted anthropology suggests that the multicultural harmony they were raised
to worship has bred a kind of self-denial.

Matt Wray, a sociologist at Temple University who is a fan of Lander's   37
humor, has observed that many of his white students are plagued by a racial-
identity crisis: "They don't care about socioeconomics; they care about culture.
And to be white is to be culturally broke. The classic thing white students say
when you ask them to talk about who they are is, 'I don't have a culture.' They
might be privileged, they might be loaded socioeconomically, but they feel bank-
rupt when it comes to culture ... They feel disadvantaged, and they feel margin-
alized. They don't have a culture that's cool or oppositional." Wray says that this
feeling of being culturally bereft often prevents students from recognizing what
it means to be a child of privilege—a strange irony that the first wave of whiteness-studies scholars, in the 1990s, failed to anticipate.

Of course, the obvious material advantages that come with being born   38
white—lower infant-mortality rates and easier-to-acquire bank loans, for
example—tend to undercut any sympathy that this sense of marginalization
might generate. And in the right context, cultural-identity crises can turn
well-meaning whites into instant punch lines. Consider *ego trip's The (White)
Rapper Show*, a brilliant and critically acclaimed reality show that VH1 debuted
in 2007. It depicted 10 (mostly hapless) white rappers living together in a dilap-
idated house—dubbed "Tha White House"—in the South Bronx. Despite the
contestants' best intentions, each one seemed like a profoundly confused caricature, whether it was the solemn graduate student committed to fighting racism
or the ghetto-obsessed suburbanite who had, seemingly by accident, named himself after the abolitionist John Brown.

Similarly, Smirnoff struck marketing gold in 2006 with a viral music video   39
titled "Tea Partay," featuring a trio of strikingly bad, V-neck-sweater-clad white
rappers called the Prep Unit. "Haters like to clown our Ivy League educations /
But they're just jealous 'cause our families run the nation," the trio brayed, as a
pair of bottle-blond women in spiffy tennis whites shimmied behind them. There
was no nonironic way to enjoy the video; its entire appeal was in its self-aware
lampooning of WASP culture: verdant country clubs, "old money," croquet,
popped collars, and the like.

"The best defense is to be constantly pulling the rug out from underneath   40
yourself," Wray remarks, describing the way self-aware whites contend with their
complicated identity. "Beat people to the punch. You're forced as a white person
into a sense of ironic detachment. Irony is what fuels a lot of white subcultures.
You also see things like Burning Man, when a lot of white people are going into
the desert and trying to invent something that is entirely new and not a form of
racial mimicry. That's its own kind of flight from whiteness. We're going through
a period where whites are really trying to figure out: Who are we?"

The "flight from whiteness" of urban, college-educated, liberal whites isn't the   41
only attempt to answer this question. You can flee *into* whiteness as well. This
can mean pursuing the authenticity of an imagined past: think of the deliberately
white-bread world of Mormon America, where the '50s never ended, or the
anachronistic WASP entitlement flaunted in books like last year's *A Privileged
Life: Celebrating WASP Style*, a handsome coffee-table book compiled by Susanna
Salk, depicting a world of seersucker blazers, whale pants, and deck shoes. (What
the book celebrates is the "inability to be outdone," and the "self-confidence and
security that comes with it," Salk tells me. "That's why I call it 'privilege.' It's this
privilege of time, of heritage, of being in a place longer than anybody else.") But
these enclaves of preserved-in-amber whiteness are likely to be less important to
the American future than the construction of whiteness as a somewhat pissed-off
minority culture.

This notion of a self-consciously white expression of minority empowerment   42
will be familiar to anyone who has come across the comedian Larry the Cable
Guy—he of "Farting Jingle Bells"—or witnessed the transformation of Detroit-
born-and-bred Kid Rock from teenage rapper into "American Bad Ass"
southern-style rocker. The 1990s may have been a decade when multiculturalism
advanced dramatically—when American culture became "colorized," as the
critic Jeff Chang put it—but it was also an era when a very different form of identity politics crystallized. Hip-hop may have provided the decade's soundtrack, but
the highest-selling artist of the '90s was Garth Brooks. Michael Jordan and Tiger
Woods may have been the faces of athletic superstardom, but it was NASCAR
that emerged as professional sports' fastest-growing institution, with ratings second only to the NFL's.

As with the unexpected success of the apocalyptic Left Behind novels, or the   43
Jeff Foxworthy–organized Blue Collar Comedy Tour, the rise of country music
and auto racing took place well off the American elite's radar screen. (None of
Christian Lander's white people would be caught dead at a NASCAR race.)
These phenomena reflected a growing sense of cultural solidarity among lower-

middle-class whites—a solidarity defined by a yearning for American "authenticity," a folksy realness that rejects the global, the urban, and the effete in favor of nostalgia for "the way things used to be."

Like other forms of identity politics, white solidarity comes complete with its own folk heroes, conspiracy theories (Barack Obama is a secret Muslim! The U.S. is going to merge with Canada and Mexico!), and laundry lists of injustices. The targets and scapegoats vary—from multiculturalism and affirmative action to a loss of moral values, from immigration to an economy that no longer guarantees the American worker a fair chance—and so do the political programs they inspire. (Ross Perot and Pat Buchanan both tapped into this white identity politics in the 1990s; today, its tribunes run the ideological gamut, from Jim Webb to Ron Paul to Mike Huckabee to Sarah Palin.) But the core grievance, in each case, has to do with cultural and socioeconomic dislocation—the sense that the system that used to guarantee the white working class some stability has gone off-kilter. 44

Wray is one of the founders of what has been called "white-trash studies," a field conceived as a response to the perceived elite-liberal marginalization of the white working class. He argues that the economic downturn of the 1970s was the precondition for the formation of an "oppositional" and "defiant" white-working-class sensibility—think of the rugged, anti-everything individualism of 1977's *Smokey and the Bandit*. But those anxieties took their shape from the aftershocks of the identity-based movements of the 1960s. "I think that the political space that the civil-rights movement opens up in the mid-1950s and '60s is the transformative thing," Wray observes. "Following the black-power movement, all of the other minority groups that followed took up various forms of activism, including brown power and yellow power and red power. Of course the problem is, if you try and have a 'white power' movement, it doesn't sound good." 45

The result is a racial pride that dares not speak its name, and that defines itself through cultural cues instead—a suspicion of intellectual elites and city dwellers, a preference for folksiness and plainness of speech (whether real or feigned), and the association of a working-class white minority with "the real America." (In the Scots-Irish belt that runs from Arkansas up through West Virginia, the most common ethnic label offered to census takers is "American.") Arguably, this white identity politics helped swing the 2000 and 2004 elections, serving as the powerful counterpunch to urban white liberals, and the McCain-Palin campaign relied on it almost to the point of absurdity (as when a McCain surrogate dismissed Northern Virginia as somehow not part of "the real Virginia") as a bulwark against the threatening multiculturalism of Barack Obama. Their strategy failed, of course, but it's possible to imagine white identity politics growing more potent and more forthright in its racial identifications 46 in the future, as "the real America" becomes an ever-smaller portion of, well, the real America, and as the soon-to-be white minority's sense of being besieged and disdained by a multicultural majority grows apace.

This vision of the aggrieved white man lost in a world that no longer values   47
him was given its most vivid expression in the 1993 film *Falling Down*. Michael Douglas plays Bill Foster, a downsized defense worker with a buzz cut and a pocket protector who rampages through a Los Angeles overrun by greedy Korean shop-owners and Hispanic gangsters, railing against the eclipse of the America he used to know. (The film came out just eight years before California became the nation's first majority-minority state.) *Falling Down* ends with a soulful police officer apprehending Foster on the Santa Monica Pier, at which point the middle-class vigilante asks, almost innocently: *"I'm the bad guy?"*

But this is a nightmare vision. Of course most of America's Bill Fosters aren't the   48
bad guys—just as civilization is not, in the words of Tom Buchanan, "going to pieces" and America is not, in the phrasing of Pat Buchanan, going "Third World." The coming white minority does not mean that the racial hierarchy of American culture will suddenly become inverted, as in 1995's *White Man's Burden*, an awful thought experiment of a film, starring John Travolta, that envisions an upside-down world in which whites are subjugated to their high-class black oppressors. There will be dislocations and resentments along the way, but the demographic shifts of the next 40 years are likely to reduce the power of racial hierarchies over everyone's lives, producing a culture that's more likely than any before to treat its inhabitants as individuals, rather than members of a caste or identity group.

Consider the world of advertising and marketing, industries that set out to mold our desires at a subconscious level. Advertising strategy once assumed a   49
"general market"—"a code word for 'white people,'" jokes one ad executive—and smaller, mutually exclusive, satellite "ethnic markets." In recent years, though, advertisers have begun revising their assumptions and strategies in antic-ipation of profound demographic shifts. Instead of herding consumers toward a discrete center, the goal today is to create versatile images and campaigns that can be adapted to highly individualized tastes. (Think of the dancing silhouettes in Apple's iPod campaign, which emphasizes individuality and diversity without privileging—or even representing—any specific group.)

At the moment, we can call this the triumph of multiculturalism, or post-racialism. But just as *whiteness* has no inherent meaning—it is a vessel we fill   50
with our hopes and anxieties—these terms may prove equally empty in the long run. Does being post-racial mean that we are past race completely, or merely that race is no longer essential to how we identify ourselves? Karl Carter, of Atlanta's

youth-oriented GTM Inc. (Guerrilla Tactics Media), suggests that marketers and advertisers would be better off focusing on matrices like "lifestyle" or "culture" rather than race or ethnicity. "You'll have crazy in-depth studies of the white consumer or the Latino consumer," he complains. "But how do skaters feel? How do hip-hoppers feel?"

The logic of online social networking points in a similar direction. The New York University sociologist Dalton Conley has written of a "network nation," in which applications like Facebook and MySpace create "crosscutting social groups" and new, flexible identities that only vaguely overlap with racial identities. Perhaps this is where the future of identity after whiteness lies—in a dramatic departure from the racial logic that has defined American culture from the very beginning. What Conley, Carter, and others are describing isn't merely the displacement of whiteness from our cultural center; they're describing a social structure that treats race as just one of a seemingly infinite number of possible self-identifications. 51

FROM THE ARCHIVES:
The Freedmen's Bureau
(March 1901)

"The problem of the twentieth century is the problem of the color line . . ."
By W. E. B. Du Bois

The problem of the 20th century, W. E. B. DuBois famously predicted, would be the problem of the color line. Will this continue to be the case in the 21st century, when a black president will govern a country whose social networks increasingly cut across every conceivable line of identification? The ruling of *United States v. Bhagat Singh Thind* no longer holds weight, but its echoes have been inescapable: we aspire to be post-racial, but we still live within the structures of privilege, injustice, and racial categorization that we inherited from an older order. We can talk about defining ourselves by lifestyle rather than skin color, but our lifestyle choices are still racially coded. We know, more or less, that race is a fiction that often does more harm than good, and yet it is something we cling to without fully understanding why—as a social and legal fact, a vague sense of belonging and place that we make solid through culture and speech. 52

But maybe this is merely how it used to be—maybe this is already an outdated way of looking at things. "You have a lot of young adults going into a more diverse world," Carter remarks. For the young Americans born in the 1980s and 1990s, culture is something to be taken apart and remade in their own image. "We came along in a generation that didn't have to follow that path of race," he goes on. "We saw something *different.*" This moment was not the end of white America; it was not the end of anything. It was a bridge, and we crossed it. 53

Naomi Klein (1970–), feminist, activist, journalist, author and filmmaker, was born in Montreal, Quebec. Both her first and second books, *No Logos: Taking Aim at the Brand Bullies* (2000) and *The Shock Doctrine: The Rise of Disaster Capitalism* (2007), quickly became international best-sellers and both have been translated into over twenty-seven languages. Klein has also worked as a journalist and writer for *The Nation* and *The Guardian*. In 2004, she received the James Aronson Award for Social Justice Journalism for her reporting in Iraq for *Harper's* Magazine. Klein has also worked in film, producing the documentary *The Take* (2004), an exploration of Argentina's occupied factories, with her husband, director Avi Lewis. A former Milibrand Fellow at the London School of Economics, Klein also holds an honorary Doctor of Civil Law degree from the University of King's College, Nova Scotia.

The Branding of Learning: Ads in Schools and Universities

Naomi Klein

> A democratic system of education . . . is one of the surest ways of creating and greatly extending markets for goods of all kinds and especially those goods in which fashion may play a part.
> —Ex-adman James Rorty, *Our Master's Voice*, 1934

Although the brands seem to be everywhere—at kids' concerts, next to them on the couch, on stage with their heroes, in their on-line chat groups, and on their playing fields and basketball courts—for a long time one major unbranded youth frontier remained: a place where young people gathered, talked, sneaked smokes, made out, formed opinions and, most maddeningly of all, stood around looking cool for hours on end. That place is called school. And clearly, the brands had to get into the schools. 1

"You'll agree that the youth market is an untapped wellspring of new revenue. You'll also agree that the youth market spends the majority of each day inside the schoolhouse. Now the problem is, how do you reach that market?" asks a typically tantalizing brochure from the Fourth Annual Kid Power Marketing Conference. 2

As we have just seen, marketers and cool hunters have spent the better part of the decade hustling the brands back to high school and pouring them into the template of the teenage outlaw. Several of the most successful brands had even cast their corporate headquarters as private schools, referring to them as "campuses" and, at the Nike World Campus, nicknaming one edifice "the student 3

---

union building." Even the cool hunters are going highbrow; by the late nineties, the rage in the industry was to recast oneself less as a trendy club-hopper than as a bookish grad student. In fact, some insist they aren't cool hunters at all but rather "urban anthropologists."

And yet despite their up-to-the-minute outfits and intellectual pretensions, the brands and their keepers still found themselves on the wrong side of the school gate, a truly intolerable state of affairs and one that would not last long. American marketing consultant Jack Myers described the insufferable slight like this: "The choice we have in this country [the U.S.] is for our educational system to join the electronic age and communicate to students in ways they can understand and to which they can relate. Or our schools can continue to use outmoded forms of communications and become the daytime prisons for millions of young people, as they have become in our inner cities."[1] This reasoning, which baldly equates corporate access to the schools with access to modern technology, and by extension to the future itself, is at the core of how the brands have managed, over the course of only one decade, to all but eliminate the barrier between ads and education. It was technology that lent a new urgency to nineties chronic underfunding: at the same time as schools were facing ever-deeper budget cuts, the costs of delivering a modern education were rising steeply, forcing many educators to look to alternative funding sources for help. Swept up by info-tech hype, schools that couldn't afford up-to-date textbooks were suddenly expected to provide students with audiovisual equipment, video cameras, classroom computers, desktop publishing capacity, the latest educational software programs, Internet access—even, at some schools, video-conferencing.

As many education experts have pointed out, the pedagogical benefits technology brings to the classroom are dubious at best, but the fact remains that employers are clamoring for tech-trained graduates and chances are the private school down the street or across town is equipped with all the latest gadgets and toys. In this context, corporate partnerships and sponsorship arrangements have seemed to many public schools, particularly those in poorer areas, to be the only possible way out of the high-tech bind. If the price of staying modern is opening the schools to ads, the thinking goes, then parents and teachers will have to grin and bear it.

The fact that more schools are turning to the private sector to finance technology purchases does not mean that governments are relinquishing any role in supplying public schools with computers. Quite the opposite. A growing number of politicians are making a computer on every desk a key plank in their election platforms, albeit in partnership with local businesses. But in the process school boards are draining money out of programs like music and physical education to finance this high-tech dream—and here too they are opening the door to corporate sponsorships and to direct forms of brand promotion in cash—strapped cafeterias and sports programs.

As fast-food, athletic gear and computer companies step in to fill the gap,   7
they carry with them an educational agenda of their own. As with all branding projects, it is never enough to tag the schools with a few logos. Having gained a foothold, the brand managers are now doing what they have done in music, sports and journalism outside the schools: trying to overwhelm their host, to grab the spotlight. They are fighting for their brands to become not the add-on but the subject of education, not an elective but the core curriculum.

Of course the companies crashing the school gate have nothing against edu-   8
cation. Students should by all means learn, they say, but why don't they read about our company, write about our brand, research their own brand preferences or come up with a drawing for our next ad campaign? Teaching students and building brand awareness, these corporations seem to believe, can be two aspects of the same project. Which is where Channel One, owned by K-III Communications, and its Canadian counterpart, the Youth News Network, come in, perhaps the best-known example of in-school branding.

At the beginning of the decade, these self-styled in-school broadcasters   9
approached North American school boards with a proposition. They asked them to open their classrooms to two minutes of television advertising a day, sandwiched between twelve minutes of teenybopper current affairs programming. Many schools consented, and the broadcasts soon aired. Turning off the cheerful ad patter is not an option. Not only is the programming mandatory viewing for students, but teachers are unable to adjust the volume of the broadcast, especially during commercials. In exchange, the schools do not receive direct revenue from the stations but they can use the much-coveted audiovisual equipment for other lessons and, in some cases, receive "free" computers.

Channel One, meanwhile, charges advertisers top dollar for accessing its   10
pipeline to classrooms—twice as much as regular TV stations because, with mandatory attendance and no channel-changing or volume control, it can boast something no other broadcaster can: "No audience erosion." The station now boasts a presence in 12,000 schools, reaching an estimated eight million students.

When those students aren't watching Channel One or surfing with ZapMe!,   11
an in-school Internet browser first offered free to American schools in 1998, they may turn their attention to their textbooks—and those too may be sending out more messages to "Just Do It" or "CK Be." The Cover Concepts company sells slick ads that wrap around books to 30,000 U.S. schools, where teachers use them

instead of plastic or tinfoil as protective jackets. And when lunchtime arrives, more ads are literally on the menu at many schools. In 1997, Twentieth Century-Fox managed to get cafeteria menu items named after characters from its film *Anastasia* in forty U.S. elementary schools. Students could dine on "Rasputin Rib-B-Cue on Bartok Bun" and "Dimitri's Peanut Butter Fudge." Disney and Kellogg's have engaged in similar lunch-menu promotions through School Marketing, a company that describes itself as a "school-lunch ad agency."[2]

Competing with the menu sponsors are the fast-food chains themselves,   12
chains that go head-to-head with cafeterias in 13 percent of U.S. schools. In an arrangement that was unheard of in the eighties, companies like McDonald's and Burger King now set up kiosks in lunchrooms, which they advertise around the school. Subway supplies 767 schools wirh sandwiches; Pizza Hut corners the market in approximately 4,000 schools; and a staggering 20,000 schools participate in Taco Bell's "frozen burrito product line." A Subway sandwich guide about how to access the in-school market advises franchisees to pitch their brand-name food to school boards as a way to keep students from sneaking out at lunch hour and getting into trouble. "Look for situations where the local school board has a closed campus policy for lunch. If they do, a strong case can be made for branded product to keep the students on campus."[3] The argument works for administrators such as Bob Honson, the director of nutritional services for the Portland, Oregon, school district. "Kids come to us with brand preferences," he explains.[4]

Not all students' brand preferences, however, are accommodated with equal   13
enthusiasm. Since the fast-food outposts don't accept vouchers from kids on the federal lunch program and their food is usually twice as expensive as cafeteria fare, kids from poor families are stuck with mystery meat while their wealthier classmates lunch on Pizza Hut pizza and Big Macs. And they can't even look forward to days when the cafeteria serves pizza or cheeseburgers, since many schools have signed agreements with the chains that prohibit them from serving "generic versions" of fast-food items: no-name burgers, it seems, constitute "unfair competition."

Students may also find that brand wars are being waged over the pop   14
machine outside the gym. In Canada and the U.S., many school boards have given exclusive vending rights to the Pepsi-Cola Company in exchange for generally undisclosed lump sums. What Pepsi negotiates in return varies from district to district. In Toronto, it gets to fill the 560 public schools with its vending machines, to block the sales of Coke and other competitors, and to distribute "Pepsi Achievement Awards" and other goodies emblazoned with its logo. In communities like Cayuga, a rural Ontario tobacco-farming town, Pepsi buys the right to brand entire schools. "Pepsi—Official Soft Drink of Cayuga Secondary

School" reads the giant sign beside the road. At South Fork High School in Florida, there is a blunt, hard-sell arrangement: the school has a clause in its Pepsi contract committing the school to "make its best effort to maximize all sales opportunities for Pepsi-Cola products."[5]

Similarly bizarre and haphazard corporate promotions arrangements are   15 thrown together on college and university campuses around the world. At almost every university in North America, advertising billboards appear on campus bicycle racks, on benches, in hallways linking lecture halls, in libraries and even in bathroom stalls. Credit-card companies and long-distance phone carriers solicit students from the moment they receive their orientation-week information kit to the instant after they receive their degree; at some schools, diplomas come with an envelope stuffed with coupons, credit offers and advertising flyers. In the U.S. Barnes & Noble is rapidly replacing campus-owned bookstores, and Chapters has similar plans in Canada. Taco Bells, KFCs, Starbucks and Pizza Huts are already fixtures on university campuses, where they are often clumped together in food courts inside on-campus malls. Not surprisingly, in the U.S. and Canada the fiercest scholastic marketing battles are fought over high-school gym class and university athletics. The top high-school basketball teams have sponsorship deals with Nike and Adidas, which deck out teenagers in swoosh- and stripe-festooned shoes, warm-ups and gym bags. At the university level, Nike has sponsorship deals with more than two hundred campus athletics departments in the U.S. and twelve in Canada. As anyone familiar with college ball well knows, the standard arrangement gives the company the right to stamp the swoosh on uniforms, sports gear, official university merchandise and apparel, on stadium seats and, most important, on ad banners in full view of the cameras that televise high-profile games. Since student players can't get paid in amateur athletics, it is the coaches who receive the corporate money to dress their teams in the right logos, and the amounts at stake are huge. Nike pays individual coaches as much as $1.5 million in sponsorship fees at top sports universities like Duke and North Carolina, sums that make the coaches' salaries look like tokens of appreciation.

As educational institutions surrender to the manic march of branding, a new   16 language is emerging. Nike high schools and universities square off against their Adidas rivals: the teams may well have their own "official drink," either Coke or Pepsi. In its daily broadcasts, Channel One makes frequent references to the goings-on at "Channel One schools." William Hoynes, a sociologist at Vassar College who conducted a study on the broadcaster, says the practice is "part of a broader marketing approach to develop a 'brand name' consciousness of the network, including the promotion of the 'Channel One school' identity."[6]

As several critics have pointed out, Channel One isn't just hawking its   17
advertisers' sneakers and candy to school kids, it is also selling the idea that its
own programming is an invaluable educational aid, one that modernizes such
arid, outmoded educational resources as books and teachers. In the model
advanced by these broadcasters, the process of learning is little more than the
transferring of "stuff" to a student's brain. Whether that stuff happens to be about
a new blockbuster from Disney or the Pythagorean theorem, the net effect,
according to this theory, is the same: more stuff stuffed. So Fox's attempts to flog
Anastasia in schools didn't stop with lunch-menu ads; it also provided teachers
with an "*Anastasia* study guide." Jeffrey Godsick, Fox senior vice president of
publicity and promotion, explained that Fox was providing a service to the
schools, not the other way around. "Public school teachers are desperate for
materials that will excite the kids," he said.[7]

It's impossible to know which teachers use these branded materials in class   18
and which ones toss them away, but a report published by the U.S. Consumers
Union in 1995 "found that thousands of corporations were targeting school children or their teachers with marketing activities ranging from teaching videos, to
guidebooks, and posters to contests, product giveaways, and coupons."[8]

It will come as no surprise that it is the folks at the Nike World Campus who   19
have devised the most advanced hybrid of in-class advertisement, public relations exercise and faux teaching aid: the "Air-to-Earth" lesson kit. During the
1997–98 academic year, elementary school students in more than eight hundred
classrooms across the U.S. sat down at their desks to find that today's lesson was
building a Nike sneaker, complete with a swoosh and an endorsement from an
NBA star. Called a "despicable use of classroom time" by the National Education
Association and "the warping of education" by the Consumers Union, the make-
your-own-Nike exercise purports to raise awareness about the company's envi-
ronmentally sensitive production process. Nike's claim to greenness relies
heavily on the fact that the company recycles old sneakers to re-cover community center basketball courts, which, in a postmodern marketing spiral, it then
brands with the Nike swoosh.[9]

HEY, KIDS! BE A *SELF*-PROMOTER!

In a corporate climate obsessed with finding the secret recipe for cool, there are   20
still more in-school resources to tap. After all, if there is one thing the cool
hunters have taught us, it's that groups of kids aren't just lowly consumers: they
are also card-carrying representatives of their age demographic. In the eyes of the
brand managers, every lunchroom and classroom is a focus group waiting to be

focused. So getting access to schools means more than just hawking product—
it's a bona fide, bargain-basement cool-hunting opportunity.

For this reason, the in-school computer network ZapMe! doesn't merely sell   21
ad space to its sponsors; it also monitors students' paths as they surf the Net and
provides this valuable market research, broken down by the students' sex, age
and zip code, to its advertisers. Then, when students log on to ZapMe!, they are
treated to ads that have been specially "microtargeted" for them.[10] This kind of
detailed market research is exploding in North American schools: weekly focus
groups, taste tests, brand-preference questionnaires, opinion polls, panel discussions on the Internet, all are currently being used inside classrooms. And in a feat
of peer-on-peer cool hunting, some market researchers have been experimenting
with sending kids home from school with disposable cameras to take pictures of
their friends and family—returning with documented evidence, in one assignment conducted for Nike, "of their favorite place to hang out." Exercises like
these are "educational" and "empowering" the market researchers argue, and
some educators agree. In explaining the merits of a cereal taste test, the principal of Our Lady of Assumption elementary school in Lynnfield, Massachusetts,
said: "It's a learning experience. They had to read, they had to look, they had to
compare."[11]

Channel One is pushing the market-research model even further, frequently   22
enlisting "partner" teachers to develop class lessons in which students are asked
to create a new ad campaign for Snapple or to redesign Pepsi's vending machines.
In New York and Los Angeles high-school students have created thirty-second
animated spots for Starburst fruit candies, and students in Colorado Springs
designed Burger King ads to hang in their school buses.[12] Finished assignments
are passed on to the companies and the best entries win prizes and may even be
adopted by the companies—all subsidized by the taxpayer-funded school system.
At Vancouver's Laurier Annex school, students in Grades 3 and 4 designed two
new product lines for the British Columbia restaurant chain White Spot. For several months in 1997, the children worked on developing the concept and pack-
aging for "Zippy" pizza burgers, a product that is now on the kids' menu at White
Spot. The following year, they designed an entire concept for birthday parties to
be held at the chain. The students' corporate presentation included "sample
commercials, menu items, party games invented by the students and cake ideas,"
taking into account such issues as safety, possible food allergies, low costs "and
allowing for flexibility."[13] According to nine-year-old Jeffrey Ye, "It was a lot of
work."[14]

Perhaps the most infamous of these experiments occurred in 1998, when   23
Coca-Cola ran a competition asking several schools to come up with a strategy

for distributing Coke coupons to students. The school that devised the best pro-
motional strategy would win $500. Greenbriar High School in Evans, Georgia,
took the contest extremely seriously, calling an official Coke Day in late March
during which all students came to school in Coca-Cola T-shirts, posed for a pho-
tograph in a formation spelling Coke, attended lectures given by Coca-Cola
executives and learned about all things black and bubbly in their classes. It was
a little piece of branding heaven until it came to the principal's attention that in
an act of hideous defiance, one Mike Cameron, a nineteen-year-old senior, had
come to school wearing a T-shirt with a Pepsi logo. He was promptly suspended
for the offense. "I know it sounds bad—'Child suspended for wearing Pepsi shirt
on Coke Day,'" said principal Gloria Hamilton. "It really would have been
acceptable . . . if it had just been in-house, but we had the regional president here
and people flew in from Atlanta to do us the honor of being resource speakers.
These students knew we had guests."[15]

Though all public institutions are starved for new sources of income, most   24
schools and universities do try to set limits. When York University's Atkinson
College sent out a call to donors in 1997 stating that "for a gift of $10,000 . . .
you or your corporation can become the official sponsor for the development and
design of one of our new multi-media, high-tech courses," the college insisted
that only the courses' names were for sale—not their content. Rogel Trull, who
brokers deals with corporations at Ontario's McMaster University, explains
where he draws the line: "They have to be things that don't impact on academics," meaning only extracurricular sponsorship. Besides, many point out that
before lunchrooms and letter-man sweaters went brand-name, school weren't
exactly corporate-free turf. Advertising historian Stuart Ewen writes that as early
as the 1920s, teaching kids to consume was seen as just another way of promot-
ing patriotism and economic well-being. Back then, toothbrush companies visited American schools to conduct "toothpaste drills" and cocoa producers made
cameos in science class to demonstrate "the various stages in the production of
cocoa."[16]

And in more recent history, commercialism had already become a major part   25
of campus life before the brands even arrived. For instance, U.S. college sports is
a big business in its own right with sales of merchandise generating $2.75 billion
in 1997, a higher figure than the merchandising sales of the National Basketball
Association, Major League Baseball and the National Hockey League. And well
before the fast-food invasion, many cafeterias had already been contracted out to
companies like Marriott and Cara, which also specialize in providing airlines and
hospitals with institutional glop.

For these catering giants, however, faceless and generic was their calling   26
card—the very antithesis of branding. When the prima-donna brands arrived on
campus, they brought their preening and posturing values with them, introduc-
ing to schools new concepts like corporate image control, logo visibility, brand-
extension opportunities and the fierce protection of trade secrets. And this
collision of the dictates of academia with the dictates of branding often proves
uncomfortable. At the University of British Columbia, for instance, students
have been unable to find out what is in the text of an agreement between their
school and the Coca-Cola Company. Despite the fact that UBC is a publicly
funded institution, the soft-drink company demanded that the amount it paid for
the vending rights be kept secret for reasons of corporate competitiveness.
(Coca-Cola also refused to cooperate with requests for information for this book,
claiming that all of its campus activities—including the precise number of campuses with which it has agreements—are confidential "for competitive purposes.")

In May 1996, students and faculty at the University of Wisconsin at   27
Madison did find out what was in the text of a sponsorship deal their administration was about to sign with Reebok—and they didn't like what they discovered. The deal contained a "non-disparagement" clause that prohibited members
of the university community from criticizing the athletic gear company. The
clause stated: "During and for a reasonable time after the term, the University
will not issue any official statement that disparages Reebok. Additionally, the
University will promptly take all reasonable steps necessary to address any
remark by any University employee, agent or representative, including a Coach,
that disparages Reebok, Reebok's products or the advertising agency or others
connected with Reebok."[17] Reebok agreed to nix the demand after students and
faculty members launched an educational campaign about the company's patchy
record on labor rights in Southeast Asia. What was exceptional about the
Wisconsin clause is that the university community found out about it before the
deal was signed. This has not been the case at other universities where athletic
departments have quietly entered into multimillion-dollar deals that contained
similar gag orders. The University of Kentucky's deal with Nike, for instance, has
a clause that states that the company has the right to terminate the five-year $25
million contract if the "University disparages the Nike brand . . . or takes any
other action inconsistent with the endorsement of Nike products."[18] Nike denies
that its motivation is to stifle campus critics.[19]

Regardless of the intentions when the deals are inked, the fact is that cam-   28
pus expression is often stifled when it conflicts with the interests of a corporate
sponsor. For example, at Kent State University—one of the U.S. campuses at

which Coca-Cola has exclusive vending rights—members of the Amnesty International chapter advocated a boycott of the soft drink because Coca-Cola did business with the since-ousted Nigerian dictatorship. In April 1998, the activists made a routine application to their student council for funding to bring in a human-rights speaker from the Free Nigeria Movement. "Is he going to speak negatively about Coca-Cola?" a council member asked. "Because Coca-Cola does a lot of positive things on our campus like helping organizations and sports." The representatives from Amnesty replied that the speaker would indeed have some negative comments to make about the company's involvement in Nigeria and funding for the event was denied.[20]

On some university campuses, protests critical of a corporate sponsor have   29
been effectively blocked. In August 1996, Tennis Canada hosted the DuMaurier Tennis Open Tournament, sponsored by Imperial Tobacco, at York University. Concerned that neither a university nor a sporting event should be seen to be endorsing tobacco products, an anti-smoking group, the Grim Reaper Society, asked York for permission to pass out pamphlets to students and tournament goers near the university stadium. Susan Mann, the president of York University, refused the request, saying the school did not "normally" allow "interest groups" on campus "unless for University purposes." Activists handed out cards and leaflets to motorists at a traffic light just outside the entrance to York and, on the last day of the tournament, they staged a clever culture-jam: the leaflets they handed out were shaped like fans. Clearly amused, many of the tournament goers brought their fans inside the tennis stadium, cooling themselves off with anti-tobacco slogans. After a few hours, police officers hired by the tournament approached the peaceful, off-site protest and, citing traffic problems, ticketed two of the activists and seized all the remaining fans.

These are extreme examples of how corporate sponsorship deals re-engineer   30
some of the fundamental values of public universities, including financial transparency and the right to open debate and peaceful protest on campus. But the subtle effects are equally disturbing. Many professors speak of the slow encroachment of the mall mentality, arguing that the more campuses act and look like malls, the more students behave like consumers. They tell stories of students filling out their course-evaluation forms with all the smug self-righteousness of a tourist responding to a customer-satisfaction form at a large hotel chain. "Most of all I dislike the attitude of calm consumer expertise that pervades the responses. I'm disturbed by the serene belief that my function—and more important, Freud's, or Shakespeare's, or Blake's—is to divert, entertain, and interest," writes University of Virginia professor Mark Edmundson in *Harper's* magazine.[21]

A professor at Toronto's York University, where there is a full-fledged mall on campus, tells me that his students slip into class slurping grande lattes, chat in the back and slip out. They're cruising, shopping, disengaged.

BRANDING U

While brands slowly transform the experience of campus life for undergraduates, another kind of takeover is under way at the institutional research level. All over the world, university campuses are offering their research facilities, and priceless academic credibility, for the brands to use as they please. And in North America today, corporate research partnerships at universities are used for everything: designing new Nike skates, developing more efficient oil extraction techniques for Shell, assessing the Asian market's stability for Disney, testing the consumer demand for higher bandwidth for Bell or measuring the relative merits of a brand-name drug compared with a generic one, to name just a few examples.

Dr. Betty Dong, a medical researcher at the University of California at San Francisco (UCSF), had the misfortune of taking on that last assignment—testing a brand-name drug with brand-name money. Dong was the director of a study sponsored by the British pharmaceutical company Boots (now called Knoll) and UCSF. The fate of that partnership does much to illuminate precisely how the mandate of universities as sites for public-interest research is often squarely at odds with the interests of branded fact-finding missions.

Dr. Dong's study compared the effectiveness of Boots' thyroid drug, Synthroid, with a generic competitor. The company hoped that the research would prove that its much higher priced drug was better or at least substantially different from the generic one—a claim that, if legitimized by a study from a respected university, would increase Synthroid sales. Instead, Dr. Dong found that the opposite was true. The two drugs were bio-equivalent, a fact that represented a potential saving of $365 million a year for the eight million Americans who were taking the name-brand drug, and a potential loss to Boots of $600 million (the revenue from Synthroid). After the results were reviewed by her peers, Dr. Dong's findings were slated to be published in the *Journal of the American Medical Association* on January 25, 1995. At the last minute, however, Boots successfully halted publication of the article, pointing to a clause in the partnership contract that gave the company veto rights over the publication of findings. The university, fearing a costly lawsuit, sided with the drug company and the article was yanked. After the whole ordeal was exposed in *The Wall Street Journal*, Boots backed off and the paper was finally published in April 1997, two years behind schedule.[22] "The victim is obvious: the university," wrote Dorothy S. Zinberg, a faculty member at Harvard's Center fot Science and International Affairs. "Each

31

32

33

infringement on its unwritten contract with society to avoid secrecy whenever possible and maintain its independence from government or corporate pressure weakens its integrity."[23]

In 1998, a similar case ripped through the University of Toronto and the affiliated Hospital for Sick Children—only this time, the researcher found that the drug being tested might actually be harmful to patients. Dr. Nancy Olivieri, a world-renowned scientist and expert on the blood disorder thalassemia, entered into a research contract with the drug-company giant Apotex. The company wanted Olivieri to test the effectiveness of the drug deferiprone on her young patients suffering from thalassemia major. When Olivieri found evidence that, in some cases, the drug might have life-threatening side effects, she wanted to warn the patients participating in the trial and to alert other doctors in her field. Apotex pulled the plug on the study and threatened to sue Olivieri if she went public, pointing to an overlooked clause in the research contract that gave it the right to suppress findings for one year after the trials ended. Olivieri went ahead and published in *The New England Journal of Medicine* and, once again, the administration of both her university and her hospital failed to defend the sanctity of academic research conducted in the public interest. Adding further insult, in January 1999, they demoted Olivieri from her top-level research position at the hospital.[24] (After a long and public battle, the doctor eventually got her job back.)

Perhaps the most chilling of these cases involves an associate professor at Brown University in Rhode Island, who worked as an occupational health physician at the university-affiliated Memorial Hospital of Rhode Island in Pawtucket. Dr. David Kern was commissioned by a local textile factory to investigate two cases of lung disease that he had treated at the hospital. He found six more cases of the disease in the 150-person plant, a startling occurrence since its incidence in the general population is one in 40,000. Like Dr. Dong and Dr. Olivieri, Dr. Kern was set to present a paper on his finding~ when the textile company threatened to sue, citing a clause in the agreement that prevented the publication of "trade secrets." Once again, the university and the hospital administration sided squarely with the company, forbidding Dr. Kern to publish his findings and shutting down the one-person clinic where he conducted his research.[25]

The only element out of the ordinary in these three cases of stifled research is that they involved academics with the personal integrity and the dogged tenacity to publicly challenge their corporate "partners" and their own employers— factors that eventually led to the truth coming out through the press. But relying on crusading individuals to protect the integrity of academic research does not provide a foolproof safeguard in every case. According to a 1994 study conducted on industry research partnerships at U.S. universities, most corporate interference occurs quietly and with no protest. The study found that companies maintained the right to block the publication of findings in 35 percent of cases, while 53 percent of the academics surveyed agreed that "publication can be delayed."[26]

> Kmart's attitude always has been: What did we get from you this year? . . . Many people at Kmart thought I was employed by Kmart.
>
> —J. Patrick Kelly, Kmart Chair of Marketing at Wayne State University,
> *The Chronicle of Higher Education*, April 1998

There is also a more insidious level of interference that takes place at universities every day, interference that occurs before research even begins, prior, even, to proposals being committed to paper. As John V. Lombardi, president of the University of Florida at Gainesville, says: "We have taken the great leap forward and said: 'Let's pretend we're a corporation.'"[27] What such a leap means back on the ground is that studies are designed to fit the mandate of corporate-endowed research chairs with such grand names as the Taco Bell Distinguished Professor of Hotel and Restaurant Administration at Washington State University, the Yahoo! Chair of Information-Systems Technology at Stanford University and the Lego Professorship of Learning Research at Massachusetts Institute of Technology. J. Patrick Kelly, the professor who holds the Kmart Chair of Marketing at Wayne State, estimates that his research has saved Kmart "many more times" the amount of the $2 million donation that created his position.[28] The professor who holds the Kmart-endowed chair at West Virginia University, meanwhile, has such a hands-on relationship with the retailer that he or she is required by contract to spend a minimum of thirty days a year training assistant managers.

WHERE WAS THE OPPOSITION?

Many people, upon learning of the advanced stage of branded education, want to know where the university faculty, teachers, school boards and parents were while this transformation was taking place. At the elementary and high-school level, this is a difficult question to answer—particularly since one is hard-pressed to find anyone but the advertisers who is actively *in favor* of allowing ads into schools. Over the course of the decade, all the large teachers' unions in North America have been quite vocal about the threat to independent instruction posed by commercialization, and many concerned parents have formed groups like Ralph Nader's Commercial Alert to make their opposition heard. Despite this, however, there was never one big issue on which parents and educators could band together to fight—and possibly win—a major policy battle on classroom commercialization.

Unlike the very public standoffs over prayer in schools or over explicit sex   39
education, the move to allow advertisements did not take the form of one sweeping decision but, rather, of thousands of little ones. Usually these were made on
an ad hoc, school-by-school basis, frequently with no debate, no notice, no public scrutiny at all, because advertising agencies were careful to fashion school promotions that could slip between the cracks of standard school-board regulations.

However, when Channel One and the Youth News Network wanted to   40
bring ads directly into classrooms, there *was* some debate: genuine, heated discussions took place at the school-board level, and most boards across Canada
decided to block YNN. Channel One, though far more successful, particularly in
poorer districts, has also had to swallow its share of board refusals.

There is, however, another, more ingrained cultural factor that has helped   41
the brands get inside the schools, and it has to do with the effectiveness of branding itself. Many parents and educators could not see anything to be gained by
resistance; kids today are so bombarded by brand names that it seemed as if protecting educational spaces from commercialization was less important than the
immediate benefits of finding new funding sources. And the hawkers of in-school
advertising have not been at all shy about playing upon this sense of futility
among parents and educators. As Frank Vigil, president of ZapMe! computer systems, says: "America's youth is exposed to advertising in many aspects of their
lives. We believe students are savvy enough to discern between educational content and marketing materials."[29] Thus it became possible for many parents and
teachers to rationalize their failure to protect yet another previously public space
by telling themselves that what ads students don't see in class or on campus, they
will certainly catch on the subway, on the Net or on TV when they get home.
What's one more ad in the life of these marked-up and marked-down kids? And
then again . . . what's another?

But while this may explain the brands' inroads in high schools, it still   42
doesn't explain how this process has been able to take such a firm hold on the
university campuses. Why have university professors remained silent, passively
allowing their corporate "partners" to trample the principles of freedom of
inquiry and discourse that have been the avowed centerpieces of academic life?
More to the point, aren't our campuses supposed to be overflowing with trouble-
making tenured radicals? Isn't the institution of tenure, with its lifelong promise
of job security, designed to make it safe for academics to take controversial positions without fear of repercussion? Aren't these people, to borrow a term more
readily understood in the halls of academe, *counter-hegemonic*?

As Janice Newson, a York University sociology professor who has published   43
widely on this issue, has noted: "On the surface, it is easier to account for the

increasing realization of the corporate-linked university than it is to account for the lack of resistance to it." Newson, who has been sounding the alarm on the corporate threat to academic freedom for more than a decade, writes that she had (wrongly) assumed that

> members of the academic community would become actively concerned about, if not resistant to, this shift in direction. After all, a significant if not transformative pattern of institutional change has occurred over a relatively short period of time. And in many ways, these changes sharply contrast to both the idea and the practices of the university that preceded them, the university in which most current members of the academy began their careers.[30]

Newson's critique could well be expanded to include student activists, who until the mid-nineties were also mysteriously absent from the corporatization non-debate. Sadly, part of the explanation for the lack of campus mobilization is simple self-interest. Until the mid-nineties, the growing corporate influence in education and research seemed to be taking place almost exclusively in the engineering departments, management schools and science labs. Campus radicals had always been prone to dismiss these faculties as hopelessly compromised right-wing bastions: who cared what was happening on that side of campus, so long as the more traditionally progressive fields (literature, cultural studies, political science, history and fine arts) were left alone? And as long as professors and students in the arts and humanities remained indifferent to this radical shift in campus culture and priorities, they were free to pursue other interests—and there were many on offer. For instance, more than a few of those tenured radicals who were supposed to be corrupting young minds with socialist ideas were preoccupied with their own post modernist realization that truth itself is a construct. This realization made it intellectually untenable for many academics to even participate in a political argument that would have "privileged" any one model of learning (public) over another (corporate). And since truth is relative, who is to say that Plato's dialogues are any more of an "authority" than Fox's *Anastasia*?

This academic trend only accounts for a few of the missing-in-actions, however. Many other campus radicals were still up for a good old political fight, but during the key years of the corporate campus invasion they were tied up in a different battle: the all-consuming gender and race debates of the so-called political correctness wars. As we will see in the next chapter, if the students allowed themselves to be turned into test markets, it was partly because they had other things on their minds. They were busy taking on their professors on the merits of the canon and the need for more stringent campus sexual-harassment policies. And if their professors failed to prevent the very principles of unfettered academic discourse from being traded in for a quick buck, this may also have been because they were too preoccupied with defending themselves against their own "McCarthyite" students. So there they all were, fighting about women's studies and the latest backlash book while their campuses were being sold out from under their feet. It wasn't until the politics of personal representation were themselves co-opted by branding that students and professors alike began to turn away from their quarrels with each other, realizing they had a more powerful foe.

But by then, much had already been lost. More fundamentally than some-   45
what antiquated notions of "pure" education and research, what is lost as schools "pretend they are corporations" (to borrow a phrase from the University of Florida) is the very idea of unbranded space. In many ways, schools and universities remain our culture's most tangible embodiment of public space and collective responsibility. University campuses in particular—with their residences, libraries, green spaces and common standards for open and respectful discourse—play a crucial, if now largely symbolic, role: they are the one place left where young people can see a genuine public life being lived. And however imperfectly we may have protected these institutions in the past, at this point in our history the argument against transforming education into a brand-extension exercise is much the same as the one for national parks and nature reserves: these quasi-sacred spaces remind us that unbranded space is still possible.

ENDNOTES

1. Myers, *Abashing*, 151.
2. *Wall Street Journal*, 24 November 1998.
3. "A La Carte Service in the School Lunch Program," fact sheet prepared for Subway by Giuffrida Associates, Washington, D.C.
4. *Wall Street Journal*, 15 September 1997.
5. The Center for Commercial-Free Public Education, Oakland, California, 9 October 1997 release.
6. *Extra! The magazine of Fairness and Accuracy in Reporting*, May/June 1997 10, no. 3.
7. *Wall Street Journal*, 24 November 1997, B1.
8. "Captive Kids: Commercial Pressures on Kids at School" Consumers Union paper, 1995.
9. Josh Feit, "Nike in the Classroom: Nike's effort to teach kids about treading lightly on Mother Nature meet with skepticism from educators and consumer watchdogs," *Willamette Week*, 15 April 1998.
10. "ZapMe! Sparks Battle Over Ads," Associated Press, 6 December 1998.
11. "Schools Profit from Offering Pupils for Market Research," *New York Times*, 5 April 1999.

12. *Advertising Age*, 14 August 1995.
13. Kim Bolan, *Vancouver Sun*, 20 June 1998, B5.
14. Ibid.
15. Associated Press, 25 March 1998.
16. Stuart Ewen, *Captains of Consciousness* (New York: McGraw-Hill, 1976), 90.
17. *Wisconsin State Journal*, 21 May 1996.
18. *Kentucky Gazette*, 17 June 1997.
19. Associated Press, 13 April 1996.
20. Both quotations come from personal interviews with participants in the Kent State incident.
21. Mark Edmundson, *Harper's*, September 1997.
22. *Science*, vol. 273, 26 July 1996, and *Science*, vol. 276, 25 April 1997.
23. "A Cautionary Tale," *Science*, vol. 273.
24. Michael Valpy. "Science Friction," *Elm Street*, December 1998.
25. *Science*, vol. 276, 25 April 1997.
26. W. Cohen, R. Florida, W.R. Goe, "University-Industry Research Centers in the United States" (Pittsburgh: Carnegie Mellon University Press, 1994).
27. *Business Week*, 22 December 1947.
28. Julianne Basinger, "Increase in Number of Chairs Endowed by Corporations Prompt New Concerns," *Chronicle of Higher Education*, 24 April 1998, A51.
29. "ZapMe! Invites Ralph Nader Back to School," PR Newswire, 10 December 1998.
30. Janice Newson, "Technical Fixes and Other Priorities of the Corporate Linked University: The Humanists' Challenge," paper presented to the Humanities Research Group of the University of Windsor, October 1995.

Steven **D. Levitt** (1967–) is an American economist. His book, *Freakonomics: Rogue Economist Explores the Hidden Side of Everything* (co-authored with Stephen J. Dubner, 2005), became an international best-seller. The success of *Freakonomics* spawned its sequel, *Superfreakonomics: Global Cooling, Patriotic Prostitutes and Why Suicide Bombers Should Buy Life Insurance* (2009), which also became an immediate sensation. Prior to the *Freakonomics* franchise, Levitt was already quite successful. In 2003, he was awarded the John Bates Clark Medal, given bi-annually to the most promising U.S. economist under forty years old. Levitt is also known for his work on crime, especially for his argument that the legalization of abortion in 1973 led to a reduction in crime. Levitt proposed that this drop in crime was attributable to fewer unwanted children being born. For his body of work, *Time* Magazine named him one of its "100 People Who Shape the World" in 2006. A graduate of both Harvard and M.I.T., Levitt is currently the William B. Ogden Distinguished Service Professor of Economics at the University of Chicago and is also the Director of The Becker Center on Price Theory at the University of Chicago's Booth School of Business.

Stephen **J. Dubner** (1963–) is a journalist and writer who co-authored the international best-seller *Freakonomics: Rogue Economist Explores the Hidden Side of Everything* (2005) with Steven D. Levitt. A graduate of Appalachian State University (1984), Dubner was an editor and writer for the *New York Times Magazine* from 1994–1999. He has also written for the *New Yorker* and the *Washington Post*, is a correspondent for PBS and a regular contributor to ABC News. Dubner lives in New York City with his wife and five children.

What Do Schoolteachers and Sumo Wrestlers Have In Common?

Steven D. Levitt and Stephen J. Dubner

Imagine for a moment that you are the manager of a day-care center. You have 1
a clearly stated policy that children are supposed to be picked up by 4 p.m. But very often parents are late. The result: at day's end, you have some anxious children and at least one teacher who must wait around for the parents to arrive. What to do?

A pair of economists who heard of this dilemma—it turned out to be a 2
rather common one—offered a solution: fine the tardy parents. Why, after all, should the day-care center take care of these kids for free?

The economists decided to test their solution by conducting a study of ten 3
day-care centers in Haifa, Israel. The study lasted twenty weeks, but the fine was

---

not introduced immediately. For the first four weeks, the economists simply kept track of the number of parents who came late; there were, on average, eight late pickups per week per day-care center. In the fifth week, the fine was enacted. It was announced that any parent arriving more than ten minutes late would pay $3 per child for each incident. The fee would be added to the parents' monthly bill, which was roughly $380.

After the fine was enacted, the number of late pickups promptly went . . .   4
up. Before long there were twenty late pickups per week, more than double the original average. The incentive had plainly backfired.

Economics is, at root, the study of incentives: how people get what they   5
want, or need, especially when other people want or need the same thing. Economists love incentives. They love to dream them up and enact them, study them and tinker with them. The typical economist believes the world has not yet invented a problem that he cannot fix if given a free hand to design the proper incentive scheme. His solution may not always be pretty—it may involve coercion or exorbitant penalties or the violation of civil liberties—but the original problem, rest assured, will be fixed. An incentive is a bullet, a lever, a key: an often tiny object with astonishing power to change a situation.

We all learn to respond to incentives, negative and positive, from the outset   6
of life. If you toddle over to the hot stove and touch it, you burn a finger. But if you bring home straight A's from school you get a new bike. If you are spotted picking your nose in class, you get ridiculed. But if you make the basketball team, you move up the social ladder. If you break curfew, you get grounded. But if you ace your SATs, you get to go to a good college. If you flunk out of law school, you have to go to work at your father's insurance company. But if you perform so well that a rival company comes calling, you become a vice president and no longer have to work for your father. If you become so excited about your new vice president job that you drive home at eighty mph, you get pulled over by the police and fined $100. But if you hit your sales projections and collect a year-end bonus, you not only aren't worried about the $100 ticket but can also afford to buy that Viking range you've always wanted—and on which your toddler can now burn her own finger.

An incentive is simply a means of urging people to do more of a good thing   7
and less of a bad thing. But most incentives don't come about organically. Someone—an economist or a politician or a parent—has to invent them. Your three-year-old eats all her vegetables for a week? She wins a trip to the toy store.

A big steel maker belches too much smoke into the air? The company is fined for each cubic foot of pollutants over the legal limit. Too many Americans aren't paying their share of income tax? It was the economist Milton Friedman who helped come up with a solution to this one: automatic tax withholding from employees' paychecks.

There are three basic flavors of incentive: economic, social, and moral. Very often a single incentive scheme will include all three varieties. Think about the anti-smoking campaign of recent years. The addition of a $3-per-pack "sin tax" is a strong economic incentive against buying cigarettes. The banning of cigarettes in restaurants and bars is a powerful social incentive. And when the U.S. government asserts that terrorists raise money by selling black-market cigarettes, that acts as a rather jarring moral incentive. 8

Some of the most compelling incentives yet invented have been put in place to deter crime. Considering this fact, it might be worthwhile to take a familiar question—why is there so much crime in modern society?—and stand it on its head: why isn't there a lot *more* crime? 9

After all, every one of us regularly passes up opportunities to maim, steal, and defraud. The chance of going to jail—thereby losing your job, your house, and your freedom, all of which are essentially economic penalties—is certainly a strong incentive. But when it comes to crime, people also respond to moral incentives (they don't want to do something they consider wrong) and social incentives (they don't want to be seen by others as doing something wrong). For certain types of misbehavior, social incentives are terribly powerful. In an echo of Hester Prynne's scarlet letter, many American cities now fight prostitution with a "shaming" offensive, posting pictures of convicted johns (and prostitutes) on websites or on local-access television. Which is a more horrifying deterrent: a $500 fine for soliciting a prostitute or the thought of your friends and family ogling you on www.HookersAndJohns.com. 10

So through a complicated, haphazard, and constantly readjusted web of economic, social and moral incentives, modern society does its best to militate against crime. Some people would argue that we don't do a very good job. But taking the long view, that is clearly not true. Consider the historical trend in homicide (not including wars), which is both the most reliably measured crime and the best barometer of a society's overall crime rate. These statistics, compiled by the criminologist Manuel Eisner, track the historical homicide levels in five European regions. 11

HOMICIDES

(per 100,000 People)

	England	Netherlands and Belgium	Scandinavia	Germany and Switzerland	Italy
13th and 14th c.	23.0	47.0	n.a.	37.0	56.0
15th c.	n.a.	45.0	46.0	16.0	73.0
16th c.	7.0	25.0	21.0	11.0	47.0
17th c.	5.0	7.5	18.0	7.0	32.0
18th c.	1.5	5.5	1.9	7.5	10.5
19th c.	1.7	1.6	1.1	2.8	12.6
1900–1949	0.8	1.5	0.7	1.7	3.2
1950–1994	0.9	0.9	0.9	1.0	1.5

The steep decline of these numbers over the centuries suggests that, for one of the gravest human concerns—getting murdered—the incentives that we collectively cook up are working better and better. 12

So what was wrong with the incentive at the Israeli day-care centers? 13

You have probably already guessed that the $3 fine was simply too small. For that price, a parent with one child could afford to be late every day and only pay an extra $60 each month—just one-sixth of the base fee. As babysitting goes, that's pretty cheap. What if the fine had been set at $100 instead of $3? That would have likely put an end to the late pickups, though it would have also engendered plenty of ill will. (Any incentive is inherently a trade-off; the trick is to balance the extremes.) 14

But there was another problem with the day-care center fine. It substituted an economic incentive (the $3 penalty) for a moral incentive (the guilt that parents were supposed to feel when they came late). For just a few dollars each day, parents could buy off their guilt. Furthermore, the small size of the fine sent a signal to the parents that late pickups weren't such a big problem. If the day-care center suffers only $3 worth of pain for each late pickup, why bother to cut short the tennis game? Indeed, when the economists eliminated the $3 fine in the seventeenth week of their study, the number of late-arriving parents didn't change. Now they could arrive late, pay no fine, *and* feel no guilt. 15

Such is the strange and powerful nature of incentives. A slight tweak can produce drastic and often unforeseen results. Thomas Jefferson noted this while reflecting on the tiny incentive that led to the Boston Tea Party and, in turn, the American Revolution: "So inscrutable is the arrangement of causes and consequences in this world that a two-penny duty on tea, unjustly imposed in a sequestered part of it, changes the condition of all its inhabitants." 16

In the 1970s, researchers conducted a study that, like the Israeli day-care   17
study, pitted a moral incentive against an economic incentive. In this case, they
wanted to learn about the motivation behind blood donations. Their discovery:
when people are given a small stipend for donating blood rather than simply
being praised for their altruism, they tend to donate *less* blood. The stipend
turned a noble act of charity into a painful way to make a few dollars, and it
wasn't worth it.

What if the blood donors had been offered an incentive of $50, or $500, or   18
$5,000? Surely the number of donors would have changed dramatically.

But something else would have changed dramatically as well, for every   19
incentive has its dark side. If a pint of blood were suddenly worth $5,000, you
can be sure that plenty of people would take note. They might literally steal
blood at knifepoint. They might pass off pig blood as their own. They might cir-
cumvent donation limits by using fake IDs. Whatever the incentive, whatever
the situation, dishonest people will try to gain an advantage by whatever means
necessary.

Or, as W. C. Fields once said; a thing worth having is a thing worth cheat-   20
ing for.

Who cheats?   21

Well, just about anyone, if the stakes are right. You might say to yourself, *I*   22
don't cheat, regardless of the stakes. And then you might remember the time you
cheated on, say, a board game. Last week. Or the golf ball you nudged out of
its bad lie. Or the time you really wanted a bagel in the office break room but
couldn't come up with the dollar you were supposed to drop in the coffee can.
And then took the bagel anyway. And told yourself you'd pay double the next
time. And didn't.

For every clever person who goes to the trouble of creating an incentive   23
scheme, there is an army of people, clever and otherwise, who will inevitably
spend even more time trying to beat it. Cheating may or may not be human
nature, but it is certainly a prominent feature in just about every human
endeavor. Cheating is a primordial economic act: getting more for less. So it isn't
just the boldface names—inside-trading CEOs and pill-popping ballplayers and
perk-abusing politicians—who cheat. It is the waitress who pockets her tips
instead of pooling them. It is the Wal-Mart payroll manager who goes into the
computer and shaves his employees' hours to make his own performance look
better. It is the third grader who, worried about not making it to the fourth grade,
copies test answers from the kid sitting next to him.

Some cheating leaves barely a shadow of evidence. In other cases, the evidence is massive. Consider what happened one spring evening at midnight in 1987: seven million American children suddenly disappeared. The worst kidnapping wave in history? Hardly. It was the night of April 15, and the Internal Revenue Service had just changed a rule. Instead of merely listing each dependent child, tax filers were now required to provide a Social Security number for each child. Suddenly, seven million children—children who had existed only as phantom exemptions on the previous year's 1040 forms—vanished representing about one in ten of all dependent children in the United States. 24

The incentive for those cheating taxpayers was quite clear. The same for the waitress, the payroll manager, and the third grader. But what about that third grader's *teacher*? Might she have an incentive to cheat? And if so, how would she do it? 25

Imagine now that instead of running a day-care center in Haifa you are running the Chicago Public Schools, a system that educates 400,000 students each year. 26

The most volatile current debate among American school administrators, teachers, parents, and students concerns "high-stakes" testing. The stakes are considered high because instead of simply testing students to measure their progress, schools are increasingly held accountable for the results. 27

The federal government mandated high-stakes testing as part of the No Child Left Behind law, signed by President Bush in 2002. But even before that law, most states gave annual standardized tests to students in elementary and secondary school. Twenty states rewarded individual schools for good test scores or dramatic improvement; thirty-two states sanctioned the schools that didn't do well. 28

The Chicago Public School system embraced high-stakes testing in 1996. Under the new policy, a school with low reading scores would be placed on probation and face the threat of being shut down, its staff to be dismissed or reassigned. The CPS also did away with what is known as social promotion. In the past, only a dramatically inept or difficult student was held back a grade. Now, in order to be promoted, every student in third, sixth, and eighth grade had to manage a minimum score on the standardized, multiple-choice exam known as the Iowa Test of Basic Skills. 29

Advocates of high-stakes testing argue that it raises the standards of learning and gives students more incentive to study. Also, if the test prevents poor students from advancing without merit, they won't clog up the higher grades and slow down good students. Opponents, meanwhile, worry that certain students 30 will be unfairly penalized if they don't happen to test well, and that teachers may concentrate on the test topics at the exclusion of more important lessons.

Schoolchildren, of course, have had incentive to cheat for as long as there have been tests. But high-stakes testing has so radically changed the incentives for teachers that they too now have added reason to cheat. With high-stakes testing, a teacher whose students test poorly can be censured or passed over for a raise or promotion. If the entire school does poorly, federal funding can be withheld; if the school is put on probation, the teacher stands to be fired. High-stakes testing also presents teachers with some positive incentives. If her students do well enough, she might find herself praised, promoted, and even richer: the state of California at one point introduced bonuses of $25,000 for teachers who produced big test-score gains. 31

And if a teacher were to survey this newly incentivized landscape and consider somehow inflating her students' scores, she just might be persuaded by one final incentive: teacher cheating is rarely looked for, hardly ever detected, and just about never punished. 32

How might a teacher go about cheating? There are any number of possibilities, from the brazen to the sophisticated. A fifth-grade student in Oakland recently came home from school and gaily told her mother that her super-nice teacher had written the answers to the state exam right there on the chalkboard. Such instances are certainly rare, for placing your fate in the hands of thirty prepubescent witnesses doesn't seem like a risk that even the worst teacher would take. (The Oakland teacher was duly fired.) There are more subtle ways to inflate students' scores. A teacher can simply give students extra time to complete the test. If she obtains a copy of the exam early—that is, illegitimately—she can prepare them for specific questions. More broadly, she can "teach to the test," basing her lesson plans on questions from past years' exams, which isn't considered cheating but certainly violates the spirit of the test. Since these tests all have multiple-choice answers, with no penalty for wrong guesses, a teacher might instruct her students to randomly fill in every blank as the clock is winding down, perhaps inserting a long string of Bs or an alternating pattern of Bs and Cs. She might even fill in the blanks for them after they've left the room. 33

But if a teacher *really* wanted to cheat—and make it worth her while—she might collect her students' answer sheets and, in the hour or so before turning them in to be read by an electronic scanner, erase the wrong answers and fill in correct ones. (And you always thought that no. 2 pencil was for the *children* to change their answers.) If this kind of teacher cheating is truly going on, how might it be detected? 34

To catch a cheater, it helps to think like one. If you were willing to erase   35
your students' wrong answers and fill in correct ones, you probably wouldn't want
to change too many wrong answers. That would clearly be a tip-off. You probably wouldn't even want to change answers on every student's test—another tip-   /
off. Nor, in all likelihood, would you have enough time, because the answer
sheets are turned in soon after the test is over. So what you might do is select a
string of eight or ten consecutive questions and fill in the correct answers for, say,
one-half or two-thirds of your students. You could easily memorize a short pattern of correct answers, and it would be a lot faster to erase and change that pattern than to go through each student's answer sheet individually. You might even
think to focus your activity toward the end of the test, where the questions tend
to be harder than the earlier questions. In that way, you'd be most likely to substitute correct answers for wrong ones.

If economics is a science primarily concerned with incentives, it is also—   36
fortunately—a science with statistical tools to measure how people respond to
those incentives. All you need are some data.

In this case, the Chicago Public School system obliged. It made available a   37
database of the test answers for every CPS student from third grade through seventh grade from 1993 to 2000. This amounts to roughly 30,000 students per
grade per year, more than 700,000 sets of test answers, and nearly 100 million
individual answers. The data, organized by classroom, included each student's
question-by-question answer strings for reading and math tests. (The actual
paper answer sheets were not included; they were habitually shredded soon after
a test.) The data also included some information about each teacher and demographic information for every student, as well as his or her past and future test
scores—which would prove a key element in detecting the teacher cheating.

Now it was time to construct an algorithm that could tease some conclusions   38
from this mass of data. What might a cheating teacher's classroom look like?

The first thing to search for would be unusual answer patterns in a given   39
classroom: blocks of identical answers, for instance, especially among the harder
questions. If ten very bright students (as indicated by past and future test scores)
gave correct answers to the exam's first five questions (typically the easiest ones),
such an identical block shouldn't be considered suspicious. But if ten poor students gave correct answers to the *last* five questions on the exam (the hardest
ones) that's worth looking into. Another red flag would be a strange pattern
within anyone student's exam—such as getting the hard questions right while
missing the easy ones—especially when measured against the thousands of students in other classrooms who scored similarly on the same test. Furthermore, the
algorithm would seek out a classroom full of students who performed far better

than their past scores would have predicted and who then went on to score significantly lower the following year. A dramatic one-year spike in test scores might initially be attributed to a *good* teacher; but with a dramatic fall to follow, there's a strong likelihood that the spike was brought about by artificial means. [Analysis of cheating in Chicago Public Schools]

Consider now the answer strings from the students in two sixth-grade   40
Chicago classrooms who took the identical math test. Each horizontal row represents one student's answers. The letter a, b, c, or d indicates a correct answer; a number indicates a wrong answer, with 1 corresponding to a, 2 corresponding to b, and so on. A zero represents an answer that was left blank. One of these classrooms almost certainly had a cheating teacher and the other did not. Try to tell the difference—although be forewarned that it's not easy with the naked eye.

. . .

If it strikes you as disgraceful that Chicago schoolteachers and University of   41
Georgia professors will cheat—a teacher, after all, is meant to instill values along with the facts—then the thought of cheating among sumo wrestlers may also be deeply disturbing. In Japan, sumo is not only the national sport but also a repository of the country's religious, military, and historical emotion. With its purification rituals and its imperial roots, sumo is sacrosanct in a way that American sports can never be. Indeed, sumo is said to be less about competition than about honor itself.

It is true that sports and cheating go hand in hand. That's because cheating   42
is more common in the face of a bright-line incentive (the line between winning and losing, for instance) than with a murky incentive. Olympic sprinters and weightlifters, cyclists in the Tour de France, football linemen and baseball sluggers: they have all been shown to swallow whatever pill or powder may give them an edge. It is not only the participants who cheat. Cagey baseball managers try to steal an opponent's signs. In the 2002 Winter Olympic figure-skating competition, a French judge and a Russian judge were caught trying to swap votes to make sure their skaters medaled. (The man accused of orchestrating the vote swap, a reputed Russian mob boss named Alimzhan Tokhtakhounov, was also suspected of rigging beauty pageants in Moscow.)

An athlete who gets caught cheating is generally condemned, but most fans   43
at least appreciate his motive: he wanted so badly to win that he bent the rules. (As the baseball player Mark Grace once said, "If you're not cheating, you're not trying.") An athlete who cheats *to lose*, meanwhile, is consigned to a deep circle of sporting hell. The 1919 Chicago White Sox, who conspired with gamblers to throw the World Series (and are therefore known forever as the Black Sox), retain a stench of iniquity among even casual baseball fans. The City College of

New York's championship basketball team, once beloved for its smart and scrappy play, was instantly reviled when it was discovered in 1951 that several players had taken mob money to shave points—intentionally missing baskets to help gamblers beat the point spread. Remember Terry Malloy, the tormented former boxer played by Marlon Brando in *On the Waterfront?* As Malloy saw it, all his troubles stemmed from the one fight in which he took a dive. Otherwise, he could have had class; he could have been a contender.

If cheating to lose is sport's premier sin, and if sumo wrestling is the premier   44
sport of a great nation, cheating to lose couldn't possibly exist in sumo. Could it?

Once again, the data can tell the story. As with the Chicago school tests, the   45
data set under consideration here is surpassingly large: the results from nearly every official sumo match among the top rank of Japanese sumo wrestlers between January 1989 and January 2000, a total of 32,000 bouts fought by 281 different wrestlers.

The incentive scheme that rules sumo is intricate and extraordinarily pow-   46
erful. Each wrestler maintains a ranking that affects every slice of his life: how much money he makes, how large an entourage he carries, how much he gets to eat, sleep, and otherwise take advantage of his success. The sixty-six highest-ranked wrestlers in Japan, comprising the *makuuchi* and *juryo* divisions, make up the sumo elite. A wrestler near the top of this elite pyramid may earn millions and is treated like royalty. Any wrestler in the top forty earns at least $170,000 a year. The seventieth-ranked wrestler in Japan, meanwhile, earns only $15,000 a year. Life isn't very sweet outside the elite. Low-ranked wrestlers must tend to their superiors, preparing their meals and cleaning their quarters and even soaping up their hardest-to-reach body parts. So ranking is everything.

A wrestler's ranking is based on his performance in the elite tournaments   47
that are held six times a year. Each wrestler has fifteen bouts per tournament, one per day over fifteen consecutive days. If he finishes the tournament with a winning record (eight victories or better), his ranking will rise. If he has a losing record, his ranking falls. If it falls far enough, he is booted from the elite rank entirely. The eighth victory in any tournament is therefore critical, the difference between promotion and demotion; it is roughly four times as valuable in the rankings as the typical victory.

So a wrestler entering the final day of a tournament on the bubble, with a   48
7–7 record, has far more to gain from a victory than an opponent with a record of 8–6 has to lose.

Is it possible, then, that an 8–6 wrestler might allow a 7–7 wrestler to beat   49
him? A sumo bout is a concentrated flurry of force and speed and leverage, often lasting only a few seconds. It wouldn't be very hard to let yourself be tossed. Let's

imagine for a moment that sumo wrestling is rigged. How might we measure the data to prove it?

The first step would be to isolate the bouts in question: those fought on a tournament's final day between a wrestler on the bubble and a wrestler who has already secured his eighth win. (Because more than half of all wrestlers end a tournament with either seven, eight, or nine victories, hundreds of bouts fit these criteria.) A final-day match between two 7–7 wrestlers isn't likely to be fixed, since both fighters badly need the victory. A wrestler with ten or more victories probably wouldn't throw a match either, since he has his own strong incentive to win: the $100,000 prize for overall tournament champion and a series of $20,000 prizes for the "outstanding technique" award, "fighting spirit" award, and others.

Let's now consider the following statistic, which represents the hundreds of matches in a which a 7–7 wrestler faced an 8–6 wrestler on a tournament's final day. The left column tallies the probability, based on all past meetings between the two wrestlers fighting that day, that the 7–7 wrestler will win. The right column shows how often the 7–7 wrestler actually did win.

7–7 Wrestler's Predicted Win Percentage Against 8–6 Opponent	7–7 Wrestler's Actual Win Percentage Against 8–6 Opponent
48.7	79.6

So the 7–7 wrestler, based on past outcomes, was expected to win just less than half the time. This makes sense; their records in this tournament indicate that the 8-6 wrestler is slightly better. But in actuality, the wrestler on the bubble won *almost eight out of ten* matches against his 8–6 opponent. Wrestlers on the bubble also do astonishingly well against 9–5 opponents:

7–7 Wrestler's Predicted Win Percentage Against 9–5 Opponent	7–7 Wrestler's Actual Win Percentage Against 9–5 Opponent
47.2	73.4

As suspicious as this looks, a high winning percentage alone isn't enough to prove that a match is rigged. Since so much depends on a wrestler's eighth win, he should be expected to fight harder in a crucial bout. But perhaps there are further clues in the data that prove collusion.

It's worth thinking about the incentive a wrestler might have to throw a match. Maybe he accepts a bribe (which would obviously not be recorded in the data). Or perhaps some other arrangement is made between the two wrestlers.

50

51

52

53

54

Keep in mind that the pool of elite sumo wrestlers is extraordinarily tight-knit. Each of the sixty-six elite wrestlers fights fifteen of the others in a tournament every two months. Furthermore, each wrestler belongs to a stable that is typically managed by a former sumo champion, so even the rival stables have close ties. (Wrestlers from the same stable do not wrestle one another.)

Now let's look at the win-loss percentage between the 7–7 wrestlers and the   55
8-6 wrestlers the *next* time they meet, when neither one is on the bubble. In this case, there is no great pressure on the individual match. So you might expect the wrestlers who won their 7–7 matches in the previous tournament to do about as well as they had in earlier matches against these same opponents—that is, winning roughly 50 percent of the time. You certainly wouldn't expect them to uphold their 80 percent clip.

As it turns out, the data show that the 7–7 wrestlers win only 40 percent of   56
the rematches. Eighty percent in one match and 40 percent in the next? How do you make sense of that?

The most logical explanation is that the wrestlers made a quid pro quo   57
agreement: you let me win today, when I really need the victory, and I'll let you win the next time. (Such an arrangement wouldn't preclude a cash bribe.) It's especially interesting to note that by the two wrestlers' *second* subsequent meeting, the win percentages revert to the expected level of about 50 percent, suggesting that the collusion spans only two matches.

And it isn't only the individual wrestlers whose records are suspect. The col-   58
lective records of the various sumo stables are similarly aberrational. When one stable's wrestlers fare well on the bubble against wrestlers from a second stable, they tend to do especially *poorly* when the second stable's wrestlers are on the bubble. This indicates that some match rigging may be choreographed at the highest level of the sport—much like the Olympic skating judges' vote swapping.   59

No formal disciplinary action has ever been taken against a Japanese sumo wrestler for match rigging. Officials from the Japanese Sumo Association typically dismiss any such charges as fabrications by disgruntled former wrestlers. In fact, the mere utterance of the words "sumo" and "rigged" in the same sentence can cause a national furor. People tend to get defensive when the integrity of their national sport is impugned.

Still allegations of match rigging do occasionally find their way into the   60
Japanese media. These occasional media storms offer one more chance to measure possible corruption in sumo. Media scrutiny, after all, creates a powerful incentive: if two sumo wrestlers or their stables *have* been rigging matches, they might be leery to continue when a swarm of journalists and TV cameras descend upon them.

So what happens in such cases? The data show that in the sumo tourna- 61
ments held immediately after allegations of match rigging, 7–7 wrestlers win only
50 percent of their final-day matches against 8–6 opponents instead of the typical 80 percent. No matter how the data are sliced, they inevitably suggest one
thing: it is hard to argue that sumo wrestling isn't rigged.

Several years ago, two former sumo wrestlers came forward with extensive 62
allegations of match rigging—and more. Aside from the crooked matches, they
said, sumo was rife with drug use and sexcapades, bribes and tax evasion, and
close ties to the *yakuza*, the Japanese mafia. The two men began to receive
threatening phone calls; one of them told friends he was afraid he would be killed
by the *yakuza*. Still, they went forward with plans to hold a press conference at
the Foreign Correspondents' Club in Tokyo. But shortly beforehand, the two
men died—hours apart, in the same hospital, of a similar respiratory ailment.
The police declared there had been no foul play but did not conduct an investigation. "It seems very strange for these two people to die on the same day at the
same hospital," said Mitsuru Miyake, the editor of a sumo magazine. "But no one
has seen them poisoned, so you can't prove the skepticism."

Whether or not their deaths were intentional, these two men had done what 63
no other sumo insider had previously done: named names. Of the 281 wrestlers
covered in the data cited above, they identified 29 crooked wrestlers and 11 who
were said to be incorruptible.

What happens when the whistle-blowers' corroborating evidence is factored 64
into the analysis of the match data? In matches between two supposedly corrupt
wrestlers, the wrestler who was on the bubble won about 80 percent of the time.
In bubble matches against a supposedly clean opponent, meanwhile, the bubble
wrestler was no more likely to win than his record would predict. Furthermore,
when a supposedly corrupt wrestler faced an opponent whom the whistle-
blowers did not name as either corrupt or clean, the results were nearly as skewed
as when two corrupt wrestlers met—suggesting that most wrestlers who *weren't*
specifically named were also corrupt.

So if sumo wrestlers, schoolteachers, and day-care parents all cheat, are we to 65
assume that mankind is innately and universally corrupt? And if so, how corrupt?

The answer may lie in . . . bagels. Consider the true story of a man named 66
Paul Feldman.

Once upon a time, Feldman dreamed big dreams. Trained as an agricultural 67
economist, he wanted to tackle world hunger. Instead, he took a job in
Washington, analyzing weapons expenditures for the U.S. Navy. This was in
1962. For the next twenty-odd years, he did more of the same. He held senior-

level jobs and earned good money, but he wasn't fully engaged in his work. At the office Christmas party, colleagues would introduce him to their wives not as "the head of the public research group" (which he was) but as "the guy who brings in the bagels."

The bagels had begun as a casual gesture: a boss treating his employees 68 whenever they won a research contract. Then he made it a habit. Every Friday, he would bring in some bagels, a serrated knife, and cream cheese. When employees from neighboring floors heard about the bagels, they wanted some too. Eventually he was bringing in fifteen dozen bagels a week. In order to recoup his costs, he set out a cash basket and a sign with the suggested price. His collection rate was about 95 percent; he attributed the underpayment to over-sight, not fraud.

In 1984, when his research institute fell under new management, Feldman 69 took a look at his career and grimaced. He decided to quit his job and sell bagels. His economist friends thought he had lost his mind, but his wife supported him. The last of their three children was finishing college, and they had retired their mortgage.

Driving around the office parks that encircle Washington, he solicited cus- 70 tomers with a simple pitch: early in the morning, he would deliver some bagels and a cash basket to a company's snack room; he would return before lunch to pick up the money and the leftovers. It was an honor-system commerce scheme, and it worked. Within a few years, Feldman was delivering 8,400 bagels a week to 140 companies and earning as much as he had ever made as a research analyst. He had thrown off the shackles of cubicle life and made himself happy.

He had also—quite without meaning to—designed a beautiful economic 71 experiment. From the beginning, Feldman kept rigorous data on his business. So by measuring the money collected against the bagels taken, he found it possible to tell, down to the penny, just how honest his customers were. Did they steal from him? If so, what were the characteristics of a company that stole versus a company that did not? Under what circumstances did people tend to steal more, or less?

As it happens, Feldman's accidental study provides a window onto a form of 72 cheating that has long stymied academics: white-collar crime. (Yes, shorting the bagel man is white-collar crime, writ however small.) It might seem ludicrous to address as large and intractable a problem as white-collar crime through the life of a bagel man. But often a small and simple question can help chisel away at the biggest problems.

Despite all the attention paid to rogue companies like Enron, academics 73 know very little about the practicalities of white-collar crime. The reason? There are no good data. A key fact of white-collar crime is that we hear about only the very slim fraction of people who are *caught* cheating. Most embezzlers lead quiet and theoretically happy lives; employees who steal company property are rarely detected.

With street crime, meanwhile, that is not the case. A mugging or a burglary 74 or a murder is usually tallied whether or not the criminal is caught. A street crime has a victim, who typically reports the crime to the police, who generate data, which in turn generate thousands of academic papers by criminologists, sociologists, and economists. But white-collar crime presents no obvious victim. From whom, exactly, did the masters of Enron steal? And how can you measure something if you don't know to whom it happened, or with what frequency, or in what magnitude?

Paul Feldman's bagel business was different. It did present a victim. The vic- 75 tim was Paul Feldman.

When he started his business, he expected a 95 percent payment rate, based on 76 the experience at his own office. But just as crime tends to be low on a street where a police car is parked, the 95 percent rate was artificially high: Feldman's presence had deterred theft. Not only that, but those bagel eaters knew the provider and had feelings (presumably good ones) about him. A broad swath of psychological and economic research has shown that people will pay different amounts for the same item depending on who is providing it. The economist Richard Thaler, in his 1985 "Beer on the Beach" study, showed that a thirsty sunbather would pay $2.65 for a beer delivered from a resort hotel but only $1.50 for the same beer if it came from a shabby grocery store.

In the real world, Feldman learned to settle for less than 95 percent. He 77 came to consider a company "honest" if its payment rate was above 90 percent. He considered a rate between 80 and 90 percent "annoying but tolerable." If a company habitually paid below 80 percent, Feldman might post a hectoring note, like this one:

> The cost of bagels has gone up dramatically since the beginning of the year. Unfortunately, the number of bagels that disappear without being paid for has also gone up. Don't let that continue. I don't imagine that you would teach your children to cheat, so why do it yourselves?

In the beginning, Feldman left behind an open basket for the cash, but too 78 often the money vanished. Then he tried a coffee can with a money slot in its plastic lid, which also proved too tempting. In the end, he resorted to making small plywood boxes with a slot cut into the top. The wooden box has worked well. Each year he drops off about seven thousand boxes and loses, on average, just one to theft. This is an intriguing statistic: the same people who routinely steal more than 10 percent of his bagels almost never stoop to stealing his money box—a tribute to the nuanced social calculus of theft. From Feldman's perspective, an office worker who eats a bagel without paying is committing a crime; the office worker probably doesn't think so. This distinction probably has less to do with the admittedly small amount of money involved (Feldman's bagels cost one dollar each, cream cheese included) than with the context of the "crime." The same office worker who fails to pay for his bagel might also help himself to a long slurp of soda while filling a glass in a self-serve restaurant, but he is very unlikely to leave the restaurant without paying.

So what do the bagel data have to say? In recent years, there have been two   79
noteworthy trends in the overall payment rate. The first was a long, slow decline that began in 1992. By the summer of 2001, the overall rate had slipped to about 87 percent. But immediately after September 11 of that year, the rate spiked a full 2 percent and hasn't slipped much since. (If a 2 percent gain in payment doesn't sound like much, think of it this way: the nonpayment rate fell from 13 to 11 percent, which amounts to a 15 percent decline in theft.) Because many of Feldman's customers are affiliated with national security, there may have been a patriotic element to this 9/11 Effect. Or it may have represented a more general surge in empathy.

The data also show that smaller offices are more honest than big ones. An   80
office with a few dozen employees generally outpays by 3 to 5 percent an office with a few hundred employees. This may seem counterintuitive. In a bigger office, a bigger crowd is bound to convene around the bagel table, providing more witnesses to make sure you drop your money in the box. But in the big-office/small-office comparison, bagel crime seems to mirror street crime. There is far less street crime per capita in rural areas than in cities, in large part because a rural criminal is more likely to be known (and therefore caught). Also, a smaller community tends to exert greater social incentives against crime, the main one being shame.

The bagel data also reflect how much personal mood seems to affect honesty.   81
Weather, for instance, is a major factor. Unseasonably pleasant weather inspires people to pay at a higher rate. Unseasonably cold weather, meanwhile, makes people cheat prolifically; so do heavy rain and wind. Worst are the holidays. The week of Christmas produces a 2 percent drop in payment rates—again, a 15 percent increase in theft, an effect on the same magnitude, in reverse, as that of 9/11. Thanksgiving is nearly as bad; the week of Valentine's Day is also lousy, as is the week straddling April 15. There are, however, a few good holidays: the weeks that include the Fourth of July, Labor Day, and Columbus Day. The dif-

ference in the two sets of holidays? The low-cheating holidays represent little more than an extra day off from work. The high-cheating holidays are fraught with miscellaneous anxieties and the high expectations of loved ones.

Feldman has also reached some of his own conclusions about honesty, based more on his experience than the data. He has come to believe that morale is a big factor—that an office is more honest when the employees like their boss and their work. He also believes that employees further up the corporate ladder cheat more than those down below. He got this idea after delivering for years to one company spread out over three floors—an executive floor on top and two lower floors with sales, service, and administrative employees. (Feldman wondered if perhaps the executives cheated out of an overdeveloped sense of entitlement. What he didn't consider is that perhaps cheating was how they got to *be* executives.)

If morality represents the way we would like the world to work and economics represents how it actually does work, then the story of Feldman's bagel business lies at the very intersection of morality and economics. Yes, a lot of people steal from him, but the vast majority, even though no one is watching over them, do not. This outcome may surprise some people—including Feldman's economist friends who counseled him twenty years ago that his honor-system scheme would never work. But it would not have surprised Adam Smith. In fact, the theme of Smith's first book, *The Theory of Moral Sentiments*, was the innate honesty of mankind. "How selfish soever man may be supposed," Smith wrote, "there are evidently some principles in his nature, which interest him in the fortune of others, and render their happiness necessary to him, though he derives nothing from it, except the pleasure of seeing it."

There is a tale, "The Ring of Gyges," that Feldman sometimes tells his economist friends. It comes from Plato's *Republic*. A student named Glaucon offered the story in response to a lesson by Socrates—who, like Adam Smith, argued that people are generally good even without enforcement. Glaucon, like Feldman's economist friends, disagreed. He told of a shepherd named Gyges who stumbled upon a secret cavern with a corpse inside that wore a ring. When Gyges put on the ring, he found that it made him invisible. With no one able to monitor his behavior, Gyges proceeded to do woeful things—seduce the queen, murder the king, and so on. Glaucon's story posed a moral question: could any man resist the temptation of evil if he knew his acts could not be witnessed? Glaucon seemed to think the answer was no. But Paul Feldman sides with Socrates and Adam Smith—for he knows that the answer, at least 87 percent of the time, is yes.

82

83

84

Scott McCloud (1960–) is an illustrator and writer based in California, best known as a leading "comics theorist" investigating how readers and illustrators process a narrative's events and arguing that comics operate in a nonlinear way. His *Understanding Comics* (1993) analyzed the medium of comics in all its forms, from vocabulary to history. In *Reinventing Comics* (2000), McCloud identifies twelve steps artists need to take to remain relevant. His latest book, *Making Comics* (2006) investigates comics story-telling techniques. All three works are written in comic form. Prior to these publications, McCloud enjoyed success with his strip *Zot!*, a science fiction/superhero comic. McCloud is also a champion of artists' rights. In 1988, he authored the "Creator's Bill of Rights," which attempts to protect comics writers from various forms of exploitation.

Blood in the Gutter

Scott McCloud

Chapter 3, "Blood in the Gutter" (pp. 60-90), from *Understanding Comics* by Scott McCloud. Copyright © 1993, 1994 by Scott McCloud. Reprinted by permission of HarperCollins Publishers.

JUST WHAT IS **GOING ON** HERE?

IN THE *VISUAL ARTS*, THE IMPACT OF EASTERN IDEAS WAS BOTH POWERFUL AND *LASTING*.

THE TRADITIONAL EMPHASIS IN WESTERN ART UPON THE PRIMACY OF *FOREGROUND* SUBJECTS AND *CONTINUOUSNESS* OF *TONES* GAVE WAY TO *FRAGMENTATION* AND A NEW AWARENESS OF THE *PICTURE PLANE*.

FACSIMILE OF 'FIGURE' BY PABLO PICASSO 1948

WHAT DO YOU THINK THIS PAINTING BY AL HELD IS CALLED?*

IN THEATRE, THE IDEA THAT *"LESS IS MORE"* HAS REAL *PRACTICAL IMPLICATIONS*. ONE OF THE MOST SUCCESSFUL SHOWS IN HISTORY IS *THE FANTASTICKS* -- A PLAY WHOSE ENTIRE *SET* CAME IN *THREE PIECES* -- A TATTERED BANNER, A STICK AND A CARDBOARD MOON.

*ANSWER: "THE BIG 'N'" [SEE PAGE 216]

THE MASTERY OF *ANY* MEDIUM USING MINIMAL ELEMENTS HAS LONG BEEN CONSIDERED A *NOBLE ASPIRATION*.

READERS FACED WITH PANELS LIKE THESE WILL HAVE SUBSTANTIALLY DIFFERENT INTERPRETATIONS.
CLAK! CLAK! CLAK!
BY CONSTRUCTING WHOLE IMAGES BASED ON THESE FRAGMENTS, READERS ARE PERFORMING CLOSURE, JUST AS--
WHOOSH!
Splip Splip
?
Ding! Ding!
UH--JUST AS READERS COMPLETE AN ACTION OR IDEA BETWEEN--
OW!
OW!
Ding! Ding!
AHEM! I SAY, JUST AS READERS COMPLETE--
--AN ACTION OR-- OW! OW!
STOP THAT!
Ding! Ding!
OW!
Ding! Ding!
OW!

BUT REALISTIC IMAGES HAVE A BUMPIER RIDE. THEIRS IS A PRIMARILY VISUAL EXISTENCE WHICH DOESN'T PASS EASILY INTO THE REALM OF IDEAS.
HI!
AND SO, WHAT SEEMED LIKE A CONTINUOUS SERIES OF MOMENTS IN THE LAST EXAMPLE, HERE LOOKS A LITTLE MORE LIKE A SERIES OF STILL PICTURES...
...TO ME ANYWAY. THESE THINGS ARE ALL SUBJECTIVE!
SIMILARLY, I THINK WHEN COMICS ART VEERS CLOSER TO CONCERNS OF THE PICTURE PLANE, CLOSURE CAN BE MORE DIFFICULT TO ACHIEVE, THOUGH FOR DIFFERENT REASONS.
HI!
NOW IT'S THE UNIFYING PROPERTIES OF DESIGN THAT MAKE US MORE AWARE OF THE PAGE AS A WHOLE, RATHER THAN ITS INDIVIDUAL COMPONENTS, THE PANELS.
A GOOD RULE OF THUMB IS THAT IF READERS ARE PARTICULARLY AWARE OF THE ART IN A GIVEN STORY--
--THEN CLOSURE IS PROBABLY NOT HAPPENING WITHOUT SOME EFFORT.
OF COURSE, MAKING THE READER WORK A LITTLE MAY BE JUST WHAT THE ARTIST IS TRYING TO DO. ONCE AGAIN, IT'S ALL A MATTER OF PERSONAL TASTE.

Mark Sagoff is a senior research scholar at the Institute for Philosophy and Public Policy at the University of Maryland and the author of two books: *The Economy of the Earth: Philosophy, Law, and the Environment* (1988) and *Price, Principle, and the Environment* (2004). He has also published over 100 articles on a range of subjects including the environment, biotechnology, morality, and economics. He previously taught at Cornell, Princeton, and the University of Wisconsin at Madison and has won grants from various foundations, including the National Endowment for the Humanities. He is a former president of the International Society for Environmental Ethics, has been a member of the Science Advisory Board of the Committee on the Valuation of Ecosystem Services in the Environmental Protection Agency since 2003, and has been a fellow of the American Association for the Advancement of Science since 2000.

ZUCKERMAN'S DILEMMA: A PLEA FOR ENVIRONMENTAL ETHICS

Mark Sagoff

Many of us recall from childhood—or from reading to our own children— E. B. White's story of the spider Charlotte and her campaign to save Wilbur, a barnyard pig.[1] Charlotte wove webs above Wilbur's sty proclaiming the pig's virtues in words—"TERRIFIC," "RADIANT," and "HUMBLE"—she copied from newspaper advertisements salvaged by a helpful rat. Wilbur won a special prize at the county fair. Moved by these events, Zuckerman, the farmer who owned Wilbur, spared him from being sent to market. Charlotte saved Wilbur's life.   1

"Why did you do all this for me?" the pig asks at the end of Charlotte's Web. "I don't deserve it. I've never done anything for you."   2

"You have been my friend," Charlotte replied. "That in itself is a tremendous thing. I wove my webs for you because I liked you. After all, what's a life, anyway? We're born, we live a little while, we die. A spider's life can't help being something of a mess, what with all this trapping and eating flies. By helping you, perhaps I was trying to lift up my life a little. Heaven knows, anyone's life can stand a little of that" (p. 164).   3

Charlotte's Web illustrates three ways we value nature. First, nature benefits us. Nature is useful: it serves a purpose, satisfies a preference, or meets a need. This is the instrumental good. Traders have this kind of value in mind when they bid on pork belly futures. Price is the usual measure of the instrumental good.   4

Mark Sagoff, "Zuckerman's Dilemma: A Plea for Environmental Ethics." © The Hastings Center. Reprinted by permission. This article originally appeared in *The Hastings Center Report*, vol. 21, no. 5 (1991).

Second, we may value nature as an object of knowledge and perception. 5
This is the aesthetic good.[2] While the basis of instrumental value lies in our
wants and inclinations, the basis of aesthetic value lies in the object itself—in
qualities that demand an appreciative response from informed and discriminat-
ing observers. The judges who awarded Wilbur a prize recognized in him superb
qualities—qualities that made him a pig to be appreciated rather than a pig to
be consumed.

Third, we may regard an object (as Charlotte did Wilbur) with love or 6
affection. Charlotte's love for Wilbur included feelings of altruism, as we would
expect, since anyone who loves a living object (we might include biological systems and communities) will take an interest in its well-being or welfare. Love
might also attach to objects that exemplify ideals, aspirations, and commitments that "lift up" one's life by presenting goals that go beyond one's own welfare. We might speak of "love of country" in this context. Objects of our love
and affection have a moral good, and, if they are living, a good of their own.

Aesthetic value depends on qualities that make an object admirable of its 7
kind; when these qualities change, the aesthetic value of the object may change
with them. With love, it is different. Shakespeare wrote that love alters not
where it alteration finds, and even if this is not strictly true, love still tolerates
better than aesthetic appreciation changes that may occur in its object.

Although love is other-regarding in that it promotes the well-being of its 8
object, it does not require actions to be entirely altruistic. Only saints are completely selfless, and it is hardly obvious that we should try to be like them.[3]
Nevertheless, anyone's life can stand some dollop of idealistic or altruistic
behavior, as Charlotte says.

When we regard an object with appreciation or with love, we say it has 9
intrinsic value, by which we mean that we value the object itself rather than just
the benefits it confers on us. This essay concerns the intrinsic value of nature in
its relation to environmental policy. The two forms of intrinsic value—aesthetic
and moral—differ in important ways, as one would expect, since moral value
arises in the context of action, while aesthetic value has to do with perception. I
shall touch on these differences, but I do not have space to explicate them here.
Those of us who wish to protect estuaries, forests, species, and other aspects of
nature may give any of three kinds of arguments—instrumental, aesthetic, or
moral—to support our conviction. We might argue on instrumental grounds, for
example, that we should save species for their possible medicinal applications, or
rain forests because they add to global oxygen budgets. An aesthetic argument,
in contrast, would point to the magnificent qualities a ten-thousand-year-old forest or estuary may possess. In nature we find perhaps for the last time in history
objects commensurate with our capacity to wonder.

A moral argument describes obligations we have toward objects of nature   10
insofar as we regard them with reverence, affection, and respect. Such an argument may contend that humanity confronts a great responsibility in learning to
share the world with other species. Love of or respect for the natural world
increases our stature as moral beings, and it may teach us to be critical of and to
change our preferences and desires. By taking an interest in the welfare of some
creature beside herself, Charlotte too found there is more to life than "all this
trapping and eating flies."

Within the next decade or two, we shall decide the fate of many estuaries,   11
forests, species, and other wonderful aspects of the natural world. How can we
justify efforts to protect them? Will instrumental or prudential arguments do the
trick? If not, how will we justify the sacrifices we must make to save our evolutionary and ecological heritage?

Why Save the Whales?   Consider, as a real-world example, whales. Two centuries   12
ago, whale oil fetched a high price because people used it in lamps. Whales had
instrumental value. Electric lights are better and cheaper than oil lamps;
accordingly, there is little or no market for whale oil today.

Why, then, do so many people care about saving whales? Is it for instru-   13
mental reasons? Are they concerned about maintaining a strategic reserve of
blubber? Do they worry that the seas might fill up with krill? No; as whales have
lost their instrumental value, their aesthetic and moral worth has become all
the more evident.

Whale oil has substitutes in a way that whales do not. We get along easily   14
without whale oil because electricity lights our lamps. The extinction of whales,
in contrast, represents an aesthetic and moral loss—something like the destruction of a great painting or the death of a friend. Life goes on, of course, but we
mourn such a loss and, if we caused it, we should feel guilty or ashamed of it. No
one cares about the supply of whale oil, but we do care about the abundance of
whales. Aesthetic and moral value attaches to those animals themselves rather
than to any function they serve or benefit they confer on us. When they perish,
all that was valuable about them will perish with them.

Fungibility as the Mark of the Instrumental.   Insofar as we care about an object for   15
instrumental reasons, we would accept a substitute—for example, ball point
pens in place of quills—if it performs the same function at a lower cost. The
market price of any object should in theory not exceed that of the cheapest
substitute.

With intrinsic value, it is different. When we see, for example, a Jacques   16
Cousteau film about the ability of humpback whales to communicate with each
other over hundreds of miles, we are properly moved to admire this impressive

species. That we can fax junk mail faster and farther is irrelevant. We admire the ability of these whales to do what they do. It is this species we admire; its qualities demand admiration and attention.

Similarly, love is not transferable but attaches to the individuals one hap-   17
pens to love. At one time, people had children, in part, because they needed them as farm hands. Today, we think the relation between parents and children should be primarily moral rather than instrumental. One can purchase the serv-ices of farmhands and even of sexual partners, but our relationship to hired labor or sex is nothing like our relationship to children or spouses. We would not think of trading a child, for example, for a good tractor.

Technology, though still in its infancy, promises to do for many aspects of   18
nature what it has done for whales and for children, namely, to make us eco-nomically less dependent on them. This need not concern us. That we no longer require whales for oil or children for tending bobbins does not imply that we cease to value them. The less we depend on nature economically, the more we may find that the reasons to value species, forests, estuaries, and other aspects of nature are not instrumental but aesthetic and moral.

Why Protect the Natural Environment?   We undertake many environmental programs   19
primarily to protect the well-being of nature, even if we defend them as neces-sary to promote the welfare of human beings. Why, for example, did the Envi-ronmental Protection Agency ban DDT in the 1970s? The pesticide killed peli-cans and other wildlife; that was the reason to prohibit its use. EPA banned it, however, as a human carcinogen—which it is not.[4] Today we should make no such pretense.[5] The new Clean Air Act undertakes an expensive program to control acid rain. The law does not pretend that acid rain causes cancer. It answers directly to moral and aesthetic concerns about what coal-burning power plants are doing to trees and fish.

We environmentalists often appeal to instrumental arguments for instru-   20
mental reasons, i.e., not because we believe them, but because we think that they work. I submit, however, that advances in technology will continue to undermine these arguments. The new biotechnologies, for example, seem poised to replace nature as the source of many cultural commodities. As one environmentalist observes: "In the years to come, an increasing number of agri-cultural activities are going to be taken indoors and enclosed in vats and cal-drons, sealed off from the outside world."[6]

When machinery replaced child labor in mills and mines, people did not   21
stop raising children. Society found it possible to treat children as objects of love rather than as factors of production. As biotechnology industrializes agriculture, we may protect farmland for its aesthetic and symbolic value rather than for its

products. We may measure wealth not in terms of what we can consume but in terms of what we can do without—what we treasure for its own sake.

Poverty is one of today's greatest environmental and ecological problems. This is because people who do not share in the wealth technology creates must live off nature; in their need to exploit the natural commons, they may destroy it. Analogously, in an urban context, poor people have had to send their children to work in sweat shops—to survive. The problem, of course, is not that poor people have the wrong values. Extreme and deplorable inequalities in the distribution of wealth lead to the mistreatment of children and to the destruction of the environment.   22

Accordingly, I question the adequacy of the argument environmentalists often make that we must protect nature to provide for the welfare of human beings. I think it is also true that we must provide for the welfare of human beings if we are to protect the natural environment.   23

Zuckerman's Dilemma

Zuckerman faced a dilemma. He had to choose whether to butcher Wilbur (the slaughterhouse would have paid for the pig) or on moral and aesthetic grounds to spare his life.   24

What reasons have we to preserve biodiversity, protect rain forests, and maintain the quality of lakes, rivers, and estuaries? I should like to suggest that we confront Zuckerman's dilemma with respect to many of the most wonderful aspects of nature. As we come to depend on nature less and less for instrumental reasons, we may recognize more and more the intrinsic reasons for preserving it.   25

Water Pollution.   Consider, as an example, the problem of water pollution. The question I wish to ask here is whether instrumental arguments would justify the expenditure of the roughly $200 billion Americans invested between 1970 and 1984 in controlling water pollution.[7] Did this investment pay off in terms of our health, safety, or welfare? Could we conclude that, in this instance, instrumental as well as intrinsic values justify the protection of the environment?   26

I think it fair to say that the large public investment in water pollution control cannot be justified on instrumental grounds alone. The same money put into public clinics, education, or antismoking campaigns might have led to greater improvements in public safety and health. This is true in part because the major uses of water—commercial, industrial, agricultural, and municipal— are not very sensitive to water quality. Drinking water can be treated very cheaply and thus can tolerate many common pollutants. "Much of what has been said about the need for high quality water supplies," two experts write, "is more a product of emotion than logic . . . [A] plant at Dusseldorf, Germany,   27 withdraws water from the Rhine River, which is of far lower quality than the Delaware, the Hudson, or the Missouri, treats it . . . and produces quite potable drinking water."[8]

The Value of an Estuary.   In the Chesapeake Bay, as in other prominent aquatic   28
ecosystems, pollution must concern us deeply for moral and aesthetic reasons. It is not clear, however, that the harm pollution does to nature translates into damage to human health, safety, or welfare. Indeed, more pollution might be better from a strictly instrumental point of view.

The reason is that the major uses of the Bay are fairly insensitive to water   29
quality. The Chesapeake possesses instrumental value as a liquid highway (Baltimore is a major port), as a sewer (tributaries drain several major cities), and as a site for a huge naval base (Norfolk). These uses affect but are not greatly affected by water quality or, for that matter, by the biological health, integrity, richness, or diversity of the Chesapeake ecosystem.

How does pollution affect the health of commercial and recreational fish-   30
eries in estuaries? Consider rockfish (striped bass). Environmentalists for many years deplored the pollution of the Hudson off Manhattan; they pronounced that portion of the estuary—one of the most degraded in the world—biologically dead. Developers of the Westway Project, who wished to fill the offshore waters to build condos, hired scientists who confirmed that rockfish did not and probably could not visit the polluted lower Hudson.

Environmentalists were able to stop the project, however, by arguing in the   31
nick of time that even though the "interpier" area may be the most polluted ecosystem in the world, it functions as perhaps the most important, healthy, and thriving hatchery for rockfish on the Atlantic coast. The well-being of fish populations—at least as we view it—can have more to do with politics than with pollution.[9]

In the Chesapeake, rockfish populations rebounded after a moratorium on   32
fishing. One might surmise, then, that while fisheries have been hurt by over-harvesting, the effects of pollution are harder to prove. Bluefish, crabs, and other "scavengers" abound in polluted waters, including the Chesapeake. And organic pollutants, primarily compounds of nitrogen and phosphorus, could support oysters and other filter feeders if their populations (depleted by overfishing and natural disease) returned to the Bay.

Maryland's former director of tidal fisheries, recognizing the benefits of   33
genetic engineering, argued that the Chesapeake Bay "should be run more like a farm than a wilderness."[10] He believed that the state should subsidize efforts to fabricate fish the way Frank Perdue manufactures chickens. Many experts agree that industrial mariculture, by pushing fish populations far beyond the carrying capacity of ecosystems, will render capture fisheries obsolete.[11]

Pollution at present levels hardly bothers boaters, which is why there are so   34
many "stinkpots" out there. Even in a "sick" estuary, a 347 Evinrude outboard
gives people what they apparently want: plenty of noise and plenty of wake.
Many recreational fish remain plentiful, and biotechnologists are engineering
others to withstand pollutants to which they now succumb. They have perfected a nonmigrating rockfish that need not transit the anoxic stem of the Bay.
(They have also perfected an acid-tolerant trout that does well in acidified
lakes.) It may not be efficient to regulate pollution to accommodate species. It
may be cheaper to regulate species to accommodate pollution.

Since a nasty jellyfish occurring naturally in the Bay makes swimming too   35
painful, recreational interest in the Chesapeake is limited in any case. Most
vacationers experience the Bay from bridges, where they sit in terrific traffic
jams on their way to resorts on the Atlantic shore. They seem willing to pay a
lot to visit the Ho Jos, discos, go gos, peep shows, and condos that stretch from
Atlantic City to Virginia Beach. If you are looking for recreational benefits people are willing to pay for, look for them there.

Why Not Pollute?   We may find acts of environmental destruction to be aestheti-   36
cally and morally outrageous even if they do no damage to human health,
safety, or welfare. News reports tell us that Prince William Sound, now
"sparkling with sea life and renewed health," has produced a record salmon
catch a little more than a year after the tragic Valdez spill.[12] From a strictly
instrumental point of view, that spill was not nearly so detrimental as many
environmentalists thought. The immediate victims, more than 36,000 water-
fowl, at least 1,016 sea otters, and 144 bald eagles, have no commercial value.
Populations of wildlife will be detrimentally affected probably forever. These
animals have enormous aesthetic and moral—but little instrumental—worth.

I do not mean to suggest that water pollution, especially when it is illegal or   37
careless, is anything but morally and aesthetically outrageous. I do not mean to
minimize the harm it does. I am arguing only that pollution may represent a
failure in aesthetic appreciation and moral responsibility without representing a
market failure, that is, without impairing any of the uses we make of an estuary.
The Chesapeake will perform its major economic tasks: to function as a sewer, a
liquid highway, and a place for boating. If it were only the beneficial use rather
than the intrinsic value of the Bay that concerned us, controlling pollution further might not be worth the cost.

The Problem of Scale

"What's wrong with this argument," a reader might object, "is that it leaves out   38
the question of scale. We can get away with polluting an estuary here and there

if elsewhere healthy ecosystems support the global processes essential to life. At a local scale, an instrumental calculus may argue for industrializing a particular environment. The problem, though, is that when we apply the same calculus to every ecosystem, we end up by destroying the crucial services nature provides."

This argument has weight with respect to activities that affect the atmos-   39
phere. Scientists have shown a connection between the use of CFCs and changes in stratospheric ozone. Likewise, the excessive combustion of coal and oil threatens to change the world's climate. That we should follow policies that prudence recommends, I have no doubt. The Montreal Protocol concerning CFCs represents an important first step. Prudence also recommends that we reach similar international agreements to decrease the amount of fuel we burn and, perhaps, to increase our reliance on those forms of energy that do not involve combustion.

While it is urgent that we limit atmospheric pollution, this does not give us a   40
reason to protect intrinsically valuable species or ecosystems. The pollution, degradation, and exploitation of the Chesapeake Bay, for example, has no cogniz-able effect on global biochemical processes. One may argue, indeed, that the more eutrophic the Bay becomes, the more carbon it will store, thus helping to counter the "greenhouse" effect. By solving the problems of the Chesapeake, we do little to solve the problems of the atmosphere. The two sets of problems arise from dif-ferent causes, involve different sorts of values, and require different solutions.

Rain Forests.   Consider the rain forests, which seem doomed by economic   41
progress. One can argue persuasively that humanity has no more important eth-ical or aesthetic task than to keep these magnificent ecosystems from being turned into particle boards and disposable diapers. Popular arguments to the effect that rain forests store net carbon or add to global oxygen budgets, how-ever, may not be convincing.

Since rain forests are climax ecosystems, they absorb through the cold   42
burning of decay as much oxygen as they release through respiration; thus the popular belief that these forests add to global oxygen budgets betrays a naivete about how climax ecosystems work.[13] One way to get a rain forest to store net carbon may be to chop it down and plant instead of trees fast-growing crops genetically designed to do very nicely in the relevant soil and climatic condi-tions. (The biologist Dan Janzen has described this dreadful possibility.)[14] The trees could be used to make disposable diapers which, after use, would go to landfills where they would store carbon nearly forever.

Biodiversity.   Anyone with any moral or aesthetic sense must agree that another   43
of humanity's greatest responsibilities today is to arrest shameful and horrendous rates of extinction. Yet one is hard pressed to find credible instrumental argu-

ments for protecting endangered species in their habitats. The reason that we produce Thanksgiving turkeys by the millions while letting the black-footed boobie become extinct is that one bird has instrumental value while the other has not. The boobie had no ecological function; it was epiphenomenal even in its own habitat. Its demise in no way contributed, for example, to the loss of stratospheric ozone or to the "greenhouse" effect.

Environmentalists, to justify their efforts to protect biological diversity,   44
sometimes speculate that exotic species might prove useful for medical purposes, for instance. No public health professional, as far as I know, has vouched for this proposition. Pharmaceutical companies are not known for contributing to the Nature Conservancy or for otherwise encouraging efforts to preserve biodiversity. They are interested in learning from folk medicine, but they cannot even think of tracking down, capturing, and analyzing the contents of millions of species (many of them unidentified) each of which may contain thousands of compounds.

If pharmaceutical companies wanted to mine exotic species, they would not   45
preserve them in their habitats. They might trap and freeze them or sequence their genes for later reconstruction. Seed companies would likewise store germ tissue in banks, not leave it in the wild. Capturing and freezing specimens, not preserving habitats, would be the way to go, to make biodiversity benefit us.

Even a single endangered species enlists our respect and admiration, since   46
(as one observer has said) it would require another heaven and earth to produce such a being. The grand diversity of life, particularly the existence of rare and exotic species, presents a profound moral obligation for civilization, which is to share the earth peaceably with other species. This obligation exists whether or not we can defend the preservation of species on grounds of self-interest rather than morality. The destruction of biodiversity may be immoral, even sinful, without being irrational or imprudent.

A Plea for Environmental Ethics

In an old movie, a character played by W. C. Fields, having, it appears, negli-   47
gently killed a baby, confronts its hysterical mother. Eyeing her youthful figure, he says: "No matter, madam; I would be happy to get you with another."

What we find chilling in this scene is Fields's appeal wholly to instrumental   48
value. He sees nothing wrong with killing a baby as long has he can "get" its mother with another child who, one day, will be equally capable of supporting her in her old age. To Fields, objects have only instrumental value; we can evaluate all our actions in terms of costs and benefits. They have no other meaning.

Moral Value—a Benefit or Cost?   The scene in the movie might remind us of the   49
way the EXXON Corporation dealt with public outrage over the recent

unpleasantness in Prince William Sound. The corporation assured everyone that the salmon fishery would bounce back. If anyone was out of pocket, EXXON would lavishly compensate them. EXXON said to the outraged public: "No matter, madam; we will be happy to make you at least as well off."

From the point of view of instrumental value alone, both Fields and EXXON   50 were correct. They could replace whatever was lost with equally beneficial or useful substitutes. Another baby could grow up to plow land or tend bobbins as well as the first. The mother's income in old age would not decrease. EXXON too would make up lost income. Isn't it irrational, then, for people to complain when children are killed or wildlife is destroyed? From the point of view of instrumental value, they aren't worth much. They may have meaning, but they confer few benefits on us. They make demands on us. They are mostly costs.

Indeed, raising children, preserving nature, cherishing art, and practicing   51 the virtues of civil life are all costs—the costs of being the people we are. Why do we pay these costs? We can answer only that these costs are benefits; these actions justify themselves; these virtues are their own reward.

I wonder, therefore, whether we environmentalists do well to argue for   52 environmental protection primarily on instrumental rather than on moral and aesthetic grounds. Are the possible medicinal or agricultural uses of rare and endangered species really what we care about? We might as well argue that we should protect whales for the sake of their oil or sea otters to harvest their teeth. I think the destruction and extinction of wildlife would horrify us even if we knew sea otter, murres, and eagles would never benefit us. How do we differ from Charlotte, then, who saved Wilbur even though he did nothing for her?

Preference versus Judgment.   "The distinction between instrumental and intrinsic   53 value," someone may object, "lies beside the point of environmental policy, since a cost-benefit analysis, based in willingness-to-pay estimates, can take both sorts of preferences into account. Whether people are willing to pay to protect wildlife for moral, aesthetic, or self-interested reasons (hunting, for example) is their business; all the policy maker needs to know is what their preferences are and how much they are willing to pay to satisfy them."

This objection misses the crucial importance of the way we choose to make   54 decisions. Consider, for example, how we determine whether a person is innocent or guilty of a crime. We might do this by sending questionnaires to a random sample of citizens to check off whether they prefer a guilty or innocent verdict and, perhaps, how much they are willing to pay for each. This method of reaching a verdict would be "rational" in the sense that it aggregates "given" preferences (data) to mathematical principles laid down in advance. The method is also "neutral" in that it translates a data set into a social choice without itself entering, influencing, or affecting the outcome.

On the other hand, we may trust the finding of innocence or guilt to a jury who are steeped in the evidence, who hear the arguments, and then, by deliberation, reach a collective judgment. This procedure, since it involves discussion and even persuasion, would not proceed from "given" preferences according to rules laid down in advance. The process or method itself is supposed to affect the result.

Which model would be most appropriate for environmental policy? Consider erosion. Public officials must assess instrumental reasons for protecting soil: they must determine how much arable land we need for crops, how much we are losing, and how best to conserve what we have. They also weigh intrinsic values, for example, what soil and its protection expresses about us or means to us as a community. Our policy, presumably, should be based not on the revealed or expressed preferences of a random sample of people, no matter how rigorous our techniques of sampling and aggregating may be, but on the judgment of responsible authorities after appropriate public consideration and debate.

Similarly, policies for civil rights, education, the arts, child labor, and the environment depend on judgment—often moral and aesthetic judgment—concerning facts about the world and about ourselves, that is, about our goals and intentions as a community. People who believe we ought to save the whales, for example, do not tell us simply what they prefer; rather, they call for the reasoned agreement or disagreement of others. That is why public policy is always argued in public terms—in terms of what we ought to do, not what I happen to want.

With respect to aesthetic experience, anyone can tell you what he or she likes, but not everyone can tell you what is worth appreciating. A person judges aesthetically not for himself or herself only but on the basis of reasons, arguments, or ideas that he or she believes would lead others to the same conclusion. Knowledge, experience, sensitivity, discernment—these distinguish judgments of taste from expressions of preference.

To be sure, we enjoy objects we appreciate, but we do not value these objects because we enjoy them. Rather, we enjoy them because we find them valuable or, more precisely, enjoyment is one way of perceiving their value. To enjoy ecological communities aesthetically or to value them morally is to find directly in them or in their qualities the reasons that justify their protection. This is not a matter of personal preference. It is a matter of judgment and perception, which one might believe correct or mistaken, and thus argue for or against, within an open political process.

The contrast I have drawn between instrumental and intrinsic value borrows   60
a great deal, of course, from Kant, who summed up the distinction as follows.
"That which is related to general human inclination and needs has a market
price . . . But that which constitutes . . . an end in itself does not have a mere
relative worth, i.e., a price, but an intrinsic worth, i.e., a dignity."[15] Kant believed
that dignity attaches to objects because of what they are and, therefore, how we
judge them. The discovery of what things are—whether it is their moral, aesthetic, or scientific properties—has to do with knowledge. Like any form of
knowledge it is inter-subjective: it represents not the preference of individuals but
the will, the perception, or the considered opinion of a community.

Are Values Relative?   While many Americans may share an environmental   61
ideology—the United States has been described as Nature's Nation[16]—this does
not apply everywhere. Even if the love of nature belongs to most cultures, moreover, it might express itself in different ways. The Japanese may not experience
whales as we do; *Moby Dick* is one of our classics. Italians, who treasure their
artistic heritage, might as soon eat as listen to a song bird. How can we expect
other cultures to respond to nature in the ways we do?

This kind of question may lead environmentalists to suppose that instru-   62
mental arguments for protecting nature have a universality that intrinsic arguments do not. Yet instrumental arguments depend on interpretations of fact—
models of climate change, for example—that invite all kinds of disagreement.
And ethical issues arise, moreover, even when instrumental concerns are para-
mount, such as when determining how much industrialized and developing
nations should cut back combustion to counter global warming. It may be easier
to persuade, attract, or cajole other nations to cooperate (if not agree) with our
moral and aesthetic concerns than with our reading of prudence or self-interest.
The process of reaching agreement is the same, however, whether instrumental
or intrinsic values are at stake.

Living with Nature.   I have argued that we ought to preserve nature for its sake and   63
not simply our benefit. How far, however, should we go? The Chesapeake Bay
commends itself to us for intrinsic but also for instrumental reasons. How can
we balance our need to use with our desire to protect this ecosystem?

We confront this kind of question, I believe, also in relation to people   64
whom we love and whose freedom and spontaneity we respect but with whom
we have to live. Children are examples. We could treat our children—as we
might treat nature—completely as means to our own ends. We would then simply use them to take out the empties, perform sexual favors, tend bobbins, or
whatever it is that benefits us. This would be despicable as well as criminal. We

know that morality requires that we treat our children as ends in themselves and not merely as means to our own ends.

At the same time, we have to live with our kids, and this allows us to make   65
certain demands on them, like not to wake us up too early in the morning, no matter how much we love them for their own sake. While we insist on protecting our children's innate character, independence, and integrity, we have to socialize the little devils or they will destroy us and themselves. I think this is true of nature: we can respect the integrity of ecosystems even if we change them in ways that allow us all to share the same planet.

No clear rules determine how far one should go in disciplining one's chil-   66
dren or in modifying their behavior; socialization may have fairly broad limits. But there are limits; we recognize child abuse when we see it. Have we such a conception of the abuse of nature? I think we need one. At least we should regard as signs of environmental abuse the typical results of egregious assaults on ecosystems, such as eutrophication, pandemic extinctions, and so on. We might then limit changes we make in nature by keeping this notion of ecological health—or disease—in mind.

Zuckerman's Response

William Reilly, administrator of the Environmental Protection Agency,   67
recently wrote: "Natural ecosystems . . . have intrinsic values independent of human use that are worthy of protection." He cited an advisory scientific report that urged the agency to attach as much importance to intrinsic ecological values as to risks to human health and welfare. Mr. Reilly added:

> Whether it is Long Island Sound or Puget Sound, San Francisco Bay or the Chesapeake, the Gulf of Mexico or the Arctic tundra, it is time to get serious about protecting what we love. Clearly we do love our great water bodies: . . . They are part of our heritage, part of our consciousness. Let us vow not to let their glory pass from this good Earth.[17]

In 1991 the State of Maryland offered anyone registering an automobile the   68
option of paying $20 (which would go to an environmental fund) to receive a special license plate bearing the motto: "Treasure the Chesapeake." A surprising number of registrants bought the plate. How many of us would have ponied up the $20 for a plate that read: "Use the Chesapeake Efficiently" or "The Chesapeake: It Satisfies Your Revealed and Expressed Preferences"?

To treasure the Chesapeake is to see that it has a good of its own—and   69
therefore a "health" or "integrity"—that we should protect even when to do so does not benefit us. "Why did you do all this for me?" Wilbur asked. "I've never

done anything for you." Even when nature does not do anything for us—one might think, for example, of the eagles and otters destroyed in Prince William Sound—we owe it protection for moral and aesthetic reasons. Otherwise our civilization and our lives will amount to little more than the satisfaction of private preferences: what Charlotte described as "all this trapping and eating flies."

In this essay, I have proposed that we may lift up our lives a little by seeing   70
nature as Charlotte did, not just as an assortment of resources to be managed and consumed, but also as a setting for collective moral and aesthetic judgment. I have also suggested that our evolutionary heritage—the diversity of species, the miracle of life—confronts us with the choice Zuckerman had to make: whether to butcher nature for the market or to protect it as an object of moral attention and aesthetic appreciation.

If Zuckerman had not learned to appreciate Wilbur for his own sake, he   71
would have converted the pig to bacon and chops. Likewise, if we do not value nature for ethical and aesthetic reasons, then we might well pollute and degrade it for instrumental ones. If a spider could treat a pig as a friend, however, then we should be able to treat a forest, an estuary, or any other living system in the same way.

REFERENCES

1. E. B. White, *Charlotte's Web* (New York: Harper & Row, 1952).
2. In defining the instrumental and aesthetic good, I follow the analysis of Georg Henrik von Wright, *The Varieties of Goodness* (London: Routledge & Kegan Paul, 1963), pp. 19–40. Von Wright, however, uses the term technical good where I use the term aesthetic good.
3. See Susan Wolf, "Moral Saints," *Journal of Philosophy* 79 (1982): 419–39.
4. During the early 1970s an enormous investment in research led to completely inconclusive findings based on animal studies, although one prominent pharmacologist summed up the available evidence by saying that at then-current levels DDT was not a human carcinogen. For documentation, see Thomas R. Dunlap, *DDT: Scientists, Citizens, and Public Policy* (Princeton: Princeton University Press, 1981), esp. pp. 214–17. Oddly, there have been few epidemiological studies during the 1980s, but those that were ~one show no clear link between DDT exposure and cancer risk. For a review with citations, see Harold M. Schmeck, Jr., "Study Finds No Link Between Cancer Risk and DDT Exposure," *New York Times*, 14 February 1989, reporting a decade-long study of nearly 1,000 people with higher than average exposure to DDT; it found no statistically significant link between the amount of DDT in their bodies and the risk of death by cancer.

5. Scholars argue correctly, I believe, that "in the 1970s, the prevention of cancer risks was accepted as a proxy for all environmental damage." A. Dan Tarlock, "Earth and Other Ethics: The Institutional Issues," *Tennessee Law Review* 56, no. 1 (1988): 63 (citing the DDT controversy as an example). See also, Regulating Pesticides, National Academy of Sciences (Washington, D.C.: NAS Press, National Research Council, 1980), pp. 18–28.

6. Jeremy Rifkin, *Biosphere Politics: A New Consciousness for a New Century* (New York: Crown, 1991), p. 69.

7. Office of Policy Analysis, EPA, The Cost of Clean Air and Water, Executive Summary (1984), p. 3. For an overview of the disappointing results of water quality protection, see William Pedersen, "Turning the Tide on Water Quality," *Ecology Law Quarterly* 15 (1988): 69–73.

8. A. Kneese and B. Bower, *Managing Water Quality: Economics, Technology, Institutions* (Baltimore: John Hopkins Press, Resources for the Future, 1968), p. 125.

9. For details about the Westway Project, see The Westway Project: A Study of Failure of Federal/State Relations, Sixty-Sixth Report by the Committee on Government Operations, 98th Cong. 2d Sess., HR 98–1166, Washington, D.C., U.S.G.P.O.,1984. See also Action for a Rational Transit v. West Side Highway Project, 536 F. Supp.1225 (S.D.N.Y.1982); Sierra Club v. U.S. Army Corps of Engineers, 541 F.Supp. 1327 (S.D.N.Y 1982) and 701 F.2d 1011 (2d Cir.1983). For another case history exemplifying the same point farther up the Hudson, see L. W. Barnhouse et al., "Population Biology in the Courtroom: The Hudson River Controversy," *BioScience* 34, no. 1 (1984): 14–19.

10. George Krantz is quoted in the *Washington Post*, 26 September 1984.

11. See, for example, Harold Webber, "Aquabusiness," in *Biotechnology and the Marine Sciences*, ed. R. Colwell, A. Sinskey, and E. Pariser (New York: Wiley, 1984), pp. 115–16. Webber believes we depend on traditional fisheries only because the "results of recent research and development in the biotechnological sciences have not yet been integrated into the broader context of large scale, vertically integrated, high technology, centrally controlled, aquabusiness food production systems." He calls the substitution of industrial for "natural" methods of fish production in aquatic environments "Vertically Integrated Aquaculture (VIA)."

12. Jay Mathews, "In Alaska, Oil Spill Has Lost Its Sheen," *Washington Post*, 9 February 1991.

13. For discussion, see T. C. Whitmore, "The Conservation of Tropical Rain Forests," in *Conservation Biology: An Evolutionary Perspective*, ed.

M. Soule and B. A. Wilcox (Sunderland, Mass.: Sinauer, 1980), p. 313: "The suggestion, sometimes made, that atmospheric oxygen levels would be lowered by the removal of tropical rain forests rests on a mistaken view of climax ecosystems."

14. See William Allen, "Penn Prof Views Biotechnology as Potential Threat to Tropical Forests," *Genetic Engineering News 7*, no. 10 (1987): 10. The article quotes a letter by Janzen: "Tropical wildlands and most of the earth's contemporary species still exist because humanity has not had organisms capable of converting all tropical land surfaces to profitable agriculture and animal husbandry. Within one to three decades, organisms modified through genetic engineering will be capable of making agriculture or animal husbandry, or both, profitable on virtually any land surface. Agricultural inviability, the single greatest tropical conservation force, will be gone."

Some commentators have speculated that transpiration from rain forests may play some role in the atmosphere. Since more that 85 percent of water absorbed into the atmosphere comes from the oceans, however, the marginal difference—if any—in transpiration between natural and biotech species in rain forests is unlikely to be consequential.

15. Immanuel Kant, *Foundations of the Metaphysics of Morals*, ed. R. P. Wolff, trans. L. W. Beck (Indianapolis: Bobbs-Merrill, 1959), p. 53. Emphasis in original.

16. Perry Miller, *Nature's Nation* (Cambridge, Mass.: Harvard University Press, 1967).

17. William K. Reilly, "A Strategy to Save the Great Water Bodies," *EPA Journal 16*, no. 6 (1990): 4.

Margaret Talbot, a *New Yorker* staff writer since 2003, specializes in the coverage of social policy, especially prominent legal battles on issues such as gay marriage and the teaching of creationism. She also writes on issues related to psychology, family life, and manners and morals. She previously wrote for the *New York Times Magazine* and *The Atlantic Monthly* and was a founding editor of *Lingua Franca* and, from 1995 to 1999, an editor at *The New Republic*. She now serves as a senior fellow at the New America Foundation, a nonprofit, nonpartisan public policy institute in Washington, D.C. Anthologies featuring her essays include *The Best American Science Writing* (2002) and *Because I Said So: 33 Mothers Write about Children, Sex, Men, Aging, Faith, Race, and Themselves* (2005). In 1999, she received the Whiting Writer's Award.

Brain Gain

Margaret Talbot

A young man I'll call Alex recently graduated from Harvard. As a history major,   1
Alex wrote about a dozen papers a semester. He also ran a student organization, for which he often worked more than forty hours a week; when he wasn't on the job, he had classes. Weeknights were devoted to all the schoolwork that he couldn't finish during the day, and weekend nights were spent drinking with friends and going to dance parties. "Trite as it sounds," he told me, it seemed important to "maybe appreciate my own youth." Since, in essence, this life was impossible, Alex began taking Adderall to make it possible.

    Adderall, a stimulant composed of mixed amphetamine salts, is commonly   2
prescribed for children and adults who have been given a diagnosis of attention-deficit hyperactivity disorder. But in recent years Adderall and Ritalin, another stimulant, have been adopted as cognitive enhancers: drugs that high-functioning, overcommitted people take to become higher-functioning and more overcommitted. (Such use is "off label," meaning that it does not have the approval of either the drug's manufacturer or the Food and Drug Administration.) College campuses have become laboratories for experimentation with neuroenhancement, and Alex was an ingenious experimenter. His brother had received a diagnosis of A.D.H.D., and in his freshman year Alex obtained an Adderall prescription for himself by describing to a doctor symptoms that he knew were typical of the disorder. During his college years, Alex

took fifteen milligrams of Adderall most evenings, usually after dinner, guaranteeing that he would maintain intense focus while losing "any ability to sleep for approximately eight to ten hours." In his sophomore year, he persuaded the doctor to add a thirty-milligram "extended release" capsule to his daily regimen.

Alex recalled one week during his junior year when he had four term papers due. Minutes after waking on Monday morning, around seven-thirty, he swallowed some "immediate release" Adderall. The drug, along with a steady stream of caffeine, helped him to concentrate during classes and meetings, but he noticed some odd effects; at a morning tutorial, he explained to me in an e-mail, "I alternated between speaking too quickly and thoroughly on some subjects and feeling awkwardly quiet during other points of the discussion." Lunch was a blur: "It's always hard to eat much when on Adderall." That afternoon, he went to the library, where he spent "too much time researching a paper rather than actually writing it—a problem, I can assure you, that is common to all intellectually curious students on stimulants." At eight, he attended a two-hour meeting "with a group focussed on student mental-health issues." Alex then "took an extended-release Adderall" and worked productively on the paper all night. At eight the next morning, he attended a meeting of his organization; he felt like "a zombie," but "was there to insure that the semester's work didn't go to waste." After that, Alex explained, "I went back to my room to take advantage of my tired body." He fell asleep until noon, waking "in time to polish my first paper and hand it in."

I met Alex one evening last summer, at an appealingly scruffy bar in the New England city where he lives. Skinny and bearded, and wearing faded hipster jeans, he looked like the lead singer in an indie band. He was ingratiating and articulate, and smoked cigarettes with an ironic air of defiance. Alex was happy enough to talk about his frequent use of Adderall at Harvard, but he didn't want to see his name in print; he's involved with an Internet start-up, and worried that potential investors might disapprove of his habit.

After we had ordered beers, he said, "One of the most impressive features of being a student is how aware you are of a twenty-four-hour work cycle. When you conceive of what you have to do for school, it's not in terms of nine to five but in terms of what you can physically do in a week while still achieving a variety of goals in a variety of realms—social, romantic, sexual, extracurricular, résumé-building, academic commitments." Alex was eager to dispel the notion that students who took Adderall were "academic automatons who are using it in order to be first in their class, or in order to be an obvious admit to law school or the first accepted at a consulting firm." In fact, he said, "it's often people"—mainly guys—"who are looking in some way to compensate for activities that are detrimental to their performance." He explained, "At Harvard, at least, most people are to some degree realistic about it. . . . I don't think people who take Adderall are aiming to be the top person in the class. I think they're aiming to be among the best. Or maybe not even among the best. At the most basic level, they aim to do better than they would have otherwise." He went on, "Everyone is aware of the fact that if you were up at 3 A.M. writing this paper it isn't going to be as good as it could have been. The fact that you were partying all weekend, or spent the last week being high, watching 'Lost'—that's going to take a toll."

Alex's sense of who uses stimulants for so-called "nonmedical" purposes is borne out by two dozen or so scientific studies. In 2005, a team led by Sean Esteban McCabe, a professor at the University of Michigan's Substance Abuse Research Center, reported that in the previous year 4.1 per cent of American undergraduates had taken prescription stimulants for off-label use; at one school, the figure was twenty-five per cent. Other researchers have found even higher rates: a 2002 study at a small college found that more than thirty-five per cent of the students had used prescription stimulants nonmedically in the previous year.   6

Drugs such as Adderall can cause nervousness, headaches, sleeplessness, and decreased appetite, among other side effects. An F.D.A. warning on Adderall's label notes that "amphetamines have a high potential for abuse" and can lead to dependence. (The label also mentions that adults using Adderall have reported serious cardiac problems, though the role of the drug in those cases is unknown.) Yet college students tend to consider Adderall and Ritalin benign, in part because they are likely to know peers who have taken the drugs since childhood for A.D.H.D. Indeed, McCabe reports, most students who use stimulants for cognitive enhancement obtain them from an acquaintance with a prescription. Usually, the pills are given away, but some students sell them.   7

According to McCabe's research team, white male undergraduates at highly competitive schools—especially in the Northeast—are the most frequent collegiate users of neuroenhancers. Users are also more likely to belong to a fraternity or a sorority, and to have a G.P.A. of 3.0 or lower. They are ten times as likely to report that they have smoked marijuana in the past year, and twenty times as likely to say that they have used cocaine. In other words, they are decent students at schools where, to be a great student, you have to give up a lot more partying than they're willing to give up.   8

The BoredAt Web sites—which allow college students to chat idly while they're ostensibly studying—are filled with messages about Adderall. Posts like these, from the BoredAtPenn site, are typical: "I have some Adderall—I'm sitting by room 101.10 in a grey shirt and headphones"; "I have Adderall for sale 20mg for $15"; "I took Adderall at 8 p.m., it's 6:30 a.m. and I've barely blinked."   9

On the Columbia site, a poster with an e-mail address from CUNY complains that her friends take Adderall "like candy," adding, "I don't want to be at a disadvantage to everyone else. Is it really that dangerous? Will it fuck me up? My grades weren't that great this year and I could do with a bump." A Columbia student responds, "It's probably not a good idea if you're not prescribed," but offers practical advice anyway: "Keep the dose normal and don't grind them up or snort them." Occasional dissents ("I think there should be random drug testing at every exam") are drowned out by testimonials like this one, from the BoredAtHarvard site: "I don't want to be a pusher or start people on something bad, but Adderall is AMAZING."

Alex remains enthusiastic about Adderall, but he also has a slightly jaundiced critique of it. "It only works as a cognitive enhancer insofar as you are dedicated to accomplishing the task at hand," he said. "The number of times I've taken Adderall late at night and decided that, rather than starting my paper, hey, I'll organize my entire music library! I've seen people obsessively cleaning their rooms on it." Alex thought that generally the drug helped him to bear down on his work, but it also tended to produce writing with a characteristic flaw. "Often, I've looked back at papers I've written on Adderall, and they're verbose. They're belaboring a point, trying to create this airtight argument, when if you just got to your point in a more direct manner it would be stronger. But with Adderall I'd produce two pages on something that could be said in a couple of sentences." Nevertheless, his Adderall-assisted papers usually earned him at least a B. They got the job done. As Alex put it, "Productivity is a good thing."

Last April, the scientific journal *Nature* published the results of an informal online poll asking whether readers attempted to sharpen "their focus, concentration, or memory" by taking drugs such as Ritalin and Provigil—a newer kind of stimulant, known generically as modafinil, which was developed to treat narcolepsy. One out of five respondents said that they did. A majority of the fourteen hundred readers who responded said that healthy adults should be permitted to take brain boosters for nonmedical reasons, and sixty-nine per cent said that mild side effects were an acceptable risk. Though a majority said that such drugs should not be made available to children who had no diagnosed medical condition, a third admitted that they would feel pressure to give "smart drugs" to their kids if they learned that other parents were doing so.

Such competitive anxieties are already being felt in the workplace. Recently, an advice column in *Wired* featured a question from a reader worried about "a rising star at the firm" who was "using unprescribed modafinil to work crazy hours. Our boss has started getting on my case for not being as productive." And on Internet forums such as ImmInst, whose members share a nerdy passion for tweaking their cognitive function through drugs and supplements, people trade advice about dosages and "stacks"—improvised combinations—of neuroenhancers. ("Cut a tablet into fourths and took 25 mg every four hours, 4 times today, and had a great and productive day—with no side effects.") In one recent post, a fifty-two-year-old—who was working full time, studying for an advanced degree at night, and "married, etc."—wrote that after experimenting with modafinil he had settled on two daily doses of a hundred milligrams each. He believed that he was "performing a little better," adding, "I also feel slightly more animated when in discussion."

Not long ago, I met with Anjan Chatterjee, a neurologist at the University   13
of Pennsylvania, in his office, which is tucked inside the labyrinthine Penn hospital complex. Chatterjee's main research interests are in subjects like the neurological basis of spatial understanding, but in the past few years, as he has heard more about students taking cognitive enhancers, he has begun writing about the ethical implications of such behavior. In 2004, he coined the term "cosmetic neurology" to describe the practice of using drugs developed for recognized medical conditions to strengthen ordinary cognition. Chatterjee worries about cosmetic neurology, but he thinks that it will eventually become as acceptable as cosmetic surgery has; in fact, with neuroenhancement it's harder to argue that it's frivolous. As he notes in a 2007 paper, "Many sectors of society have winner-take-all conditions in which small advantages produce disproportionate rewards." At school and at work, the usefulness of being "smarter," needing less sleep, and learning more quickly are all "abundantly clear." In the near future, he predicts, some neurologists will refashion themselves as "quality-of-life consultants," whose role will be "to provide information while abrogating final responsibility for these decisions to patients." The demand is certainly there: from an aging population that won't put up with memory loss; from overwrought parents bent on giving their children every possible edge; from anxious employees in an efficiency-obsessed, BlackBerry-equipped office culture, where work never really ends.

Chatterjee told me that many people who come to his clinic are cognitively   14
preoccupied versions of what doctors call the "worried well." The day I visited his office, he had just seen a middle-aged woman, a successful Philadelphia lawyer, who mentioned having to struggle a bit to come up with certain names. "Here's an example of someone who by most measures is doing perfectly fine," Chatterjee said. "She's not having any trouble at work. But she notices she's having some problems, and it's very hard to know how much of that is just getting older." Of course, people in her position could strive to get regular exercise and plenty of intellectual stimulation, both of which have been shown to help maintain cognitive function. But maybe they're already doing so and want a bigger

mental rev-up, or maybe they want something easier than sweaty workouts and Russian novels: a pill.

Recently, I spoke on the phone with Barbara Sahakian, a clinical neuropsy- 15 chologist at Cambridge University, and the co-author of a December, 2007, article in *Nature*, "Professor's Little Helper." Sahakian, who also consults for several pharmaceutical companies, and her co-author, Sharon Morein-Zamir, reported that a number of their colleagues were using prescription drugs like Adderall and Provigil. Because the drugs are easy to buy online, they wrote, it would be difficult to stop their spread: "The drive for self-enhancement of cognition is likely to be as strong if not stronger than in the realms of 'enhancement' of beauty and sexual function." (In places like Cambridge, at least.)

When I spoke with Sahakian, she had just flown from England to Scottsdale, 16 Arizona, to attend a conference, and she was tired. She might, justifiably, have forgone distractions like me, but she had her cell phone with her, and though it was a weekend morning some industrious person in the Cambridge news office had reached Sahakian in her hotel room, after she got out of the shower and before she had to rush to the first session. "We may be healthy and high-functioning, and think of ourselves that way, but it's very rare that we are actually functioning at our *optimal* level," Sahakian said. "Take me. I'm over here, and I've got jet lag and I've got to give a talk tonight and perform well, in what will be the middle of the night, U.K. time." She mentioned businessmen who have to fly back and forth across the Atlantic: "The difference between making a deal and not is huge and they sometimes only have one meeting to try and do it." She sympathized with them, but, she added, "we are a society that so wants a quick fix that many people are happy to take drugs."

For the moment, people looking for that particular quick fix have a limited 17 choice of meds. But, given the amount of money and research hours being spent on developing drugs to treat cognitive decline, Provigil and Adderall are likely to be joined by a bigger pharmacopoeia. Among the drugs in the pipeline are ampakines, which target a type of glutamate receptor in the brain; it is hoped that they may stem the memory loss associated with diseases like Alzheimer's. But ampakines may also give healthy people a palpable cognitive boost. A 2007 study of sixteen healthy elderly volunteers found that five hundred milligrams of one particular ampakine "unequivocally" improved short-term memory, though it appeared to detract from episodic memory—the recall of past events. Another class of drugs, cholinesterase inhibitors, which are already being used with some success to treat Alzheimer's patients, have also shown promise as neuroenhancers. In one study, the drug donepezil strengthened the performance of pilots on flight simulators; in another, of thirty healthy young male volunteers, it improved verbal and visual episodic memory. Several pharmaceutical companies are working on drugs that target nicotine receptors in the brain, in the hope that they can replicate the cognitive uptick that smokers get from cigarettes.

Zack and Casey Lynch are a young couple who, in 2005, launched   18
NeuroInsights, a company that advises investors on developments in brain-science technology. (Since then, they've also founded a lobbying group, the Neurotechnology Industry Organization.) Casey and Zack met as undergraduates at U.C.L.A.; she went on to get a master's degree in neuroscience at U.C.S.F., and he became an executive at a software company. Last summer, I had coffee with them in the Noe Valley neighborhood of San Francisco, and they both spoke with casual certainty about the coming market for neuroenhancers. Zack, who has a book being published this summer, called "The Neuro Revolution," said, "We live in an information society. What's the next form of human society? The *neuro*-society." In coming years, he said, scientists will understand the brain better, and we'll have improved neuroenhancers that some people will use therapeutically, others because they are "on the borderline of needing them therapeutically," and others purely "for competitive advantage."

Zack explained that he didn't really like the term "enhancement": "We're   19
not talking about superhuman intelligence. No one's saying we're coming out with a pill that's going to make you smarter than Einstein! . . . What we're really talking about is *enabling* people." He sketched a bell curve on the back of a napkin. "Almost every drug in development is something that will take someone who's working at, like, forty per cent or fifty per cent, and take them up to eighty," he said.

New psychiatric drugs have a way of creating markets for themselves.   20
Disorders often become widely diagnosed after drugs come along that can alter a set of suboptimal behaviors. In this way, Ritalin and Adderall helped make A.D.H.D. a household name, and advertisements for antidepressants have helped define shyness as a malady. If there's a pill that can clear up the wavering focus of sleep-deprived youth, or mitigate the tip-of-the-tongue experience of middle age, then those rather ordinary states may come to be seen as syndromes. As Casey put it, "The drugs get better, and the markets become bigger."

"Yes," Zack said. "We call it the lifestyle-improvement market."   21

The Lynches said that Provigil was a classic example of a related phenome-   22
non: mission creep. In 1998, Cephalon, the pharmaceutical company that manufactures it, received government approval to market the drug, but only for "excessive daytime sleepiness" due to narcolepsy; by 2004, Cephalon had obtained permission to expand the labelling, so that it included sleep apnea and "shift-work sleep disorder." Net sales of Provigil climbed from a hundred and

ninety-six million dollars in 2002 to nine hundred and eighty-eight million in 2008.

Cephalon executives have repeatedly said that they do not condone off-label use of Provigil, but in 2002 the company was reprimanded by the F.D.A. for distributing marketing materials that presented the drug as a remedy for tiredness, "decreased activity," and other supposed ailments. And in 2008 Cephalon paid four hundred and twenty-five million dollars and pleaded guilty to a federal criminal charge relating to its promotion of off-label uses for Provigil and two other drugs. Later this year, Cephalon plans to introduce Nuvigil, a longer-lasting variant of Provigil. Candace Steele, a spokesperson, said, "We're exploring its possibilities to treat excessive sleepiness associated with schizophrenia, bipolar depression, traumatic injury, and jet lag." Though she emphasized that Cephalon was not developing Nuvigil as a neuroenhancer, she noted, "As part of the preparation for some of these other diseases, we're looking to see if there's improvement in cognition."

Unlike many hypothetical scenarios that bioethicists worry about—human clones, "designer babies"—cognitive enhancement is already in full swing. Even if today's smart drugs aren't as powerful as such drugs may someday be, there are plenty of questions that need to be asked about them. How much do they actually help? Are they potentially harmful or addictive? Then, there's the question of what we mean by "smarter." Could enhancing one kind of thinking exact a toll on others? All these questions need proper scientific answers, but for now much of the discussion is taking place furtively, among the increasing number of Americans who are performing daily experiments on their own brains.

Paul Phillips was unusual for a professional poker player. When he joined the circuit, in the late nineties, he was already a millionaire: a twenty-something tech guy who had started off writing software, helped found an Internet portal called go2net, and cashed in at the right moment. He was cerebral and, at times, brusque. His nickname was Dot Com. On the international poker-tournament scene—where the male players tend to be either unabashedly schlumpy or sharply dressed in the manner of a Vegas hotel manager—Phillips cultivated a geeky New Wave style. He wore vintage shirts in wild geometric patterns; his hair was dyed orange or silver one week, shaved off the next. Most unusual of all, Phillips talked freely about taking prescription drugs—Adderall and, especially, Provigil—in order to play better cards.

He first took up the game in 1995, when he was in college, at U.C. San Diego. He recalled, "It was very mathematical, but you could also inject yourself into the game and manipulate the other guy with words"—more so than in a game like chess. Phillips soon felt that he had mastered the strategic aspects of poker. The key variable was execution. At tournaments, he needed to be able to stay focussed for fourteen hours at a stretch, often for several days, but he found it difficult to do so. In 2003, a doctor gave him a diagnosis of A.D.H.D., and he began taking Adderall. Within six months, he had won $1.6 million at poker events—far more than he'd won in the previous four years. Adderall not only helped him concentrate; it also helped him resist the impulse to keep playing losing hands out of boredom. In 2004, Phillips asked his doctor to give him a prescription for Provigil, which he added to his Adderall regimen. He took between two hundred and three hundred milligrams of Provigil a day, which, he felt, helped him settle into an even more serene and objective state of mindfulness; as he put it, he felt "less like a participant than an observer—and a very effective one." Though Phillips sees neuroenhancers as essentially steroids for the brain, they haven't yet been banned from poker competitions.

Last summer, I visited Phillips in the high-desert resort town of Bend, Oregon, where he lives with his wife, Kathleen, and their two daughters, Ivy and Ruby. Phillips, who is now thirty-six, seemed a bit out of place in Bend, where people spend a lot of time skiing and river rafting. Among the friendly, faithfully recycling locals, he was making an effort to curb his caustic side. Still, when I first sent Phillips an e-mail asking him to explain, more precisely, how Provigil affected him, he couldn't resist a smart-ass answer: "More precisely: after a pill is consumed, tiny molecules are absorbed into the bloodstream, where they eventually cross the blood-brain barrier and influence the operation of the wetware up top." 27

In person, he was more obliging. He picked me up at the Bend airport driving a black convertible BMW, and we went for coffee at a cheery café called Thump. Phillips wore shorts and flip-flops and his black T-shirt displayed an obscure programming joke. "Poker is about sitting in one place, watching your opponents for a long time, and making better observations about them than they make about you," he said. With Provigil, he "could process all the information about what was going on at the table and do something about it." Though there is no question that Phillips became much more successful at poker after taking neuroenhancers, I asked him if his improvement could be explained by a placebo effect, or by coincidence. He doubted it, but allowed that it could. Still, he said, "there's a sort of clarity I get with Provigil. With Adderall, I'd characterize the effect as correction—correction of an underlying condition. Provigil feels like enhancement." And, whereas Adderall made him "jittery," Provigil's effects were "completely limited to my brain." He had "zero difficulty sleeping." 28

On the other hand, Phillips said, Provigil's effects "have attenuated over time. The body is an amazing adjusting machine, and there's no upside that I've been able to see to just taking more." A few years ago, Phillips tired of poker, and 29 started playing competitive Scrabble. He was good, but not that good. He was older than many of his rivals, and he needed to undertake a lot of rote memorization, which didn't come as easily as it once had. "I stopped short of memorizing the entire dictionary, and to be really good you have to get up to eight- and nine-letter words," he told me. "But I did learn every word up to five letters, plus maybe ten thousand seven- and eight-letter words." Provigil, he said, helped with the memorization process, but "it's not going to make you smarter. It's going to make you better able to use the tools you have for a sustained period."

⟲ Similarly, a journalist I know, who takes the drug when he has to stay up all   30
night on deadline, says that it doesn't help in the phase when he's trying to figure out what he wants to say or how to structure a story; but, once he's arrived at those insights, it helps him stay intent on completing a draft. Similarly, a seventy-four-year-old who published a letter in *Nature* last year offered a charmingly specific description of his modafinil habit: "Previously, I could work competently on the fracture-mechanics of high-silica stone (while replicating ancient tool-flaking techniques) for about an hour. With modafinil, I could continue for almost three hours."

Cephalon, the Provigil manufacturer, has publicly downplayed the idea that   31
the drug can be used as a smart pill. In 2007, the company's founder and C.E.O., Frank Baldino, Jr., told a reporter from the trade journal *Pharmaceutical Executive*, "I think if you're tired, Provigil will keep you awake. If you're not tired, it's not going to do anything." But Baldino may have been overly modest. Only a few studies have been done of Provigil's effects on healthy, non-sleep-deprived volunteers, but those studies suggest that Provigil does provide an edge, at least for some kinds of challenges. In 2002, researchers at Cambridge University gave sixty healthy young male volunteers a battery of standard cognitive tests. One group received modafinil; the other got a placebo. The modafinil group performed better on several tasks, such as the "digit span" test, in which subjects are asked to repeat increasingly longer strings of numbers forward, then backward. They also did better in recognizing repeated visual patterns and on a spatial-planning challenge known as the Tower of London task. (It's not nearly as fun as it sounds.) Writing in the journal *Psychopharmacology*, the study's authors said the results suggested that "modafinil offers significant potential as a cognitive enhancer."

Phillips told me that, much as he believes in neuroenhancers, he did not   32
want to be "the poster boy for smart-in-a-pill." At one point, he said, "We really don't know the possible implications for long-term use of these things." (He recently stopped taking Provigil every day, replacing it with another prescription stimulant.) He found the "arms-race aspect" of cognitive enhancement distaste-

ful, and didn't like the idea that parents might force their kids to take smart pills. He sighed when I suggested that adults, too, might feel coerced into using the drugs. "Yeah, in a competitive field—if suddenly a quarter of the people are more equipped, but you don't want to take the risks with your body—it could begin to seem terribly unfair," he said. "I don't think we need to be turning up the crank another notch on how hard we work. But the fact is, the baseline competitive level is going to reorient around what these drugs make possible, and you can choose to compete or not."

In the afternoon, we drove over to Phillips's house—a big place, handsome and new, with a sweeping deck overhanging the Deschutes River. Inside, toys were strewn across the shag carpeting. Phillips was waiting for his wife and daughters to come home from the swimming pool, and, sitting in his huge, high-ceilinged living room, he looked a little bored. He told me that he had recently decided to apply to graduate school in computer programming. It was going to be hard—getting out all those applications, convincing graduate programs that he was serious about returning to school. But he had, as he put it, "exhausted myself on all forms of leisure," and felt nostalgic for his last two years of college, when he had discovered computer programming. "That was the most purely intellectually satisfying period of my whole life," he said. "It transformed my brain from being all over the place to a reasonable edifice of knowledge about something." Back then, he hadn't taken any smart pills. "I would have been a freakin' dynamo in college if I'd been taking them," he said. "But, still, I had to *find* computers. That made a bigger difference than anything else—finding something I just couldn't get enough of." 33

Provigil may well confer a temporary advantage on healthy people, but this doesn't mean that it's ready to replace your morning espresso. Anjan Chatterjee told me that there "just aren't enough studies of these drugs in normal people." He said, "In the situations where they do help, do they come with a cost?" As he wrote in a recent letter to *Nature*, "Most seasoned physicians have had the sobering experience of prescribing medications that, despite good intentions, caused bad outcomes." Given that cognitive enhancement is a choice, not a necessity, the cost-benefit calculation for neuroenhancers should probably be different than it is for, say, heart medications. 34

Provigil can be habit-forming. In a study published recently in the *Journal of the American Medical Association*, a group led by Nora Volkow, the director of the National Institute on Drug Abuse, scanned the brains of ten men after they had been given a placebo, and also after they had been given a dose of modafinil. The modafinil appeared to lead to an increase in the brain chemical dopamine. "Because drugs that increase dopamine have the potential for abuse," Volkow's 35 report concluded, "these results suggest that risk for addiction in vulnerable persons merits heightened awareness." (Cephalon, in a response to the report, notes that Provigil's label urges physicians to monitor patients closely, especially those with a history of drug abuse.) On the Web site Erowid, where people vividly, and anonymously, report their experiences with legal and illegal drugs, some modafinil users have described a dependency on the drug. One man, who identified himself as a former biochemistry student, said that he had succeeded in kicking cocaine and opiate habits but couldn't stop using modafinil. Whenever he ran out of the drug, he said, "I start to freak out." After "4–5 days" without it, "the head fog starts to come back."

Eliminating foggy-headedness seems to be the goal of many users of neu- 36 roenhancers. But can today's drugs actually accomplish this? I recently posed this question to Anjan Chatterjee's colleague Martha Farah, who is a psychologist at Penn and the director of its Center for Cognitive Neuroscience. She has been writing about neuroenhancers for several years from a perspective that is deeply fascinated and mildly critical, but basically in favor—with the important caveat that we need to know much more about how these drugs work. I spoke with her one afternoon at her research center, which is in a decidedly unfuturistic-looking Victorian house on Walnut Street, in Philadelphia. Farah, who is an energetic conversationalist, had bought canned espresso drinks for us. Though she does not take neuroenhancers, she has found that her interest in them has renewed her romance with the next best thing: caffeine.

Farah had just finished a paper in which she reviewed the evidence on pre- 37 scription stimulants as neuroenhancers from forty laboratory studies involving healthy subjects. Most of the studies looked at one of three types of cognition: learning, working memory, and cognitive control. A typical learning test asks subjects to memorize a list of paired words; an hour, a few days, or a week later, they are presented with the first words in the pairs and asked to come up with the second. The studies on learning showed that neuroenhancers did improve retention. The benefits were more apparent in studies where subjects had been asked to remember information for several days or longer.

Working memory has been likened to a mental scratch pad: you use it to 38 keep relevant data in mind while you're completing a task. (Imagine a cross-examination, in which a lawyer has to keep track of the answers a witness has given, and formulate new questions based on them.) In one common test, subjects are shown a series of items—usually letters or numbers—and then presented with challenges: Was this number or letter in the series? Was this one? In the working-memory tests, subjects performed better on neuroenhancers, though several of the studies suggested that the effect depended on how good a subject's working memory was to begin with: the better it was, the less benefit the drugs provided.

The third category that the studies examined was cognitive control—how   39
effectively you can check yourself in circumstances where the most natural
response is the wrong one. A classic test is the Stroop Task, in which people are
shown the name of a color (let's say orange) written in a different color (let's say
purple). They're asked to read the word (which is easy, because our habitual
response to a word is to read it) or to name the ink color (which is harder,
because our first impulse is to say "orange"). These studies presented a more
mixed picture, but over all they showed some benefit "for most normal healthy
subjects"—especially for people who had inherently poorer cognitive control.

Farah told me, "These drugs will definitely help some technically normal   40
people—that is, people who don't meet the diagnostic criteria for A.D.H.D. or
any kind of cognitive impairment." But, she emphasized, "they will help people in
the lower end of the ability range more than in the higher end." One explanation
for this phenomenon might be that, the more adept you are at a given task, the
less room you have to improve. Farah has a hunch that there may be another reason that existing drugs, so far, at least, don't offer as much help to people with
greater intellectual abilities. Drugs like Ritalin and Adderall work, in part, by ele-
vating the amount of dopamine in the brain. Dopamine is something you want
just enough of: too little, and you may not be as alert and motivated as you need
to be; too much, and you may feel overstimulated. Neuroscientists have discovered that some people have a gene that leads the brain to break down dopamine
faster, leaving less of it available; such people are generally a little worse at certain
cognitive tasks. People with more available dopamine are generally somewhat
better at the same tasks. It makes sense, then, that people with naturally low
dopamine would benefit more from an artificial boost.

Of course, learning, working memory, and cognitive control represent just a   41
few aspects of thinking. Farah concluded that studies looking at other kinds of
cognition—verbal fluency, for instance—were too few and too contradictory to
tell us much. And the effects of neuroenhancers on some vital forms of intellectual activity, such as abstract thought and creativity, have barely been studied at
all. Farah said that the extant literature was concerned with "fairly boring kinds
of thinking—how long can you stay vigilant while staring at a screen and waiting for a little light to blink." She added, "It would be great to have studies of
more flexible kinds of thought."

Both Chatterjee and Farah have wondered whether drugs that heighten   42
users' focus might dampen their creativity. After all, some of our best ideas come
to us not when we sit down at a desk but, rather, when we're in the shower or
walking the dog—letting our minds roam. Jimi Hendrix reported that the inspiration for "Purple Haze" came to him in a dream; the chemist Friedrich August
Kekule claimed that he discovered the ring structure of benzene during a reverie

in which he saw the image of a snake biting its tail. Farah told me, "Cognitive psychologists have found that there is a trade-off between attentional focus and creativity. And there is some evidence that suggests that individuals who are better able to focus on one thing and filter out distractions tend to be less creative."

Farah and Chatterjee recently completed a preliminary study looking at the effect of one ten-milligram dose of Adderall on sixteen students doing standard laboratory tests of creative thinking. They did not find that this low dose had a detrimental effect, but both believe that this is only the beginning of the vetting that must be done. "More and more of our young people are using these drugs to help them work," Farah said. "They've got their laptop, their iPhone, and their Adderall. This rising generation of workers and leaders may have a subtly different style of thinking and working, because they're using these drugs or because they learned to work using these drugs, so that even if you take the drugs away they'll still have a certain approach. I'm a little concerned that we could be raising a generation of very focussed accountants." 43

Farah has also been considering the ethical complications resulting from the rise of smart drugs. Don't neuroenhancers confer yet another advantage on the kind of people who already can afford private tutors and prep courses? At many colleges, students have begun calling the off-label use of neuroenhancers a form of cheating. Writing last year in the *Cavalier Daily*, the student newspaper of the University of Virginia, a columnist named Greg Crapanzano argued that neuroenhancers "create an unfair advantage for the users who are willing to break the law in order to gain an edge. These students create work that is dependent on the use of a pill rather than their own work ethic." Of course, it's hard to imagine a university administration that would require students to pee in a cup before they get their blue books. And though secretly taking a neuroenhancer for a three-hour exam does seem unfair, condemning the drugs' use seems extreme. Even with the aid of a neuroenhancer, you still have to write the essay, conceive the screenplay, or finish the grant proposal, and if you can take credit for work you've done on caffeine or nicotine, then you can take credit for work produced on Provigil. 44

Farah questions the idea that neuroenhancers will expand inequality. Citing the "pretty clear trend across the studies that say neuroenhancers will be less helpful for people who score above average," she said that cognitive-enhancing pills could actually become levellers, if they are dispensed cheaply. A 2007 discussion paper published by the British Medical Association also makes this point: "Equality of opportunity is an explicit goal of our education system, giving individuals the best chance of achieving their full potential and of competing on equal terms with their peers. Selective use of neuroenhancers amongst those with lower intellectual capacity, or those from deprived backgrounds who do not have 45 the benefit of additional tuition, could enhance the educational opportunities for those groups." If the idea of giving a pill as a substitute for better teaching seems repellent—like substituting an I.V. drip of synthetic nutrition for actual food—it may nevertheless be preferable to a scenario in which only wealthy kids receive a frequent mental boost.

Farah was one of several scholars who contributed to a recent article in   46
Nature, "Towards Responsible Use of Cognitive Enhancing Drugs by the Healthy." The optimistic tone of the article suggested that some bioethicists are leaning toward endorsing neuroenhancement. "Like all new technologies, cognitive enhancement can be used well or poorly," the article declared. "We should welcome new methods of improving our brain function. In a world in which human workspans and lifespans are increasing, cognitive enhancement tools—including the pharmacological—will be increasingly useful for improved quality of life and extended work productivity, as well as to stave off normal and pathological age-related cognitive declines. Safe and effective cognitive enhancers will benefit both the individual and society." The British Medical Association report offered a similarly upbeat observation: "Universal access to enhancing interventions would bring up the base-line level of cognitive ability, which is generally seen to be a good thing."

And yet when enthusiasts share their vision of our neuroenhanced future it   47
can sound dystopian. Zack Lynch, of NeuroInsights, gave me a rationale for smart pills that I found particularly grim. "If you're a fifty-five-year-old in Boston, you have to compete with a twenty-six-year-old from Mumbai now, and those kinds of pressures are only going to grow," he began. Countries other than the U.S. might tend to be a little looser with their regulations, and offer approval of new cognitive enhancers first. "And if you're a company that's got forty-seven offices worldwide, and all of a sudden your Singapore office is using cognitive enablers, and you're saying to Congress, 'I'm moving all my financial operations to Singapore and Taiwan, because it's legal to use those there,' you bet that Congress is going to say, 'Well, O.K.' It will be a moot question then. It would be like saying, 'No, you can't use a cell phone. It might increase productivity!' "

If we eventually decide that neuroenhancers work, and are basically safe,   48
will we one day enforce their use? Lawmakers might compel certain workers—emergency-room doctors, air-traffic controllers—to take them. (Indeed, the Air Force already makes modafinil available to pilots embarking on long missions.) For the rest of us, the pressure will be subtler—that queasy feeling I get when I remember that my younger colleague is taking Provigil to meet deadlines. All this may be leading to a kind of society I'm not sure I want to live in: a society where we're even more overworked and driven by technology than we already

are, and where we have to take drugs to keep up; a society where we give children academic steroids along with their daily vitamins.

Paul McHugh, a psychiatrist at Johns Hopkins University, has written skeptically about cosmetic neurology. In a 2004 essay, he notes that at least once a year in his private practice he sees a young person—usually a boy—whose parents worry that his school performance could be better, and want a medication that will assure it. In most of these cases, "the truth is that the son does not have the superior I.Q. of his parents," though the boy may have other qualities that surpass those of his parents—he may be "handsome, charming, athletic, graceful." McHugh sees his job as trying to get the parents to "forget about adjusting him to their aims with medication or anything else." When I spoke with him on the phone, McHugh expanded on this point: "Maybe it's wrong-footed trying to fit people into the world, rather than trying to make the world a better place for people. And if the idea is that the only college your child can go to is Harvard, well, maybe *that's* the idea that needs righting."

If Alex, the Harvard student, and Paul Phillips, the poker player, consider their use of neuroenhancers a private act, Nicholas Seltzer sees his habit as a pursuit that aligns him with a larger movement for improving humanity. Seltzer has a B.A. from U.C. Davis and a master's degree in security policy from George Washington University. But the job that he obtained with these credentials—as a researcher at a defense-oriented think tank, in northern Virginia—has not left him feeling as intellectually alive as he would like. To compensate, he writes papers in his spare time on subjects like "human biological evolution and warfare." He also primes his brain with artificial challenges; even when he goes to the rest room at the office, he takes the opportunity to play memory or logic games on his cell phone. Seltzer, who is thirty, told me that he worried that he "didn't have the mental energy, the endurance, the—I don't know what to properly call this—the *sponginess* that I seem to recall having when I was younger."

Suffice it to say that this is not something you notice when you talk to Seltzer. And though our memory is probably at its peak in our early twenties, few thirty-year-olds are aware of a deficit. But Seltzer is the Washington-wonk equivalent of those models and actors in L.A. who discern tiny wrinkles long before their agent does. His girlfriend, a technology consultant whom he met in a museum, is nine years younger, and he was already thinking about how his mental fitness would stand up next to hers. He told me, "She's twenty-one, and I want to stay young and vigorous and don't want to be a burden on her later in life." He didn't worry about visible signs of aging, but he wanted to keep his mind "nimble and healthy for as long as possible."

Seltzer considers himself a "transhumanist," in the mold of the Oxford   52
philosopher Nick Bostrom and the futurist writer and inventor Ray Kurzweil.
Transhumanists are interested in robots, cryogenics, and living a really, really
long time; they consider biological limitations that the rest of us might accept,
or even appreciate, as creaky obstacles to be aggressively surmounted. On the
ImmInst forums—"ImmInst" stands for "Immortality Institute"—Seltzer and
other members discuss life-extension strategies and the potential benefits of cognitive enhancers. Some of the forum members limit themselves to vitamin and
mineral supplements. Others use Adderall or modafinil or, like Seltzer, a drug
called piracetam, which was first marketed by a Belgian pharmaceutical company
in 1972 and, in recent years, has become available in the U.S. from retailers that
sell supplements. Although not approved for any use by the F.D.A., piracetam
has been used experimentally on stroke patients—to little effect—and on
patients with a rare neurological condition called progressive myoclonus
epilepsy, for whom it proved helpful in alleviating muscle spasms. Data on piracetam's benefits for healthy people are virtually nonexistent, but many users
believe that the drug increases blood flow to the brain.

From the time I first talked to Seltzer, it was clear that although he felt cog-   53
nitive enhancers were of practical use, they also appealed to him on an aesthetic
level. Using neuroenhancers, he said, "is like customizing yourself—customizing
your brain." For some people, he went on, it was important to enhance their
mood, so they took antidepressants; but for people like him it was more important "to increase mental horsepower." He added, "It's fundamentally a choice
you're making about how you want to experience consciousness." Whereas the
nineties had been about "the personalization of technology," this decade was
about the personalization of the brain—what some enthusiasts have begun to
call "mind hacking."

Of course, the idea behind mind-hacking isn't exactly new. Fortifying one's   54
mental stamina with drugs of various kinds has a long history. Sir Francis Bacon
consumed everything from tobacco to saffron in the hope of goosing his brain.
Balzac reputedly fuelled sixteen-hour bouts of writing with copious servings of
coffee, which, he wrote, "chases away sleep, and gives us the capacity to engage
a little longer in the exercise of our intellects." Sartre dosed himself with speed
in order to finish "Critique of Dialectical Reason." My college friends and I wrote
term papers with the sweaty-palmed assistance of NoDoz tablets. And, before
smoking bans, entire office cultures chugged along on a collective nicotine
buzz—at least, if "Mad Men" is to be believed. Seltzer and his interlocutors on
the ImmInst forum are just the latest members of a seasoned cohort, even if they
have more complex pharmaceuticals at their disposal.

I eventually met Seltzer in an underground food court not far from the   55
Pentagon. We sat down at a Formica table in the dim light. Seltzer was slim, had
a shaved head, and wore metal-frame glasses; matching his fastidious look, he
spoke precisely, rarely stumbling over his words. I asked him if he had any ethical worries about smart drugs. After a pause, he said that he might have a concern if somebody popped a neuroenhancer before taking a licensing exam that
certified him as, say, a brain surgeon, and then stopped using the drug. Other
than that, he couldn't see a problem. He said that he was a firm believer in the
idea that "we should have a fair degree of liberty to do with our bodies and our
minds as we see fit, so long as it doesn't impinge on the basic rights, liberty, and
safety of others." He argued, "Why would you *want* an upward limit on the intellectual capabilities of a human being? And, if you have a very nationalist view-
point, why wouldn't you want our country to have the advantage over other
countries, particularly in what some people call a knowledge-based economy?"
He went on, "Think about the complexity of the intellectual tasks that people
need to accomplish today. Just trying to understand what Congress is doing is not
a simple thing! The complexity of understanding the gamut of scientific and
technical and social issues is difficult. If we had a tool that enabled more people
to understand the world at a greater level of sophistication, how can we prejudice ourselves against the notion, simply because we don't like athletes to do it?
To me, it doesn't seem like the same question. And it deserves its own debate."

Seltzer had never had a diagnosis of any kind of learning disorder. But he   56
added, "Though I wouldn't say I'm dyslexic, sometimes when I type prose, after
I look back and read it, I've frequently left out words or interposed words, and
sometimes I have difficulty concentrating." In graduate school, he obtained a
prescription for Adderall from a doctor who didn't ask a lot of questions. The
drug helped him, especially when his ambitions were relatively low. He recalled,
"I had this one paper, on nuclear strategy. The professor didn't look favorably on
any kind of creative thinking." On Adderall, he pumped out the paper in an
evening. "I just bit my tongue, regurgitated, and got a good-enough grade."

On the other hand, Seltzer recalled that he had taken piracetam to write an   57
essay on "the idea of harmony as a trope in Chinese political discourse"—it was
one of the papers he was proudest of. He said, "It was really an intellectual challenge to do. I felt that the piracetam helped me to work within the realm of the
abstract, and make the kind of associations that I needed—following this idea of
harmony from an ancient religious belief as it was translated throughout the centuries into a very important topic in political discourse."

After a hiatus of several years, Seltzer had recently resumed taking neuroen-   58
hancers. In addition to piracetam, he took a stack of supplements that he

thought helped his brain functioning: fish oils, five antioxidants, a product called ChocoMind, and a number of others, all available at the health-food store. He was thinking about adding modafinil, but hadn't yet. For breakfast every morning, he concocted a slurry of oatmeal, berries, soy milk, pomegranate juice, flaxseed, almond meal, raw eggs, and protein powder. The goal behind the recipe was efficiency: to rely on "one goop you could eat or drink that would have everything you need nutritionally for your brain and body." He explained, "Taste was the last thing on my mind; I wanted to be able to keep it down—that was it." (He told me this in the kitchen of his apartment; he lives with a roommate, who walked in while we were talking, listened perplexedly for a moment, then put a frozen pizza in the oven.)

Seltzer's decision to take piracetam was based on his own online reading, 59 which included medical-journal abstracts. He hadn't consulted a doctor. Since settling on a daily regimen of supplements, he had sensed an improvement in his intellectual work and his ability to engage in stimulating conversation. He continued, "I feel I'm better able to articulate my thoughts. I'm sure you've been in the zone—you're having a really exciting debate with somebody, your brain feels alive. I feel that more. But I don't want to say that it's this profound change."

I asked him if piracetam made him feel smarter, or just more alert and con- 60 fident—a little better equipped to marshal the resources he naturally had. "Maybe," he said. "I'm not sure what being smarter means, entirely. It's a difficult quality to measure. It's the gestalt factor, all these qualities coming together—not only your ability to crunch some numbers, or remember some figures or a sequence of numbers, but also your ability to maintain a certain emotional state that is conducive to productive intellectual work. I do feel I'm more intelligent with the drugs, but I can't give you a number of I.Q. points."

The effects of piracetam on healthy volunteers have been studied even less 61 than those of Adderall or modafinil. Most peer-reviewed studies focus on its effects on dementia, or on people who have suffered a seizure or a concussion. Many of the studies that look at other neurological effects were performed on rats and mice. Piracetam's mechanisms of action are not understood, though it may increase levels of the neurotransmitter acetylcholine. In 2008, a committee of the British Academy of Medical Sciences noted that many of the clinical trials of piracetam for dementia were methodologically flawed. Another published review of the available studies of the drug concluded that the evidence "does not support the use of piracetam in the treatment of people with dementia or cognitive impairment," but suggested that further investigation might be warranted. I asked Seltzer if he thought he should wait for scientific ratification of piracetam. He laughed. "I don't want to," he said. "Because it's working."

It makes no sense to ban the use of neuroenhancers. Too many people are 62 already taking them, and the users tend to be educated and privileged people who proceed with just enough caution to avoid getting into trouble. Besides, Anjan Chatterjee is right that there is an apt analogy with plastic surgery. In a consumer society like ours, if people are properly informed about the risks and benefits of neuroenhancers, they can make their own choices about how to alter their minds, just as they can make their own decisions about shaping their bodies.

Still, even if you acknowledge that cosmetic neurology is here to stay, there 63 is something dispiriting about the way the drugs are used—the kind of aspirations they open up, or don't. Jonathan Eisen, an evolutionary biologist at U.C. Davis, is skeptical of what he mockingly calls "brain doping." During a recent conversation, he spoke about colleagues who take neuroenhancers in order to grind out grant proposals. "It's weird to me that people are taking these drugs to write grants," he said. "I mean, if you came up with some really interesting paper that was *spurred* by taking some really interesting drug—magic mushrooms or something—that would make more sense to me. In the end, you're only as good as the ideas you've come up with."

But it's not the mind-expanding sixties anymore. Every era, it seems, has its 64 own defining drug. Neuroenhancers are perfectly suited for the anxiety of white-collar competition in a floundering economy. And they have a synergistic relationship with our multiplying digital technologies: the more gadgets we own, the more distracted we become, and the more we need help in order to focus. The experience that neuroenhancement offers is not, for the most part, about opening the doors of perception, or about breaking the bonds of the self, or about experiencing a surge of genius. It's about squeezing out an extra few hours to finish those sales figures when you'd really rather collapse into bed; getting a B instead of a B-minus on the final exam in a lecture class where you spent half your time texting; cramming for the G.R.E.s at night, because the information-industry job you got after college turned out to be deadening. Neuroenhancers don't offer freedom. Rather, they facilitate a pinched, unromantic, grindingly efficient form of productivity.

This winter, I spoke again with Alex, the Harvard graduate, and found that, 65 after a break of several months, he had gone back to taking Adderall—a small dose every day. He felt that he was learning to use the drug in a more "disciplined" manner. Now, he said, it was less about staying up late to finish work he should have done earlier, and more "about staying focussed on work, which makes me want to work longer hours." What employer would object to that?

Hanna Rosin I was born in Israel, but when I was five, my parents moved to a working-class immigrant neighborhood in Queens, New York. It seemed like the traditional setup. My dad went to work every day as a taxi driver, and my mother took care of me and my brother.

My major writing home these days is the *Atlantic*, where I am a senior editor and write broadly about American culture. That's where I wrote the story, "The End of Men," which launched this book. After that story, I headlined the first TED women's conference, held in Washington, D.C. I also write and edit for *Slate*, and do a biweekly *DoubleX* podcast. In 2009 I was nominated for a National Magazine Award for my *Atlantic* story about transgendered children, "A Boy's Life." In 2010 I shared the award as part of a package of stories in *New York* magazine about circumcision. My stories have also been included in anthologies of Best American Magazine Writing 2009 and Best American Crime Reporting 2009. I have appeared on the *Daily Show with Jon Stewart, the Colbert Report* and the *Today Show.*

THE OVERPROTECTED KID

A preoccupation with safety has stripped childhood of independence, risk taking, and discovery—without making it safer. A new kind of playground points to a better solution.

A trio of boys tramps along the length of a wooden fence, back and forth, 1 shouting like carnival barkers. "The Land! It opens in half an hour." Down a path and across a grassy square, 5-year-old Dylan can hear them through the window of his nana's front room. He tries to figure out what half an hour is and whether he can wait that long. When the heavy gate finally swings open, Dylan, the boys, and about a dozen other children race directly to their favorite spots, although it's hard to see how they navigate so expertly amid the chaos. "Is this a junkyard?" asks my 5-year-old son, Gideon, who has come with me to visit. "Not exactly," I tell him, although it's inspired by one. The Land is a playground that takes up nearly an acre at the far end of a quiet housing development in North Wales. It's only two years old but has no marks of newness and could just as well have been here for decades. The ground is muddy in spots and, at one end, slopes down steeply to a creek where a big, faded plastic boat that most people would have thrown away is wedged into the bank. The center of the playground is dominated by a high pile of tires that is growing ever smaller as a redheaded girl and her friend roll them down the hill and into the creek. "Why are you rolling tires into the water?" my son asks. "Because we are," the girl replies.

It's still morning, but someone has already started a fire in the tin drum in the 2 corner, perhaps because it's late fall and wet-cold, or more likely because the kids here love to start fires. Three boys lounge in the only unbroken chairs around it; they are the oldest ones here, so no one complains. One of them turns on the radio— Shaggy is playing (*Honey came in and she caught me red-handed, creeping with the girl next door*)—as the others feel in their pockets to make sure the candy bars and soda cans are still there. Nearby, a couple of boys are doing mad flips on a stack of filthy mattresses, which makes a fine trampoline. At the other end of the playground, a dozen or so of the younger kids dart in and out of large structures made up of wooden pallets stacked on top of one another. Occasionally a group knocks down a few pallets—just for the fun of it, or to build some new kind of slide or fort or unnamed structure. Come tomorrow and the Land might have a whole new topography.

Other than some walls lit up with graffiti, there are no bright colors, or any-   3 thing else that belongs to the usual playground landscape: no shiny metal slide topped by a red steering wheel or a tic-tac-toe board; no yellow seesaw with a central ballast to make sure no one falls off; no rubber bucket swing for babies. There is, however, a frayed rope swing that carries you over the creek and depos- its you on the other side, if you can make it that far (otherwise it deposits you in the creek). The actual children's toys (a tiny stuffed elephant, a soiled Winnie the Pooh) are ignored, one facedown in the mud, the other sitting behind a green plastic chair. On this day, the kids seem excited by a walker that was donated by one of the elderly neighbors and is repurposed, at different moments, as a scooter, a jail cell, and a gymnastics bar.

The Land is an "adventure playground," although that term is maybe a little   4 too reminiscent of theme parks to capture the vibe. In the U.K., such playgrounds arose and became popular in the 1940s, as a result of the efforts of Lady Marjory Allen of Hurtwood, a landscape architect and children's advocate. Allen was dis- appointed by what she described in a documentary as "asphalt square" playgrounds with "a few pieces of mechanical equipment." She wanted to design playgrounds with loose parts that kids could move around and manipulate, to create their own makeshift structures. But more important, she wanted to encourage a "free and permissive atmosphere" with as little adult supervision as possible. The idea was that kids should face what to them seem like "really dangerous risks" and then conquer them alone. That, she said, is what builds self-confidence and courage.

The playgrounds were novel, but they were in tune with the cultural expec-   5 tations of London in the aftermath of World War II. Children who might grow up to fight wars were not shielded from danger; they were expected to meet it with assertiveness and even bravado. Today, these playgrounds are so out of sync with affluent and middle-class parenting norms that when I showed fellow parents back home a video of kids crouched in the dark lighting fires, the most common sentence I heard from them was "This is insane." (Working-class parents hold at least some of the same ideals, but are generally less controlling—out of necessity, and maybe greater respect for toughness.) That might explain why there are so few adventure playgrounds left around the world, and why a newly established one, such as the Land, feels like an act of defiance.

If a 10-year-old lit a fire at an American playground, someone would call the   6
police and the kid would be taken for counseling. At the Land, spontaneous fires are a frequent occurrence. The park is staffed by professionally trained "playwork-ers," who keep a close eye on the kids but don't intervene all that much. Claire Griffiths, the manager of the Land, describes her job as "loitering with intent." Although the playworkers almost never stop the kids from what they're doing, before the playground had even opened they'd filled binders with "risk benefits assessments" for nearly every activity. (In the two years since it opened, no one has been injured outside of the occasional scraped knee.) Here's the list of bene-fits for fire: "It can be a social experience to sit around with friends, make friends, to sing songs to dance around, to stare at, it can be a co-operative experience where everyone has jobs. It can be something to experiment with, to take risks, to test its properties, its heat, its power, to re-live our evolutionary past." The risks? "Burns from fire or fire pit" and "children accidentally burning each other with flaming cardboard or wood." In this case, the benefits win, because a playworker is always nearby, watching for impending accidents but otherwise letting the chil-dren figure out lessons about fire on their own.

> Kids once took special pride in "knowing how to get places" alone, and in finding shortcuts adults normally wouldn't use.
> "I'm gonna put this cardboard box in the fire," one of the boys says. "You know that will make a lot of smoke," says Griffiths.

"Where there's smoke, there's fire," he answers, and in goes the box. Smoke   7
instantly fills the air and burns our eyes. The other boys sitting around the fire cough, duck their heads, and curse him out. In my playground set, we would call this "natural consequences," although we rarely have the nerve to let even much tamer scenarios than this one play out. By contrast, the custom at the Land is for parents not to intervene. In fact, it's for parents not to come at all. The dozens of kids who passed through the playground on the day I visited came and went on their own. In seven hours, aside from Griffiths and the other playworkers, I saw only two adults: Dylan's nana, who walked him over because he's only 5, and Steve Hughes, who runs a local fishing-tackle shop and came by to lend some tools.

Griffiths started selling local families on the proposed playground in 2006.   8
She talked about the health and developmental benefits of freer outdoor play,

and explained that the playground would look messy but be fenced in. But mostly she made an appeal rooted in nostalgia. She explained some of the things kids might be able to do and then asked the parents to remember their own child-hoods. "Ahh, did you never used to do that?" she would ask. This is how she would win them over. Hughes moved to the neighborhood after the Land was already open, but when he stopped by, I asked how he would have answered that question. "When I was a kid, we didn't have all the rules about health and safety," he said. "I used to go swimming in the Dee, which is one of the most dangerous rivers around. If my parents had found out, they would have grounded me for life. But back then we would get up to all sorts of mischief."

Like most parents my age, I have memories of childhood so different from the way   9
my children are growing up that sometimes I think I might be making them up, or at least exaggerating them. I grew up on a block of nearly identical six-story apartment buildings in Queens, New York. In my elementary-school years, my friends and I spent a lot of afternoons playing cops and robbers in two intercon-nected apartment garages, after we discovered a door between them that we could pry open. Once, when I was about 9, my friend Kim and I "locked" a bunch of younger kids in an imaginary jail behind a low gate. Then Kim and I got hungry and walked over to Alba's pizzeria a few blocks away and forgot all about them. When we got back an hour later, they were still standing in the same spot. They never hopped over the gate, even though they easily could have; their parents never came looking for them, and no one expected them to. A couple of them were pretty upset, but back then, the code between kids ruled. We'd told them they were in jail, so they stayed in jail until we let them out. A parent's opinion on their term of incarceration would have been irrelevant.

I used to puzzle over a particular statistic that routinely comes up in arti-   10
cles about time use: even though women work vastly more hours now than they did in the 1970s, mothers—and fathers—of all income levels spend much more time with their children than they used to. This seemed impossible to me until recently, when I began to think about my own life. My mother didn't work all that much when I was younger, but she didn't spend vast amounts of time with me, either. She didn't arrange my playdates or drive me to swimming lessons or introduce me to cool music she liked. On weekdays after school she just expected me to show up for dinner; on weekends I barely saw her at all. I, on the other hand, might easily spend every waking Saturday hour with one if not all three of my children, taking one to a soccer game, the second to a theater program, the third to a friend's house, or just hanging out with them at home. When my

daughter was about 10, my husband suddenly realized that in her whole life, she had probably not spent more than 10 minutes unsupervised by an adult. Not 10 minutes in 10 years.

It's hard to absorb how much childhood norms have shifted in just one gen-   11
eration. Actions that would have been considered paranoid in the '70s—walking third-graders to school, forbidding your kid to play ball in the street, going down the slide with your child in your lap—are now routine. In fact, they are the markers of good, responsible parenting. One very thorough study of "children's independent mobility," conducted in urban, suburban, and rural neighborhoods in the U.K., shows that in 1971, 80 percent of third-graders walked to school alone. By 1990, that measure had dropped to 9 percent, and now it's even lower. When you ask parents why they are more protective than their parents were, they might answer that the world is more dangerous than it was when they were growing up. But this isn't true, or at least not in the way that we think. For example, parents now routinely tell their children never to talk to strangers, even though all available evidence suggests that children have about the same (very slim) chance of being abducted by a stranger as they did a generation ago. Maybe the real question is, how did these fears come to have such a hold over us? And what have our children lost—and gained—as we've succumbed to them?

In 1978, a toddler named Frank Nelson made his way to the top of a 12-foot slide   12
in Hamlin Park in Chicago, with his mother, Debra, a few steps behind him. The structure, installed three years earlier, was known as a "tornado slide" because it twisted on the way down, but the boy never made it that far. He fell through the gap between the handrail and the steps and landed on his head on the asphalt. A year later, his parents sued the Chicago Park District and the two companies that had manufactured and installed the slide. Frank had fractured his skull in the fall and suffered permanent brain damage. He was paralyzed on his left side and had speech and vision problems. His attorneys noted that he was forced to wear a helmet all the time to protect his fragile skull.

The Nelsons' was one of a number of lawsuits of that era that fueled a back-   13
lash against potentially dangerous playground equipment. Theodora Briggs Sweeney, a consumer advocate and safety consultant from John Carroll University, near Cleveland, testified at dozens of trials and became a public crusader for playground reform. "The name of the playground game will continue to be Russian roulette, with the child as unsuspecting victim," Sweeney wrote in a 1979 paper published in *Pediatrics*. She was concerned about many things—the heights of slides, the space between railings, the danger of loose S-shaped hooks holding

parts together—but what she worried about most was asphalt and dirt. In her paper, Sweeney declared that lab simulations showed children could die from a fall of as little as a foot if their head hit asphalt, or three feet if their head hit dirt.

A federal-government report published around that time found that tens of   14
thousands of children were turning up in the emergency room each year because of playground accidents. As a result, the U.S. Consumer Product Safety Commission in 1981 published the first "Handbook for Public Playground Safety," a short set of general guidelines—the word *guidelines* was in bold, to distinguish the contents from *requirements*—that should govern the equipment. For example, no component of any equipment should form angles or openings that could trap any part of a child's body, especially the head.

To turn up the pressure, Sweeney and a fellow consultant on playground   15
safety, Joe Frost, began cataloguing the horrors that befell children at playgrounds. Between them, they had testified in almost 200 cases and could detail gruesome specifics—several kids who had gotten their heads trapped or crushed by merry-go-rounds; one who was hanged by a jump rope attached to a deck railing; one who was killed by a motorcycle that crashed into an unfenced playground; one who fell while playing football on rocky ground. In a paper they wrote together, Sweeney and Frost called for "immediate inspection" of all equipment that had been installed before 1981, and the removal of anything faulty. They also called for playgrounds nationwide to incorporate rubber flooring in crucial areas.

In January 1985, the Chicago Park District settled the suit with the Nelsons.   16
Frank Nelson was guaranteed a minimum of $9.5 million. Maurice Thominet, the chief engineer for the Park District, told the *Chicago Tribune* that the city would have to "take a cold, hard look at all of our equipment" and likely remove all the tornado slides and some other structures. At the time, a reader wrote to the paper:

> Do accidents happen anymore? ...
>
> Can a mother take the risk of taking her young child up to the top of a tornado slide, with every good intention, and have an accident?
>
> Who is responsible for a child in a park, the park district or the parent? ... Swings hit 1-year-old children in the head, I'm sure with dire consequences in some instances. Do we eliminate swings?

But these proved to be musings from a dying age. Around the time the   17
Nelson settlement became public, park departments all over the country began removing equipment newly considered dangerous, partly because they could not afford to be sued, especially now that a government handbook could be used by litigants as proof of standards that parks were failing to meet. In anticipation of

lawsuits, insurance premiums skyrocketed. As the *Tribune* reader had intuited, the cultural understanding of acceptable risk began to shift, such that any known risk became nearly synonymous with hazard.

Over the years, the official consumer-product handbook has gone through   18
several revisions; it is now supplemented by a set of technical guidelines for manufacturers. More and more, the standards are set by engineers and technical experts and lawyers, with little meaningful input from "people who know anything about children's play," says William Weisz, a design consultant who has sat on several committees overseeing changes to the guidelines. The handbook includes specific prescriptions for the exact heights, slopes, and other angles of nearly every piece of equipment. Rubber flooring or wood chips are virtually required; grass and dirt are "not considered protective surfacing because wear and environmental factors can reduce their shock absorbing effectiveness."

"Reasonable risks are essential for children's healthy development," says Joe Frost, an influential safety crusader.

It is no longer easy to find a playground that has an element of surprise, no   19
matter how far you travel. Kids can find the same slides at the same heights and angles as the ones in their own neighborhood, with many of the same accessories. I live in Washington, D.C., near a section of Rock Creek Park, and during my first year in the neighborhood, a remote corner of the park dead-ended into what our neighbors called the forgotten playground. The slide had wooden steps, and was at such a steep angle that kids had to practice controlling their speed so they wouldn't land too hard on the dirt. More glorious, a freestanding tree house perched about 12 feet off the ground, where the neighborhood kids would gather and sort themselves into the pack hierarchies I remember from my childhood— little kids on the ground "cooking" while the bigger kids dominated the high shelter. But in 2003, nearly a year after I moved in, the park service tore down the tree house and replaced all the old equipment with a prefab playground set on rubber flooring. Now the playground can hold only a toddler's attention, and not for very long. The kids seem to spend most of their time in the sandbox; maybe they like it because the neighbors have turned it into a mini adventure playground, dropping off an odd mixing spoon or colander or broken-down toy car.

In recent years, Joe Frost, Sweeney's old partner in the safety crusade, has   20
become concerned that maybe we have gone too far. In a 2006 paper, he gives the example of two parents who sued when their child fell over a stump in a small redwood forest that was part of a playground. They had a basis for the lawsuit. After all, the latest safety handbook advises designers to "look out for tripping hazards, like exposed concrete footings, tree stumps, and rocks." But adults have

come to the mistaken view "that children must somehow be sheltered from all risks of injury," Frost writes. "In the real world, life is filled with risks—financial, physical, emotional, social—and reasonable risks are essential for children's healthy development."

At the core of the safety obsession is a view of children that is the exact opposite of Lady Allen's, "an idea that children are too fragile or unintelligent to assess the risk of any given situation," argues Tim Gill, the author of *No Fear*, a critique of our risk-averse society. "Now our working assumption is that children cannot be trusted to find their way around tricky physical or social and emotional situations."   21

What's lost amid all this protection? In the mid-1990s, Norway passed a law that required playgrounds to meet certain safety standards. Ellen Sandseter, a professor of early-childhood education at Queen Maud University College in Trondheim, had just had her first child, and she watched as one by one the playgrounds in her neighborhood were transformed into sterile, boring places. Sandseter had written her master's dissertation on young teens and their need for sensation and risk; she'd noticed that if they couldn't feed that desire in some socially acceptable way, some would turn to more-reckless behavior. She wondered whether a similar dynamic might take hold among younger kids as playgrounds started to become safer and less interesting.   22

Sandseter began observing and interviewing children on playgrounds in Norway. In 2011, she published her results in a paper called "Children's Risky Play From an Evolutionary Perspective: The Anti-Phobic Effects of Thrilling Experiences." Children, she concluded, have a sensory need to taste danger and excitement; this doesn't mean that what they do has to actually be dangerous, only that they *feel* they are taking a great risk. That scares them, but then they overcome the fear. In the paper, Sandseter identifies six kinds of risky play: (1) Exploring heights, or getting the "bird's perspective," as she calls it—"high enough to evoke the sensation of fear." (2) Handling dangerous tools—using sharp scissors or knives, or heavy hammers that at first seem unmanageable but that kids learn to master. (3) Being near dangerous elements—playing near vast bodies of water, or near a fire, so kids are aware that there is danger nearby. (4) Rough-and-tumble play—wrestling, play-fighting—so kids learn to negotiate aggression and cooperation. (5) Speed—cycling or skiing at a pace that feels too fast. (6) Exploring on one's own.   23

This last one Sandseter describes as "the most important for the children." She told me, "When they are left alone and can take full responsibility for their actions, and the consequences of their decisions, it's a thrilling experience."   24

To gauge the effects of losing these experiences, Sandseter turns to evolution-   25
ary psychology. Children are born with the instinct to take risks in play, because
historically, learning to negotiate risk has been crucial to survival; in another era,
they would have had to learn to run from some danger, defend themselves from
others, be independent. Even today, growing up is a process of managing fears
and learning to arrive at sound decisions. By engaging in risky play, children are
effectively subjecting themselves to a form of exposure therapy, in which they
force themselves to do the thing they're afraid of in order to overcome their fear.
But if they never go through that process, the fear can turn into a phobia. Paradoxically, Sandseter writes, "our fear of children being harmed," mostly in minor
ways, "may result in more fearful children and increased levels of psychopathol-
ogy." She cites a study showing that children who injured themselves falling from
heights when they were between 5 and 9 years old are less likely to be afraid of
heights at age 18. "Risky play with great heights will provide a desensitizing or
habituating experience," she writes.

We might accept a few more phobias in our children in exchange for fewer   26
injuries. But the final irony is that our close attention to safety has not in fact
made a tremendous difference in the number of accidents children have. According to the National Electronic Injury Surveillance System, which monitors hospital visits, the frequency of emergency-room visits related to playground equipment, including home equipment, in 1980 was 156,000, or one visit per 1,452
Americans. In 2012, it was 271,475, or one per 1,156 Americans. The number
of deaths hasn't changed much either. From 2001 through 2008, the Consumer
Product Safety Commission reported 100 deaths associated with playground
equipment—an average of 13 a year, or 10 fewer than were reported in 1980.
Head injuries, runaway motorcycles, a fatal fall onto a rock—most of the horrors
Sweeney and Frost described all those years ago turn out to be freakishly rare,
unexpected tragedies that no amount of safety-proofing can prevent.

Even rubber surfacing doesn't seem to have made much of a difference in the   27
real world. David Ball, a professor of risk management at Middlesex University,
analyzed U.K. injury statistics and found that as in the U.S., there was no clear
trend over time. "The advent of all these special surfaces for playgrounds has contributed very little, if anything at all, to the safety of children," he told me. Ball
has found some evidence that long-bone injuries, which are far more common
than head injuries, are actually increasing. The best theory for that is "risk com-
pensation"—kids don't worry as much about falling on rubber, so they're not as
careful, and end up hurting themselves more often. The problem, says Ball, is that
"we have come to think of accidents as preventable and not a natural part of life."

The category of risky play on Sandseter's list that likely makes this current gen-   28
eration of parents most nervous is the one involving children getting lost, or
straying from adult supervision. "Children love to walk off alone and go exploring away from the eyes of adults," she writes. They "experience a feeling of risk
and danger of getting lost" when "given the opportunity to 'cruise' on their own
exploring unknown areas; still, they have an urge to do it." Here again Sandseter
cites evidence showing that the number of separation experiences before age 9
correlates negatively with separation-anxiety symptoms at age 18, "suggesting an
'inoculation' effect."

> In all my years as a parent, I've mostly met children who take it for granted that they
> are always being *watched*.

But parents these days have little tolerance for children's wandering on   29
their own, for reasons that, much like the growing fear of playground injuries,
have their roots in the 1970s. In 1979, nine months after Frank Nelson fell off
that slide in Chicago, 6-year-old Etan Patz left his parents' downtown New York
apartment to walk by himself to the school-bus stop. Etan had been begging his
mother to let him walk by himself; many of his friends did, and that morning was
the first time she let him. But, as just about anyone who grew up in New York in
that era knows, he never came home. (In 2012, a New Jersey man was arrested for
Etan's murder.) I was nearly 10 at the time, and I remember watching the nightly
news and seeing his school picture, with a smile almost as wide as Mick Jagger's.
I also remember that, sometime during those weeks of endless coverage of the
search for Etan, the parents in my neighborhood for the first time organized a
walk pool to take us to the bus stop.

The Etan Patz case launched the era of the ubiquitous missing child, as Paula   30
Fass chronicles in *Kidnapped: Child Abduction in America*. Children's faces began
to appear on milk cartons, and Ronald Reagan chose the date of Etan's disappearance as National Missing Children's Day. Although no one knew what had
happened to Etan, a theory developed that he had been sexually abused; soon *The
New York Times* quoted a psychologist who said that the Patz case heralded an
"epidemic of sexual abuse of children." In a short period, writes Fass, Americans
came to think child molestations were very prevalent. Over time, the fear drove
a new parenting absolute: children were never to talk to strangers.

But abduction cases like Etan Patz's were incredibly uncommon a generation   31
ago, and remain so today. David Finkelhor is the director of the Crimes Against
Children Research Center and the most reliable authority on sexual-abuse and
abduction statistics for children. In his research, Finkelhor singles out a category
of crime called the "stereotypical abduction," by which he means the kind of

abduction that's likely to make the news, during which the victim disappears overnight, or is taken more than 50 miles away, or is killed. Finkelhor says these cases remain exceedingly rare and do not appear to have increased since at least the mid–'80s, and he guesses the '70s, although he was not keeping track then. Overall, crimes against children have been declining, in keeping with the general crime drop since the '90s. A child from a happy, intact family who walks to the bus stop and never comes home is still a singular tragedy, not a national epidemic.

One kind of crime that *has* increased, says Finkelhor, is family abduction   32 (which is lumped together with stereotypical abduction in FBI crime reports, accounting for the seemingly alarming numbers sometimes reported in the media). The explosion in divorce in the '70s meant many more custody wars and many more children being smuggled away by one or the other of their parents. If a mother is afraid that her child might be abducted, her ironclad rule should not be *Don't talk to strangers.* It should be *Don't talk to your father.*

The gap between what people fear (abduction by a stranger) and what's   33 actually happening (family turmoil and custody battles) is revealing. What has changed since the 1970s is the nature of the American family, and the broader sense of community. For a variety of reasons—divorce, more single-parent families, more mothers working—both families and neighborhoods have lost some of their cohesion. It is perhaps natural that trust in general has eroded, and that parents have sought to control more closely what they can—most of all, their children.

As we parents began to see public spaces—playgrounds, streets, public ball   34 fields, the distance between school and home—as dangerous, other, smaller daily decisions fell into place. Ask any of my parenting peers to chronicle a typical week in their child's life and they will likely mention school, homework, after-school classes, organized playdates, sports teams coached by a fellow parent, and very little free, unsupervised time. Failure to supervise has become, in fact, synonymous with failure to parent. The result is a "continuous and ultimately dramatic decline in children's opportunities to play and explore in their own chosen ways," writes Peter Gray, a psychologist at Boston College and the author of *Free to Learn.* No more pickup games, idle walks home from school, or cops and robbers in the garage all afternoon. The child culture from my Queens days, with its own traditions and codas, its particular pleasures and distresses, is virtually extinct.

In 1972, the British-born geography student Roger Hart settled on an unusual   35 project for his dissertation. He moved to a rural New England town and, for two years, tracked the movements of 86 children in the local elementary school, to create what he called a "geography of children," including actual maps that would show where and how far the children typically roamed away from home. Usually research on children is conducted by interviewing parents, but Hart decided he would go straight to the source. The principal of the school lent him a room, which became known as "Roger's room," and he slowly got to know the children. Hart asked them questions about where they went each day and how they felt about those places, but mostly he just wandered around with them. Even now, as a father and a settled academic, Hart has a dreamy, puckish air. Children were comfortable with him and loved to share their moments of pride, their secrets. Often they took him to places adults had never seen before—playhouses or forts the kids had made just for themselves.

Hart's methodology was novel, but he didn't think he was recording any-   36
thing radical. Many of his observations must have seemed mundane at the time. For example: "I was struck by the large amount of time children spend modifying the landscape in order to make places for themselves and for their play." But reading his dissertation today feels like coming upon a lost civilization, a child culture with its own ways of playing and thinking and feeling that seems utterly foreign now. The children spent immense amounts of time on their own, creating imaginary landscapes their parents sometimes knew nothing about. The parents played no role in their coming together—"it is through cycling around that the older boys chance to fall into games with each other," Hart observed. The forts they built were not praised and cooed over by their parents, because their parents almost never saw them.

> "There's a fear" among parents, Roger Hart told me, "an exaggeration of the dangers, a loss of trust" that isn't clearly explainable.

Through his maps, Hart discovered broad patterns: between second and third   37
grade, for instance, the children's "free range"—the distance they were allowed to travel away from home without checking in first—tended to expand significantly, because they were permitted to ride bikes alone to a friend's house or to a ball field. By fifth grade, the boys especially gained a "dramatic new freedom" and could go pretty much wherever they wanted without checking in at all. (The girls were more restricted because they often helped their mothers with chores or errands, or stayed behind to look after younger siblings.) To the children, each little addition to their free range—being allowed to cross a paved road, or go to the center of town—was a sign of growing up. The kids took special pride, Hart noted, in "knowing how to get places," and in finding shortcuts that adults wouldn't normally use.

Hart's research became the basis for a BBC documentary, which he recently   38
showed me in his office at the City University of New York. One long scene takes place across a river where the kids would go to build what they called "river

houses," structures made from branches and odds and ends they'd snuck out from home. In one scene, Joanne and her sister Sylvia show the filmmakers the "house" they made, mostly from orange and brown sheets slung over branches. The furniture has been built with love and wit—the TV, for example, is a crate on a rock with a magazine glamour shot taped onto the front. The phone is a stone with a curled piece of wire coming out from under it.

The girls should be self-conscious because they are being filmed, but they are utterly at home, flipping their hair, sitting close to each other on crates, and drawing up plans for how to renovate. Nearby, their 4-year-old brother is cutting down a small tree with a hatchet for a new addition. The girls and their siblings have logged hundreds of hours here over the years; their mother has never been here, not once, they say, because she doesn't like to get her toes wet.   39

In another scene, Andrew and Jenny, a brother and sister who are 6 and 4, respectively, explore a patch of woods to find the best ferns to make a bed with. Jenny walks around in her knee-high white socks, her braids swinging, looking for the biggest fronds. Her big brother tries to arrange them just so. The sun is shining through the dense trees and the camera stays on the children for a long time. When they are satisfied with their bed, they lie down next to each other. "Don't take any of my ferns," Jenny scolds, and Andrew sticks his tongue out. At this point, I could hear in my head the parent intervening: "Come on, kids, share. There's plenty to go around." But no parents are there; the kids have been out of their sight for several hours now. I teared up while watching the film, and it was only a few days later that I understood why. In all my years as a parent, I have never come upon children who are so inwardly focused, so in tune with each other, so utterly absorbed by the world they've created, and I think that's because in all my years as a parent, I've mostly met children who take it for granted that they are always being *watched*.   40

In 2004, Hart returned to the same town to do a follow-up study. His aim was to reconnect with any kids he had written about who still lived within 100 miles of the town and see how they were raising their own children, and also to track some of the kids who now lived in the town. But from the first day he arrived, he knew he would never be able to do the research in the same way. Hart started at the house of a boy he'd known, now a father, and asked whether he could talk to his son outside. The mother said they could go in the backyard, but she followed them, always staying about 200 yards behind them. Hart didn't get the sense that the parents were suspicious of him, more that they'd "gotten used to the idea of always being close to their children, and didn't like them going off." He realized that this time around, he could get to the children only through the adults; even the kids didn't seem that interested in talking to him alone; they got plenty of   41 adult attention already. "They were so used to having their lives organized by their parents," he told me. Meanwhile, the new principal at the school said he didn't want Hart doing any research there, because it was not directly related to the curriculum.

At one point Hart tracked down Sylvia, one of the girls he'd filmed at the   42
river house. "Roger Hart! Oh my God, my childhood existed," she screamed into the phone. "It's just that I'm always telling people what we used to do, and they don't believe me!" Sylvia was now a suburban mom of two kids (ages 5 and 4), and she and her husband had moved into a new house 30 miles away. When Hart went to visit Sylvia, he filmed the exchange. Standing outside in her back-yard, Sylvia tells him she bought this house because she wanted to give her own children the kinds of childhood experiences she'd had, and when she saw the little wooded area out back, her "heart leapt." But "there's no way they'd be out in the woods," she adds. "My hometown is now so diverse, with people coming in and out and lots of transients." Hart reminds her how she used to spend most of her time across the river, playing. "There's no river here," she tells him, then whispers, "and I'm really glad about that." There will soon be a fence around the yard—she mentions the fence several times—"so they'll be contained," and she'll always be able to see her kids from the kitchen window. As Sylvia is being inter-viewed, her son makes some halfhearted attempts to cut the hedges with a pair of scissors, but he doesn't really seem to know how to do it, and he never strays more than a few inches from his father.

When Hart shows Jenny and Andrew the film of themselves playing in the   43
ferns, they are both deeply moved, because they'd never seen a film of themselves as children, and because for them, too, the memories had receded into hazy unreal-ity. They are both parents and are still living in that New England town. Of all the people Hart caught up with, they seem to have tried the hardest to create some of the same recreational opportunities for their own children that they'd had. Jenny bought a house, with a barn, near a large patch of woods; she doesn't let her sons watch TV or play video games all that much, instead encouraging them to go to the barn and play in the hay, or tend the garden. She says she wouldn't really mind if they strayed into the woods, but "they don't want to go out of sight." Anyway, they get their exercise from the various sports teams they play on. Jenny gets some of her girlish self back when she talks about how she and the boys pile up rocks in the backyard to build a ski jump or use sticks to make a fort. But Jenny initiates these activities; the boys usually don't discover them on their own.

Among this new set of kids, the free range is fairly limited. They don't roam   44
all that far from home, and they don't seem to want to. Hart talked with a law-enforcement officer in the area, who said that there weren't all that many

transients and that over the years, crime has stayed pretty steady—steadily low. "There's a fear" among the parents, Hart told me, "an exaggeration of the dangers, a loss of trust that isn't totally clearly explainable." Hart hasn't yet published his findings from his more recent research, and he told me he's wary of running into his own nostalgia for the Rousseauean children of his memories. For example, he said he has to be honest about the things that have improved in the new version of childhood. In the old days, when children were left on their own, child power hierarchies formed fairly quickly, and some children always remained on the bottom, or were excluded entirely. Also, fathers were largely absent; now children are much closer to their dads—closer to both their parents than kids were back then. I would add that the 1970s was the decade of the divorce boom, and many children felt neglected by their parents; perhaps today's close supervision is part of a vow not to repeat that mistake. And yet despite all this, Hart can't help but wonder what disappeared with "the erosion of child culture," in which children were "inventing their own activities and building up a kind of community of their own that they knew much more about than their parents."

One common concern of parents these days is that children grow up too li fast.   45
But sometimes it seems as if children don't get the space to grow up at all; they just become adept at mimicking the habits of adulthood. As Hart's research shows, children used to gradually take on responsibilities, year by year. They crossed the road, went to the store; eventually some of them got small neighborhood jobs. Their pride was wrapped up in competence and independence, which grew as they tried and mastered activities they hadn't known how to do the previous year. But these days, middle-class children, at least, skip these milestones. They spend a lot of time in the company of adults, so they can talk and think like them, but they never build up the confidence to be truly independent and self-reliant.

　　Lately parents have come to think along the class lines defined by the Uni-   46
versity of Pennsylvania sociologist Annette Lareau. Middle-class parents see their children as projects: they engage in what she calls "concerted cultivation," an active pursuit of their child's enrichment. Working-class and poor parents, meanwhile, speak fewer words to their children, watch their progress less closely, and promote what Lareau calls the "accomplishment of natural growth," perhaps leaving the children less prepared to lead middle-class lives as adults. Many people interpret her findings as proof that middle-class parenting styles, in their totality, are superior. But this may be an overly simplistic and self-serving conclusion; perhaps each form of child-rearing has something to recommend it to the other.

When Claire Griffiths, the Land's manager, applies for grants to fund her   47
innovative play spaces, she often lists the concrete advantages of enticing children outside: combatting obesity, developing motor skills. She also talks about
the same issue Lady Allen talked about all those years ago—encouraging children
to take risks so they build their confidence. But the more nebulous benefits of
a freer child culture are harder to explain in a grant application, even though
experiments bear them out. For example, beginning in 2011, Swanson Primary
School in New Zealand submitted itself to a university experiment and agreed to
suspend all playground rules, allowing the kids to run, climb trees, slide down a
muddy hill, jump off swings, and play in a "loose-parts pit" that was like a mini
adventure playground. The teachers feared chaos, but in fact what they got was
less naughtiness and bullying—because the kids were too busy and engaged to
want to cause trouble, the principal said.

In an essay called "The Play Deficit," Peter Gray, the Boston College psy-   48
chologist, chronicles the fallout from the loss of the old childhood culture, and
it's a familiar list of the usual ills attributed to Millennials: depression, narcis-
sism, and a decline in empathy. In the past decade, the percentage of college-age
kids taking psychiatric medication has spiked, according to a 2012 study by the
American College Counseling Association. Practicing psychologists have written (in this magazine and others) about the unique identity crisis this generation
faces—a fear of growing up and, in the words of Brooke Donatone, a New York–
based therapist, an inability "to think for themselves."

In his essay, Gray highlights the work of Kyung-Hee Kim, an educational   49
psychologist at the College of William and Mary and the author of the 2011 paper
"The Creativity Crisis." Kim has analyzed results from the Torrance Tests of Creative Thinking and found that American children's scores have declined steadily
across the past decade or more. The data show that children have become:

> less emotionally expressive, less energetic, less talkative and verbally expressive, less
> humorous, less imaginative, less unconventional, less lively and passionate, less per-
> ceptive, less apt to connect seemingly irrelevant things, less synthesizing, and less
> likely to see things from a different angle.

The largest drop, Kim noted, has been in the measure of "elaboration," or the   50
ability to take an idea and expand on it in a novel way.

The stereotypes about Millennials have alarmed researchers and parents   51
enough that they've started pushing back against the culture of parental control.
Many recent parenting books have called for a retreat, among them *Duct Tape
Parenting*, *Baby Knows Best*, and the upcoming *The Kids Will Be Fine*. In her excellent new book, *All Joy and No Fun*, Jennifer Senior takes the route that parents

are making themselves miserable by believing they always have to maximize their children's happiness and success.

In the U.K., the safety paranoia is easing up. The British equivalent of the   52
Consumer Product Safety Commission recently released a statement saying it "wants to make sure that mistaken health and safety concerns do not create sterile play environments that lack challenge and so prevent children from expanding their learning and stretching their abilities." When I was in the U.K., Tim Gill, the author of *No Fear*, took me to a newly built London playground that reminded me of the old days, with long, fast slides down a rocky hill, high drops from a climbing rock, and few fenced-in areas. Meanwhile, the Welsh government has explicitly adopted a strategy to encourage active independent play, rather than book learning, among young children, paving the way for a handful of adventure playgrounds like the Land and other play initiatives.

> If a mother is afraid that her child might be abducted, her ironclad rule should not be *Don't talk to strangers*. It should be *Don't talk to your father*.

Whether Americans will pick up on the British vibe is hard to say, although   53
some hopeful signs are appearing. There is rising American interest in European-style "forest kindergartens," where kids receive little formal instruction and have more freedom to explore in nature. And in Washington, D.C., not far from where I live, we finally have our first exciting playground since the "forgotten playground" was leveled. Located at a private school called Beauvoir, it has a zip line and climbing structures that kids of all ages perceive as treacherous. I recently met someone who worked on the playground and asked him why the school board wasn't put off by safety concerns, especially since it keeps the park open to the public on weekends. He said the board was concerned about safety but also wanted an exciting playground; the safety guidelines are, after all these years, still just guidelines.

But the real cultural shift has to come from parents. There is a big difference   54
between avoiding major hazards and making every decision with the primary goal of optimizing child safety (or enrichment, or happiness). We can no more create the perfect environment for our children than we can create perfect children. To believe otherwise is a delusion, and a harmful one; remind yourself of that every time the panic rises.

As the sun set over the Land, I noticed out of the corner of my eye a gray   55
bin, like the kind you'd keep your recycling in, about to be pushed down the slope that led to the creek. A kid's head poked out of the top, and I realized it was my son's. Even by my relatively laissez-faire parenting standards, the situation seemed dicey. The light was fading, the slope was very steep, and Christian, the

kid who was doing the pushing, was only 7. Also, the creek was frigid, and I had no change of clothes for Gideon.

I hadn't seen much of my son that day. Kids, unparented, take on pack habits, so as the youngest and newest player, he'd been taken care of by the veterans of the Land. I inched close enough to hear the exchange.   56

"You might fall in the creek," said Christian.   57

"I know," said Gideon.   58

Christian had already taught Gideon how to climb up to the highest slide   59
and manage the rope swing. At this point, he'd earned some trust. "I'll push you gently, okay?" "Ready, steady, go!," Gideon said in response. Down he went, and landed in the creek. In my experience, Gideon is very finicky about water. He hates to have even a drop land on his sleeve while he's brushing his teeth. I hadn't rented a car on this trip, and the woman who'd been driving us around had left for a while. I started scheming how to get him new clothes. Could I knock on one of the neighbors' doors? Ask Christian to get his father? Or, failing that, persuade Gideon to sit a while with the big boys by the fire?

"I'm wet," Gideon said to Christian, and then they raced over to claim some   60
hammers to build a new fort.

Amanda Ripley Amanda Ripley is an investigative journalist for *Time*, *The Atlantic* and other magazines. She is the author, most recently, of *The Smartest Kids in the World–and How They Got That Way*, a *New York Times*bestseller. Her first book, *The Unthinkable: Who Survives When Disaster Strikes–and Why*, was published in 15 countries and turned into a PBS documentary.

In her books and magazine writing, Amanda explores the gap between public policy and human behavior. How does the brain learn—and how does that compare to what children do in school all day? How do people behave under extreme stress, and how can we do better?

Amanda's work has also appeared in *Slate*, the *Wall Street Journal* and the *Times of London*. Her work has helped *Time Magazine* win two National Magazine Awards. To discuss her writing, Amanda has appeared on ABC, NBC, CNN, FOX News and NPR. She has spoken at the Pentagon, the Senate, the State Department and the Department of Homeland Security, as well as conferences on leadership, public policy and education.

Before joining *Time* as a writer in 2000, Amanda covered the D.C. courts for *Washington City Paper* and Capitol Hill for *Congressional Quarterly*. She graduated from Cornell University. She currently lives in Washington, D.C., where she is an Emerson Senior Fellow.

The Case Against High-School Sports

The United States routinely spends more tax dollars per high-school athlete than per highschool math student—unlike most countries worldwide. And we wonder why we lag in international education rankings?   1

Every year, thousands of teenagers move to the United States from all over the world, for all kinds of reasons. They observe everything in their new country with fresh eyes, including basic features of American life that most of us never stop to consider.

One element of our education system consistently surprises them: "Sports   2 are a big deal here," says Jenny, who moved to America from South Korea with her family in 2011. Shawnee High, her public school in southern New Jersey, fields teams in 18 sports over the course of the school year, including golf and bowling. Its campus has lush grass fields, six tennis courts, and an athletic Hall of Fame. "They have days when teams dress up in Hawaiian clothes or pajamas just because—'We're the soccer team!,' " Jenny says. (To protect the privacy of Jenny and other students in this story, only their first names are used.)

By contrast, in South Korea, whose 15-year-olds rank fourth in the world   3
(behind Shanghai, Singapore, and Hong Kong) on a test of critical thinking in
math, Jenny's classmates played pickup soccer on a dirt field at lunchtime. They
brought badminton rackets from home and pretended there was a net. If they
made it into the newspaper, it was usually for their academic accomplishments.

Sports are embedded in American schools in a way they are not almost any-   4
where else. Yet this difference hardly ever comes up in domestic debates about
America's international mediocrity in education. (The U.S. ranks 31st on the
same international math test.) The challenges we do talk about are real ones,
from undertrained teachers to entrenched poverty. But what to make of this
other glaring reality, and the signal it sends to children, parents, and teachers
about the very purpose of school?

When I surveyed about 200 former exchange students last year, in cooper-   5
ation with an international exchange organization called AFS, nine out of 10
foreign students who had lived in the U.S. said that kids here cared more about
sports than their peers back home did. A majority of Americans who'd studied
abroad agreed.

Even in eighth grade, American kids spend more than twice the time Korean   6
kids spend playing sports, according to a 2010 study published in the *Journal of
Advanced Academics*. In countries with more-holistic, less hard-driving education
systems than Korea's, like Finland and Germany, many kids play club sports in
their local towns—outside of school. Most schools do not staff, manage, trans-
port, insure, or glorify sports teams, because, well, why would they?

When I was growing up in New Jersey, not far from where Jenny now lives, I   7
played soccer from age 7 to 17. I was relieved to find a place where girls were not
expected to sit quietly or look pretty, and I still love the game. Like most other
Americans, I can rattle off the many benefits of high-school sports: exercise, lessons in sportsmanship and perseverance, school spirit, and just plain fun. All of
those things matter, and Jenny finds it refreshing to attend a school that is about
so much more than academics. But as I've traveled around the world visiting
places that do things differently—and get better results—I've started to wonder
about the trade-offs we make.

Nearly all of Jenny's classmates at Shawnee are white, and 95 percent come   8
from middle- or upper-income homes. But in 2012, only 17 percent of the school's
juniors and seniors took at least one Advanced Placement test—compared with
the 50 percent of students who played school sports.

As states and districts continue to slash education budgets, as more kids play   9
on traveling teams outside of school, and as the globalized economy demands
that children learn higher-order skills so they can compete down the line, it's

worth reevaluating the American sporting tradition. If sports were not *central* to the mission of American high schools, then what would be?

On October 12, 1900, the Wall School of Honey Grove played St. Matthew's 10 Grammar School of Dallas in football, winning 5–0. The event was a milestone in Texas history: the first recorded football game between two highschool teams. Until then, most American boys had played sports in the haphazard way of boys the world over: ambling onto fields and into alleys for pickup games or challenging other loosely affiliated groups of students to a match. Cheating was rampant, and games looked more like brawls than organized contests.

Schools got involved to contain the madness. The trend started in elite pri- 11 vate schools and then spread to the masses. New York City inaugurated its Public Schools Athletic League in 1903, holding a track-and-field spectacular for 1,000 boys at Madison Square Garden the day after Christmas.

At the time, the United States was starting to educate its children for more 12 years than most other countries, even while admitting a surge of immigrants. The ruling elite feared that all this schooling would make Anglo-Saxon boys soft and weak, in contrast to their brawny, newly immigrated peers. Oliver Wendell Holmes Sr. warned that cities were being overrun with "stiff-jointed, softmuscled, paste-complexioned youth."

Sports, the thinking went, would both protect boys' masculinity and distract 13 them from vices like gambling and prostitution. "Muscular Christianity," fashionable during the Victorian era, prescribed sports as a sort of moral vaccine against the tumult of rapid economic growth. "In life, as in a foot-ball game," Theodore Roosevelt wrote in an essay on "The American Boy" in 1900, "the principle to follow is: Hit the line hard; don't foul and don't shirk, but hit the line hard!"

Athletics succeeded in distracting not just students but entire communities. 14 As athletic fields became the cultural centers of towns across America, educators became coaches and parents became boosters.

From the beginning, though, some detractors questioned whether tax money 15 should be spent on activities that could damage the brain, and occasionally leave students dead on the field. In 1909, New York City superintendents decided to abolish football, and *The New York Times* predicted that soccer would become the sport of choice. But officials reversed course the next year, re-allowing football, with revised rules.

The National Collegiate Athletic Association had emerged by this time, 16 as a means of reforming the increasingly brutal sport of college football. But the enforcers were unable to keep pace with the industry. Once television exponentially expanded the fan base in the mid-20th century, collegiate sports gained a spiritual and economic choke hold on America. College scholarships rewarded high-school athletes, and the search for the next star player trickled down even to grade school. As more and more Americans attended college, growing ranks of alumni demanded winning teams—and university presidents found their reputations shaped by the success of their football and basketball programs.

In 1961, the sociologist James Coleman observed that a visitor entering an   17
American high school

> would likely be confronted, first of all, with a trophy case. His examination of the trophies would reveal a curious fact: The gold and silver cups, with rare exception, symbolize victory in athletic contests, not scholastic ones ... Altogether, the trophy case would suggest to the innocent visitor that he was entering an athletic club, not an educational institution.

Last Year in Texas, whose small towns are the spiritual home of high-school   18
football and the inspiration for *Friday Night Lights*, the superintendent brought in to rescue one tiny rural school district did something insanely rational. In the spring of 2012, after the state threatened to shut down Premont Independent School District for financial mismanagement and academic failure, Ernest Singleton suspended all sports—including football.

To cut costs, the district had already laid off eight employees and closed the   19
middle-school campus, moving its classes to the high-school building; the elementary school hadn't employed an art or a music teacher in years; and the high school had sealed off the science labs, which were infested with mold. Yet the high school still turned out football, basketball, volleyball, track, tennis, cheerleading, and baseball teams each year.

Football at Premont cost about $1,300 a player. Math, by contrast, cost just   20
$618 a student. For the price of one football season, the district could have hired a full-time elementary-school music teacher for an entire year. But, despite the fact that Premont's football team had won just one game the previous season and hadn't been to the playoffs in roughly a decade, this option never occurred to anyone.

"I've been in hundreds of classrooms," says Singleton, who has spent 15 years   21
as a principal and helped turn around other struggling schools. "This was the worst I've seen in my career. The kids were in control. The language was filthy. The teachers were not prepared." By suspending sports, Singleton realized, he could save $150,000 in one year. A third of this amount was being paid to teachers as coaching stipends, on top of the smaller costs: $27,000 for athletic supplies, $15,000 for insurance, $13,000 for referees, $12,000 for bus drivers. "There are so many things people don't think about when they think of sports," Singleton told me. Still, he steeled himself for the town's reaction. "I knew the minute I announced it, it was going to be like the world had caved in on us."

First he explained his decision to Enrique Ruiz Jr., the principal of Premont's only high school: eliminating sports would save money and refocus everyone's attention on academics. Ruiz agreed. The school was making other changes, too, such as giving teachers more time for training and planning, making students wear uniforms, and aligning the curriculum with more-rigorous state standards. Suspending sports might get the attention of anyone not taking those changes seriously.

22

Then Singleton told the school's football coach, a history teacher named Richard Russell, who'd been coaching for two decades. Russell had played basketball and football in high school, and he loved sports. But he preferred giving up the team to shutting down the whole district. He told Singleton to do whatever he needed to do, then walked over to the gym and told the basketball players, who were waiting for practice to begin. At first, the students didn't seem to understand. "What? Why?" asked Nathan, then a junior and a quarterback on the football team. "Would you rather have sports or school?," Russell replied.

23

Out by the tennis courts, Daniel, a junior who was in line to become a captain of the football team, was waiting for tennis practice to start when a teacher came out and delivered the news. Daniel went home and texted his friends in disbelief, hoping there had been some kind of mistake.

24

"We were freaking out," says Mariela, a former cheerleader and tennis and volleyball player. American kids expect to participate in school sports as a kind of rite of passage. "We don't get these years back," she told me. "I'm never going to get the experience of cheering as captain under the lights."

25

As the news trickled out, reporters from all over America came to witness the unthinkable. A photographer followed Nathan around, taking pictures of him not playing football, which the *Corpus Christi Caller-Times* ran in a photo essay titled "Friday Without Football in Premont."

26

Many observers predicted that Singleton's experiment would end in disaster. Premont was a speck on the map, an hour and a half southwest of Corpus Christi. The town's population had dwindled since the oil fields had dried up, and a majority of the 282 high-school students who remained were from low-income Hispanic families. How many football players would drop out? How many cheerleaders would transfer to the next town's school? How would kids learn about grit, teamwork, and fair play?

27

Laet Fall at Premont, the first without football, was quiet—eerily so. There were no Friday-night games to look forward to, no players and their parents cheered onto the field on opening night, no cheerleaders making signs in the hallway, no football practice 10 or more hours a week. Only the basketball team was allowed to play, though its tournament schedule was diminished.

28

More than a dozen students transferred, including four volleyball players and   29
a football player. Most went to a school 10 miles away, where they could play
sports. Two teachers who had been coaches left as well. To boost morale, Principal Ruiz started holding sports-free pep rallies every Friday. Classes competed
against each other in drum-offs and team-building exercises in the school gym.

But there was an upside to the quiet. "The first 12 weeks of school were the   30
most peaceful beginning weeks I've ever witnessed at a high school," Singleton
says. "It was calm. There was a level of energy devoted to planning and lessons,
to after-school tutoring. I saw such a difference."

Nathan missed the adrenaline rush of running out onto the field and the   31
sense of purpose he got from the sport. But he began playing flag football for a
club team on the weekends, and he admitted to one advantage during the week:
"It did make you focus. There was just all this extra time. You never got behind
on your work."

That first semester, 80 percent of the students passed their classes, compared   32
with 50 percent the previous fall. About 160 people attended parent-teacher night,
compared with six the year before. Principal Ruiz was so excited that he went out
and took pictures of the parking lot, jammed with cars. Through some combina-
tion of new leadership, the threat of closure, and a renewed emphasis on academics, Premont's culture changed. "There's been a definite decline in misbehavior,"
says Desiree Valdez, who teaches speech, theater, and creative writing at Premont.
"I'm struggling to recall a fight. Before, it was one every couple of weeks."

Suspending sports was only part of the equation, but Singleton believes it   33
was crucial. He used the savings to give teachers raises. Meanwhile, communities throughout Texas, alarmed by the cancellation of football, raised $400,000
for Premont via fund-raisers and donations—money that Singleton put toward
renovating the science labs.

No one knew whether the state would make good on its threat to shut the   34
district down. But for the first time in many years, Premont had a healthy operating balance and no debt. This past spring, the school brought back baseball,
track, and tennis, with the caveat that the teams could participate in just one
travel tournament a season. "Learning is going on in 99 percent of the classrooms
now," Coach Russell told me, "compared to 2 percent before."

In many schools, sports are so entrenched that no one—not even the peo-   35
ple in charge—realizes their actual cost. When Marguerite Roza, the author of
Educational Economics, analyzed the finances of one public high school in the
Pacific Northwest, she and her colleagues found that the school was spending
$328 a student for math instruction and more than four times that much for
cheerleading—$1,348 a cheerleader. "And it is not even a school in a district

that prioritizes cheerleading," Roza wrote. "In fact, this district's 'strategic plan' has for the past three years claimed that *math* was the primary focus."

Many sports and other electives tend to have lower student-to-teacher ratios 36 than math and reading classes, which drives up the cost. And contrary to what most people think, ticket and concession sales do not begin to cover the cost of sports in the vast majority of high schools (or colleges).

Football is, far and away, the most expensive high-school sport. Many foot- 37 ball teams have half a dozen or more coaches, all of whom typically receive a stipend. Some schools hire professional coaches at full salaries, or designate a teacher as the full-time athletic director. New bleachers can cost half a million dollars, about the same as artificial turf. Even maintaining a grass field can cost more than $20,000 a year. Reconditioning helmets, a ritual that many teams pay for every year, can cost more than $1,500 for a large team. Some communities collect private donations or levy a special tax to fund new school-sports facilities.

Many of the costs are insidious, Roza has found, "buried in unidentifiable 38 places." For example, when teacher-coaches travel for game days, schools need to hire substitute teachers. They also need to pay for buses for the team, the band, and the cheerleaders, not to mention meals and hotels on the road. For home games, schools generally cover the cost of hiring officials, providing security, painting the lines on the field, and cleaning up afterward. "Logistics are a big challenge," says Jared Bigham, until recently the supervising principal of two schools in Copperhill, Tennessee, and a former teacher, coach, and player. "Even though the coaches are in charge of the budgets, I still have to oversee them and approve each expenditure. You're looking at 10 different budgets you have to manage."

That kind of constant, low-level distraction may be the greatest cost of all. 39 During football season in particular, the focus of American principals, teachers, and students shifts inexorably away from academics. Sure, high-school football players spend long, exhausting hours practicing (and according to one study, about 15 percent experience a brain injury each season), but the commitment extends to the rest of the community, from late-night band practices to elaborate pep rallies to meetings with parents. Athletics even dictate the time that school starts each day: despite research showing that later start times improve student performance, many high schools begin before 8 a.m., partly to reserve afternoon daylight hours for sports practice.

American principals, unlike the vast majority of principals around the world, 40 make many hiring decisions with their sports teams in mind—a calculus that does not always end well for students. "Every school in the entire country has done this," Marcia Gregorio, a veteran teacher in rural Pennsylvania, told me. "You hire a teacher, and you sometimes lower the standards because you need a coach."

But here's the thing: most American principals I spoke with expressed no   41
outrage over the primacy of sports in school. In fact, they fiercely defended it. "If
I could wave a magic wand, I'd have more athletic opportunities for students, not
less," Bigham, the former Tennessee principal, told me. His argument is a familiar
one: sports can be bait for students who otherwise might not care about school.
"I've seen truancy issues completely turned around once students begin playing
sports," he says. "When students have a sense of belonging, when they feel tied to
the school, they feel more part of the process."

Premontis not alone   Over the past few years, budget cuts have forced more school   42
districts, from Florida to Illinois, to scale back on sports programs. But in most
of these places, even modest cuts to athletics are viewed as temporary—and
tragic—sacrifices, not as necessary adaptations to a new reality. Many schools
have shifted more of the cost of athletics to parents rather than downsize programs. Others have cut basic academic costs to keep their sports programs intact.
Officials in Pasco County, Florida, have considered squeezing athletic budgets
for each of the past six years. They've so far agreed to cut about 700 education
jobs, and they extended winter break in 2011, but sports have been left mostly
untouched.

In these communities, the dominant argument is usually that sports lure stu-   43
dents into school and keep them out of trouble—the same argument American
educators have made for more than a century. And it remains relevant, without a
doubt, for some small portion of students.

But at this moment in history, now that more than 20 countries are pulling   44
off better high-school-graduation rates than we are, with mostly nominal athletic
offerings, using sports to tempt kids into getting an education feels dangerously
old-fashioned. America has not found a way to dramatically improve its children's academic performance over the past 50 years, but other countries have—
and they are starting to reap the economic benefits.

Andreas Schleicher, a German education scientist at the Organization for   45
Economic Cooperation and Development, has visited schools all over the world
and is an authority on different regional approaches to education. (I profiled
Schleicher for this magazine in 2011.) He is wary of the theory that sports can
encourage sustained classroom engagement. "Our analysis suggests that the most
engaging environment you can offer students is one of cognitive challenge combined with individualised pedagogical support," he told me in an e-mail. "If you
offer boring and poor math instruction and try to compensate that with interesting sport activities, you may get students interested in sports but I doubt it will do
much good to their engagement with school."

Though the research on student athletes is mixed, it generally suggests that sports do more good than harm for the players themselves. One 2010 study by Betsey Stevenson, then at the University of Pennsylvania, found that, in a given state, increases in the number of girls playing high-school sports have historically generated higher college-attendance and employment rates among women. Another study, conducted by Columbia's Margo Gardner, found that teenagers who participated in extracurriculars had higher college-graduation and voting rates, even after controlling for ethnicity, parental education, and other factors. 46

But only 40 percent of seniors participate in high-school athletics, and what's harder to measure is how the overriding emphasis on sports affects everyone who doesn't play. One study of 30,000 students at the University of Oregon found that the grades of men who did not play sports went down as the football team's performance improved. Both men and women reported that the better their football team did, the less they studied and the more they partied. 47

Exercise, without a doubt, is good for learning and living. But these benefits accrue to the athletes, who are in the minority. What about everyone else? 48

At Spelman College, a historically black, all-women's college in Atlanta, about half of last year's incoming class of some 530 students were obese or had high blood pressure, Type 2 diabetes, or some other chronic health condition that could be improved with exercise. Each year, Spelman was spending nearly $1 million on athletics—not for those students, but for the 4 percent of the student body that played sports. 49

Spelman's president, Beverly Daniel Tatum, found the imbalance difficult to justify. She told me that early last year, while watching a Spelman basketball game, "it occurred to me that none of these women were going to play basketball after they graduated. By that I don't mean play professionally—I mean even recreationally. I thought of all the black women I knew, and they did not tend to spend their recreational time playing basketball. So a little voice in my head said, *Well, let's flip it.*" 50

That April, after getting approval from her board and faculty, she gathered Spelman's athletes and coaches in an auditorium and announced that she was going to cancel intercollegiate sports after the spring of 2013, and begin spending that $1 million on a campus-wide health-and-fitness program. 51

Many of Spelman's 80 athletes were devastated, needless to say, and it is too early to tell whether the new swim, aerobics, and Zumba classes, among other offerings, will lead to healthier students on campus. But Tatum's signal was clear: lifelong health habits matter more than expensive, elite sporting competitions with rival schools. One priority has real and lasting benefits; the other is a fantasy. 52

Imagine, for a moment, if Americans transferred our obsessive inten-   53
sity about high-school sports—the rankings, the trophies, the ceremonies, the
pride—to high-school academics. We would look not so different from South
Korea, or Japan, or any of a handful of Asian countries whose hypercompeti-
tive, pressurecooker approach to academics in many ways mirrors the American
approach to sports. Both approaches can be dysfunctional; both set kids up for
stress and disappointment. The difference is that 93 percent of South Korean
students graduate from high school, compared with just 77 percent of American
students—only about 2 percent of whom receive athletic scholarships to college.

As it becomes easier and more urgent to compare what kids around the   54
world know and can do, more schools may follow Premont's lead. Basis public charter schools, located in Arizona, Texas, and Washington, D.C., are mod-
eled on rigorous international standards. They do not offer tackle football; the
founders deemed it too expensive and all-consuming. Still, Basis schools offer
other, cheaper sports, including basketball and soccer. Anyone who wants to play
can play; no one has to try out. Arizona's mainstream league is costly to join, so
Basis Tucson North belongs to an alternative league that costs less and requires
no long-distance travel, meaning students rarely miss class for games. Athletes
who want to play at an elite level do so on their own, through club teams—not
through school.

Basis teachers channel the enthusiasm usually found on football fields into   55
academic conquests. On the day of Advanced Placement exams, students at Basis
Tucson North file into the classroom to "Eye of the Tiger," the *Rocky III* theme
song. In 2012, 15-year-olds at two Arizona Basis schools took a new test designed
to compare individual schools' performance with that of schools from around the
world. The average Basis student not only outperformed the typical American
student by nearly three years in reading and science and by four years in math,
but outscored the average student in Finland, Korea, and Poland as well. The
Basis kid did better even than the average student from Shanghai, China, the
region that ranks No. 1 in the world.

"I actually believe that sports are extremely important," Olga Block, a Basis   56
cofounder, told me. "The problem is that once sports become important to the
school, they start colliding with academics."

In a column published in 1927, Roy Henderson, the athletic director of the   57
University Interscholastic League, a public-school sports organization in Texas,
articulated the challenge of keeping sports and academics in balance: "Football
cannot be defended in the high school unless it is subordinated, controlled, and
made to contribute something definite in the cause of education."

The State of Texas announced in May that the Premont Independent School District could stay open. The district has a lot of work to do before its students can feel the kind of pride in their academics that they once felt in their sports teams. But Ernest Singleton, Enrique Ruiz, the teachers, and the students have proved their ability to adapt. Nathan, the one-time quarterback, started college this fall, as did Mariela, the cheerleader—and, as it turns out, the valedictorian. This fall, Premont brought back a volleyball team and a cross-country team, in addition to basketball, baseball, track, and tennis. But for now, still no football.

William G. Staples   ill Staples grew up on the south shore of Long Island, New York. He has been a commercial fisherman, taxicab driver, plumber's apprentice, and pizza maker. He studied sociology at the University of Oregon, the University of Southern California, and UCLA. Staples is currently the 2013–14 E. Jackson Baur Professor of Sociology and founding Director of the Surveillance Studies Research Center at the University of Kansas. In addition to the first edition of EVERYDAY SURVEILLANCE his previous books include CASTLES OF OUR CONSCIENCE: SOCIAL CONTROL AND THE AMERICAN STATE, 1800–1985, a CHOICE Outstanding Academic Title, POWER, PROFITS, AND PATRIAR-CHY: THE SOCIAL ORGANIZATION OF WORK AT A BRITISH METAL TRADES FIRM, 1791–1922 (with C. L. Staples), an American Sociological Association Book Award winner as well as and the two-volume reference work, THE ENCYCLOPEDIA OF PRIVACY, also a CHOICE Outstanding Academic Title. He lives in Lawrence, Kansas

Everyday Surveillance

Throughout the United States, thousands of offenders are placed under "house 1 arrest," their movements monitored electronically by a transmitter attached to their ankle or a computer placed in their home. In a number of cities, police deploy mobile fingerprint scanners to check the immigration status and criminal records of day laborers. In several states, prison inmates are issued radio frequency ID-enabled (RFID) wristbands to track their movements in the facility. In New York City, a digitized courtroom collects myriad information about a single defendant that is kept in an electronic file. Most "clients" in community corrections programs are subjected to random drug testing.

At the same time: 2

> More than 70 percent of major U.S. employers engage in some form of electronic moni- 3
> toring of workers. At Walt Disney World in Florida, a biometric "measurement" is taken
> from the finger of "guests" to make sure that a multi-day ticket is used by only one per-
> son. School districts around the country have issued RFID student badges that monitor
> a pupil's movements on campus. A company in Arkansas has constructed the world's
> largest consumer database containing detailed information on about five hundred million
> consumers worldwide. And about 90 percent of U.S. manufacturers test workers for drugs.

These examples illustrate a blurring distinction between the surveillance 4 and social control practices of the official justice system and those existing in the everyday lives of ordinary people. How are we to understand these developments? Are they simply "advances" in our struggle against possible illegal, deviant, or problematic behavior or do they signal the rise of what might be called a "culture of surveillance"? What kind of society has produced these practices, and why do we appear so willing to adopt or permit them? The purpose of this book is to explore these and other questions about the emergence of new forms of pervasive monitoring in contemporary society.

A while ago I sat in the café section of a large, suburban bookstore talking   5
with a friend. She asked me what I was working on these days and I told her that I was writing a book about social control in contemporary life. At this she said, "You mean about crime and prisons?" "No," I said, "not really. More like the issue of surveillance." "Oh," she replied, "so you are looking into how the government spies on people?" To many of us, including my friend, issues of discipline, social control, and surveillance tend either to revolve around the criminal justice system or to invite the image of George Orwell's notorious Big Brother. Yet as important as our vast prison system and the activities of domestic "spying" organizations are, I am most interested here in the relatively small, often mundane procedures and practices, the "tiny brothers," if you will, that are increasingly present in our daily lives. These techniques exist in the shadow of large institutions; they are not ushered in with dramatic displays of state power; nor do they appear as significant challenges to constitutional democracy. The methods I want to consider are the evermore commonplace strategies used by both public and private organizations to influence our choices, change our habits, "keep us in line," monitor our performance, gather knowledge or evidence about us, assess deviations, and in some cases, exact penalties. I argue that it is these routine kinds of surveillance and monitoring activities that involve many more of us than does life in a state prison or a National Security Agency (NSA) "warrantless wiretapping" of our phone conversations.

The practices I have in mind range along a continuum. They begin on one   6
end of the spectrum with the "soft," seemingly benign and relatively inconspicuous forms of monitoring and assessment such as those used in the very bookstore where I sat with my friend. In that business, as in thousands across the United States, a "security" system chronicled our interaction with video cameras while the store's spatial arrangement was designed for optimal surveillance of customers and employees alike. Computerized checkout stations kept track of inventory, calculated store performance figures, assessed the credit worthiness of patrons through remote databases, collected personal information about customers so they could be targeted for marketing campaigns, monitored the log-on and log-off times of employees, and calculated the average number of customers those employees processed per hour. All of this was accomplished "behind the scenes" as it were, without disruption to the manufactured ambiance of soft leather chairs, the "narrowcast" background music, and the sound and smell of cappuccino brewing.

At the "hard" end of the spectrum are the most obtrusive and confrontational practices—often taking on the qualities of what I call "surveillance ceremonies"— that may begin with the assumption of guilt, are often designed to uncover the truth about someone's behavior, to test an individual's character, and, more generally, to make them consciously aware that they are indeed being watched and monitored. This element was also present at the corporate bookstore I visited with my friend since the employees there were subjected to pre-employment drug testing and we were also aware that the merchandise was "tagged" so that we could be electronically "frisked" as we walked through the observable sensor gates at the exit. Other "surveillance ceremonies" include the use of lie detectors, pre-employment integrity tests, mobile fingerprint scanning, drug and alcohol testing, electronically monitored "house arrest," and the use of metal detectors and various body scanners.

Between these soft and hard types of surveillance lies a vast array of techniques and technologies that are designed to watch our bodies, to monitor our activities, habits, and movements, and, ultimately, to shape or change our behavior.[1] These procedures are often undertaken in the name of law and order, public safety, fraud prevention, the protection of private property, or "good business practice"; other measures are initiated for an individual's "own good" or benefit. But no matter what the stated motivation, the intent is to mold, shape, and modify actions and behaviors.[2] Surveillance and social control of this type, *sans* "big brother," is not orchestrated by a few individuals; it is not part of a master plan that is simply imposed on us. Rather, in my view, *we are all involved and enmeshed within a matrix of power relations that are highly intentional and purposeful; arrangements that can be more or less unequal but are never simply one-directional.*

The subjects of this book, then, are the cultural practices that I call "meticulous rituals of power." Most generally, I include those microtechniques of surveillance and social monitoring that are often enhanced by the use of new information, communications, and medical technologies. These are knowledge-gathering strategies that involve surveillance, information and evidence collection, and analysis. I call them meticulous because they are "small" procedures and techniques that are precisely and thoroughly exercised. I see them as ritualistic because they are often embedded in organizational procedures, faithfully repeated, and quickly accepted and routinely practiced with little question or resistance. And they are about power because they are intended to entice, cajole, prod, discipline, or outright force people into behaving in ways that have been deemed appropriate, normal, beneficial, productive, or lawful.

So while these techniques may be "small," monotonous, and even seemingly trivial, they are not without effect. In this way, meticulous rituals are the specific, concrete mechanisms that help maintain unbalanced and unequal relationships between clusters of individuals (e.g., between managers and workers, teachers and students, store employees and customers, parents and children, police officers and suspects, probation officials and offenders) and, in a larger sense, between individuals and the public and private organizations where these rituals take place. Meticulous rituals often operate in such a way as to create a form of "information asymmetry" where one person, group, or organization gains important information about a person and uses it as leverage to modify their behavior. On the "softest" end of my spectrum, this information may be offered up "voluntarily," as in the case of someone who uses a geolocation social network application on their cell phone to announce to their friends their whereabouts and are then prodded by advertisers to patronize businesses in that area. At the "hardest" end of the spectrum, information may be taken on demand of formal authority such as a community corrections officer ordering a client to submit to a drug test.

"OK," you may say, "so what is really new here? Hasn't society always had   11
ways of keeping people in line? Aren't these 'meticulous rituals' just newer, perhaps more effective ways of doing what we have always done to ensure social order?" In some ways, yes, they are logical extensions of "modern" approaches to the problems of crime, deviance, and social control, and they may indeed be more efficient at accomplishing these societal goals. Yet, at the same time, they have qualities that make them fundamentally new, and, I want to argue, more *post*modern in design and implementation. That is, I see these strategies as a product of our contemporary period of history that contains profoundly new and distinctive patterns of social, cultural, and economic life. Therefore, I argue that there are at least four defining characteristics of *post*modern meticulous rituals of power and surveillance that set them apart from *modern* methods of social control. First, consider the following.

In the past, the watchful eyes of a small shopkeeper may have deterred a   12
would-be shoplifter; her surveillance was personal, not terribly systematic, and her memory, of course, was fallible. She was more likely to know her customers (and they her), to keep a "closer eye" on strangers, and to "look the other way" when she saw fit (and to make a call to say, an offending juvenile's parents later). This kind of "personal" social control was once typical of small communities or close-knit societies where people certainly watched one another very diligently and where a shared, customary culture, as well as fear of ridicule or exclusion, was a powerful inducement to conformity.[3]

By contrast, the part-time employees of the large corporate bookstore where   13
I sat with my friend have less interest in watching for thieves; their huge number of customers is an anonymous horde. Here, store management relies on subcontracted security personnel as well as the faceless and ever-ready video security

cameras positioned in the ubiquitous black domes in the ceiling. Video—one of the defining features of postmodern society—projects a hyper-vigilant "gaze," randomly scanning the entire store day and night, recording every event, and watching *all* the customers, not just the "suspicious ones." Moreover, the cameras are also positioned to watch the employees, who must now be monitored both for their productivity as workers and as potential thieves themselves. In this way, the surveillance practiced at this store has become oddly democratic; everyone is watched, and no one is trusted.

So, the first characteristic of postmodern surveillance is that it tends to be systematic, methodical, and automatic in operation. It is also likely to be impersonal in that the "observer" is rarely seen and is anonymous and often not an individual at all but rather what I call some form of "data sponge": a computerized system, video camera, scanner, barcode reader, drug-testing kit, RFID chip, or automated tracking system of some kind. Once collected, the data may become part of a permanent record in the form of a digital file of some kind. In fact, the role played by highly efficient digital databases is crucial. The storage capacity of these machines is now boundless, spatially efficient, and incredibly inexpensive. Corporate personnel files, hospital, mental health, and substance abuse agency records, as well as insurance company databanks, join all those demographic, financial, credit, and consumer habits information to create what is now called "big data"; massive conjoined datasets that can be used to create "virtual" data-based identities of us as well as new analytic tools used to "mine" these data in search of patterns and to sort people into different categories. Once created, our "virtual doppelgängers" are, as Mark Poster suggests, "capable of being acted upon by computers at many social locations without the least awareness by the individual concerned yet just as surely as if the individual were present somehow inside the computer."[4] For example, credit ratings may be destroyed or medical benefits denied without personal input or influence of the individual involved.

Second, meticulous rituals of power often involve our bodies in new and important ways, and I want to distinguish two primary tactics of bodily monitoring. I agree with Donald Lowe when he writes, "As living beings, we are more than body and mind, more than the representations and images of our body. We lead a bodily life in the world."[5] My thesis is that these bodily lives are shaped, manipulated, and controlled by a set of ongoing practices that compose our daily lives as workers, consumers, and community members.

The first tactic I want to distinguish has to do with types of surveillance and monitoring that enhances our visibility to others. We seem to be entering a state of permanent visibility where our bodies and our behaviors are being monitored, tracked, or watched continuously, anonymously, and systematically. This kind of surveillance happens when people engage in such diverse activities as driving a company truck, accessing a "free" wireless "hotspot" in a coffee shop, using a credit card, or simply walking down a public street. These instances signify different forms of visibility: the company vehicle is equipped with digital sensors that track the driver's activities and movements; the wireless access point collects historical data on how frequently a customer visits that cafe; the credit card purchase leaves a digital trail of the user's activities and whereabouts; and public and private surveillance cameras positioned along the street signify to anyone who gains access to the image, that a particular individual was on the street on a particular day at a certain time. Add to these transit swipe cards, electronic tolling devices, cell phone location beacons, card-key access points, and even smart parking meters, and our visibility—or at least our whereabouts—to others is being systematically recorded and stored. The methodical, technology-driven, impersonal gaze has become a primary mechanism of surveillance in our society, and it is fixed on our bodies and their movements.

A second tactic of bodily surveillance and social control relates to new 17 developments in science, technology, and medicine. These intersecting fields are making the human body infinitely more accessible to official scrutiny and assessment. This means that the ability of organizations to monitor, judge, or even regulate our actions and behaviors *through* our bodies is significantly enhanced. It also means that it becomes less important to trust anyone to speak the truth or to "tell us what we need to know." In this way, the body is treated as an "object" that holds proof of identity or evidence of possible deviance. On the soft side of my spectrum of social control, we see that corporations are using medical data collected on employees in their "wellness" and exercise clinics to confront the "unhealthy lifestyles" of those not conforming to prevailing standards (about, for example, tobacco use or appropriate weight). Meanwhile, at the hard end of the spectrum, DNA samples are being systematically collected on most people who come in contact with the justice system and permanently stored in a vast database. The body, I contend, is a central target of many postmodern surveillance techniques and rituals.

The third defining characteristic of postmodern meticulous rituals relates 18 to a shift in the location of surveillance and social control. Since the early nineteenth century, our primary method of dealing with lawbreakers, those thought to be insane, deviant, criminal, and even the poor, has been to isolate them *from* the everyday life of the community—as in the case of the mental asylum, reformatory, modem prison, and the poorhouse. Yet the kinds of practices I am most concerned with here attempt to impose a framework of accountability on an individual *in* everyday life. Although, obviously, removing the most "troublesome" people from society is still a significant means of formal social control (after all, in the United States, we "mass incarcerate" more people, at a rate per one hundred thousand of the population, than any country on the planet),[6] today we also attempt to regulate and "treat" a variety of behaviors, conditions, and "lifestyles" associated with substance and alcohol (ab)use, sexual offenses, "dysfunctional" families, and a host of psychological or psychiatric disorders and medical conditions.

Under this thinking, the segregative or quarantine model of social control developed in the nineteenth century, while, again, still very much with us, is increasingly considered by many to be too costly, ineffective, and outmoded. The incentive in recent years has been to develop new ways to control and "keep an eye on" the variety of problematic individuals and deviants through an evolving network of "community corrections" programs; regulatory welfare, health, and social service agencies; as well as in schools and other community institutions. And new developments in the forensic, medical, and computer and information sciences—generated by corporate research and development, universities, and the military/security industrial complex—are creating more remote, more flexible, and more efficient ways of making this happen. For example, consider the "accountability" regimes enforced through intensive supervision programs in the criminal justice system that monitor the behavior of "substance abusers" living in the community with random drug and alcohol tests. Or, we find that school truants, who were once sent to a juvenile detention center, are now ordered to carry a handheld GPS tracking device and required to key-in a numeric code five times throughout the day.

Finally, as new forms of social control are localized in everyday life, they are capable of bringing wide-ranging populations, not just the official "deviant," under their watchful gaze. As I indicated earlier, trust is becoming a rare commodity in our culture. The notion of "innocent until proven guilty" seems like a cliché when people are apt to be subjected to disciplinary rituals and surveillance ceremonies because aggregate statistical data suggests that they have a higher probability for being offenders (e.g., "flying while Muslim" or "driving while black"). Data generated through surveillance techniques can produce whole classes of individuals who are deemed "at risk" for behavior, whether any one particular individual has engaged in such behavior or not. These data, of course, are then used to justify even closer surveillance and scrutiny of this group, thereby increasing the likelihood of uncovering more offenses; and so it goes.[7] In the context of these changes, social control becomes more about predicting deviance—always assuming that it will, indeed, happen—rather than responding to a violation after it has occurred. Therefore, when put in place, ritualistic monitoring and surveillance ceremonies often blur the distinction between the official "deviant" and the "likely" or even "possible" offender. Indeed, what distinguishes the convicted felon from the college athlete from the discount store cashier if each is subjected to random drug screening? One consequence of this blurring is that we may be witnessing a historical shift from the specific punishment of the individual deviant, *postoffense*, to the generalized surveillance of us all.

So, it would seem that while these meticulous rituals are "more of the same," they are, in other respects, strikingly new; and this, I propose, is how we should come to understand them. In other words, we need to see how the world we are creating today is a product of both our modern historical past and our *postmodern* cultural present.[8] This historically grounded perspective has two advantages. First, if we connect these "new" disciplinary techniques to significant long-term processes and trends, we can see the continuity of social life and can understand that contemporary developments reflect an ongoing struggle to deal with problems and issues set in motion by the birth of the modern age. Second, by looking at how differently we have responded to the problems of social order in the past, we can also see that matters of deviance and social control are not fixed categories but are changing, socially constructed ideas. Therefore we begin to realize that what is defined as "deviant" behavior or as a "social problem" today—as well as what seems like appropriate responses to them—may not have been considered worthy of attention one hundred or even twenty years ago.   21

These long-term changes I refer to are some of the major themes that have come to characterize the period of modernity (from around the late eighteenth century until the middle of the twentieth century) and have had considerable influence on our strategies of social control. These themes include the increasing rationalization of social life; the rise of large centralized states and private organizations; and strongly held beliefs in reason, rationality, and the certainty of "progress." This modern faith in our power to shape the world was grounded in our apparent ability to control and to "know" nature through the physical sciences. This rational model of science was increasingly applied to the manipulation of "man" through the knowledge of the "human sciences" such as medicine, public health, criminology, psychology, sociology, and demography. In other words, with the birth of the modern era, human beings—our bodies, minds, and behaviors— became the *subject* or topic of scientific inquiry as well as the *object* or target of its knowledge. Thus, we see in the modern era the gradual disappearance of public torture, stigmatization, and banishment as primary means of punishment and social control, and their replacement by rationally organized reformatory institutions such as the prison, the poorhouse, and the asylum. Rather than seek retribution and public punishment, these institutions would isolate the offending   22 individual and introduce behavioral modification—the transformation of the individual criminal, deviant, or the poor—through the administration of techniques of knowledge and power; techniques frequently developed by those in the human sciences. It is this relationship—between knowledge and power—that is central to the operation of meticulous rituals. Many of these influences are still with us today and continue to shape social life.[9]

Yet, much like the fairly gradual movement from so-called *pre*modern to modern times, the character of social change in the last half of the twentieth century is such that, while elements of this older modern social order are still with us—lodged in various social institutions and practices—it has been giving way to new patterns and practices in social, cultural, and economic life. This *postmodernization* of societies, especially in the United States, originating in developments since World War II and more intensely since the early 1970s, is characterized by fragmentation and uncertainty as many of the once-taken-for-granted meanings, symbols, and institutions of modem life seemingly dissolve before our eyes. Time as well as social and geographical spaces are highly compressed by rapidly changing computer/media and advanced technologies, information storage and retrieval, and scientific and medical knowledge. Ours is a culture deeply penetrated by commodities and consumer "lifestyles." In our day, consumption rather than production has become the wellspring of society, while highly bureaucratic (although increasingly "decentralized") state agencies attempt to order and regulate social life. What is "real" in this culture is presented to us through the mass media in video imagery that has become the primary source of our cultural knowledge. In much of this media, we are offered a nonstop barrage of "crisis-level" social problems, leaving us to wonder "what the world is coming to." In turn, we are left cynically mistrusting each other and furthering the disintegration of public life and discourse. This cultural hysteria creates a fertile ground for those selling "science" and "advanced" technological fixes that they claim will ease our fears. Under these conditions, rather than trust the actions and judgments of others, we turn to more depersonalized, pervasive, and what appear to be more predictable means of surveillance and social control. In essence, we are seduced into believing that, given the apparent tide of problems we face, subjecting ourselves to more and more meticulous rituals is an unfortunate but necessary condition. The forgoing conditions form what I will refer to simply as "the everyday life of the postmodern," and it is in this cultural context, I believe, that we continue to struggle with problems and issues that arose during the early nineteenth century.

As an example of how our current disciplinary practices are a product of both our historical past and our cultural present, let us consider an incident that took place a few years back in my hometown. In this case, a school bus driver was

23

24

accused of physically restraining an unruly child on his vehicle. In short order, the driver was fired, and much debate took place in the local newspaper about the child's supposed "bad" behavior on the bus, the reported good reputation of the driver, and about the way school district administrators handled the case. It was clear that no one trusted anyone's account of what actually transpired on the bus that day. A few months later, right before the beginning of the new school year, there was an announcement that each of the district's fleet of buses would be equipped with a video camera "black box." The bus company claimed that, on any given day, just three video cameras would be rotated among all the district's buses and that, given the design of the boxes; neither the students nor the drivers would know when their bus was equipped with a camera. The bus company's manager stated that the use of the cameras would "help to improve student discipline" as well as ensure that the drivers follow "proper procedures."

Now, the principle behind the rotating camera is not new; it originates with a design by Jeremy Bentham dating from 1791 called the panopticon (from the Greek, for "all-seeing"); a design for a central guard tower inside a prison or reformatory. The tower was planned in such a way that prisoners were never quite sure whether a guard was present or not and would have to assume that they were being watched. The inmates, in effect, would watch themselves, internalizing, if you will, the watchful gaze of their keeper. It was a simple, even elegant, solution to the problem of disciplining people in an enclosed space—a dilemma brought about with the birth of the asylum, the modem "solution" to criminal behavior, madness, poverty, and the like. The evolution of this idea more than two hundred years later—deployed in a postmodern context—produces a technological design, routinely applied in the everyday life of schoolchildren and their adult supervisors, none of whom apparently are trusted to act responsibly. Inexpensive video technology—and our willingness to define schoolchildren's behavior on a bus as being so problematic that it warrants "objective" surveillance rather than personal monitoring—makes the use of this new form of social control possible. Curious about what people thought of the cameras, I casually spoke with friends and others in the community about the new policy. Most seemed shocked at the idea at first, but then, in resignation, many conceded that it was probably a "good idea" for the "safety" of everyone involved. I see the new disciplinary techniques, then, both as a product of important, long-term processes set in motion more than two centuries ago and as shaped by a newly emerging cultural context. My goal, echoed nicely by Best and Kellner in writing about their own work, is to "grasp the continuities and discontinuities with the earlier modern era, while mapping the changing threats, and promises now before us."[10]

One challenge I make to the modernist "grand narrative" of the inevitability   26
of historical progress is to assert that the last two hundred or so years of "reforming" justice practice has unequivocally produced a system that is more "just" or
more "humane" than the brutal, public punishment that came before it. In other
words, I want to challenge the idea that, simply put, we keep building a better
mousetrap. Rather, I want to argue that the modern attempt to transform, mold,
shape, and "rehabilitate" the criminal, the deviant, and the poor in the name
of more effective and even "progressive" social policy may, in fact, be seen as
a more general model for the rational ordering of the entire society—intended
or not. That is, I am concerned here with a process, set in motion in the early
nineteenth century, whereby the enforcement of ever-finer distinctions between
what is "acceptable" and "unacceptable" behavior has become part of all our daily
lives, and not just the lives of those who break the law. Ultimately, I will show
how we are building a culture of surveillance when we infuse daily life with practices that constantly assess our behavior, judge our performance, account for our
whereabouts, and challenge our personal integrity.

As I have argued in this chapter, postmodern surveillance practices, these   27
meticulous rituals of power, have four defining characteristics:

1. They are increasingly technology-based, methodical, automatic, and
    sometimes anonymously applied, and they usually generate a permanent
    record as evidence.
2. Many new techniques target and treat the body as an object that can be
    watched, assessed, and regulated.
3. The new techniques are often local, operating in our everyday lives.
4. Local or not, they manage to bring wide-ranging populations, not just
    the official "deviant" or suspect, under scrutiny.

These characteristics form an "ideal type" postmodern meticulous ritual of power.   28
An ideal type is not "ideal" as in desirable, but rather it is the "pure form" of a
social phenomenon; it is an analytical construct that serves as a benchmark to
compare the similarities and differences of concrete cases. In what follows, I use
this ideal type to identify practices that resemble this pure form of meticulous
ritual and I locate the settings where these practices take place. The location is
crucial since I argue that in recent times we are seeing the spread of disciplinary
practices throughout social life where surveillance and social control strategies
that were once aimed at people who had broken the law are now as well targeted
at those simply *capable* of transgressing social norms and laws. So, in my analysis,
I demonstrate this blurring distinction as I begin each chapter by highlighting

examples from, and sometimes move back and forth between, the world of criminal justice and our everyday postmodern lives.

The plan for the book is as follows: I begin chapter 2 by focusing on the   29
work of the late French philosopher Michel Foucault (1926–1984). It is from Foucault, a pioneering social theorist, that I take the idea to concentrate on the small, seemingly benign rituals at the intersection of power, knowledge, and the body. In his strikingly original book, *Discipline and Punish: The Birth of the Prison*, Foucault presented a political history of two basic forms of discipline: the physical torture associated with the "Age of the Sovereign" and, later, the emergence of the asylum, a product of modernity.[11] Building on Foucault's analysis, I chart the evolution of disciplinary practices and surveillance techniques from the invention of the asylum on and, by taking up where Foucault left off, I hope to extend his study of modern social control into the *post*modern era. In chapter 3, I focus on new forms of surveillance that systematically watch and monitor our bodies and behaviors; I show how our communities, homes, schools, and workplaces are increasingly infused with meticulous rituals and surveillance ceremonies. In chapter 4, I turn my attention to practices that treat the body itself as the site and source of evidence and knowledge or, alternatively, that attempt to take control of the body through the use of various technologies. In chapter 5, I consider the postmodern qualities of the Internet and examine a number of surveillance and social control practices developed for and facilitated by the Web. Finally, in chapter 6, I return to considering the important issues and questions I have raised throughout the book about these contemporary developments, assess their consequences, and modestly suggest at least one strategy should we decide to confront the culture of surveillance we are creating.

BEFORE WE MOVE ON

My goal for this book is to offer a theoretically informed description and exami-   30
nation of a variety of surveillance and disciplinary techniques that have become part of our contemporary lives. My agenda is not explicitly "for" or "against" these practices but rather to engage the reader in a process of critical thinking: I want to raise important questions and problems, express them clearly, gather relevant information, use abstract ideas to interpret that information effectively, and to come to well-reasoned conclusions about how surveillance and disciplinary practices actually operate. In my experience, the topic of this book generates passionate feelings that can lead quickly to what are called "normative judgments" or the commonplace view that some things are decidedly "better" than others. So, in this case, it might be a hasty assessment about whether, say, surveillance cameras in public places are a "good" or "bad" thing. These value-laden determinations

often turn on a crude cost-benefit analysis of perceived usefulness of the cameras versus a sense of potential harm from their installation. Although, ultimately of course, values are critically important in, for example, drafting public policy regarding the installation of video surveillance, premature normative judgments tend to close off further consideration, impede deeper analysis, and limit our ability to see the "big picture." For the sake of understanding, I encourage the reader to "suspend" their normative judgments and approach the text with a "beginner's mind," that is, with an attitude of openness and lack of predeterminations.

Let me try also to make a few other points clear from the outset. I am neither   31
a technological determinist nor a neo-Luddite. That is, I do not believe that technology "drives" social life or that it is inherently "bad." I do assume, however, that technologies are social products, created and implemented within a complex milieu of cultural, political, and economic influences.[12] In this book I attempt to uncover those influences as they relate to the actual workings of disciplinary power, its daily practices, rituals, and minute procedures, and how those workings are often bound up with the use of new technologies. Moreover, I am *not* suggesting that there is no need for social control in society or that shoplifting, drug abuse, or violent crime are not real problems with real victims. Of course they are. I lived in Los Angeles for a decade and witnessed firsthand the crime, violence, and chronic social problems that seem to define the hard edge of urban life in the United States. But the issues I am raising are of broader sociological concern and have to do with that "big picture" of where we are going as a culture and with the balance of power, if you will, within that larger society. In other words, I want to look at the evolution of surveillance as an entry point to observing and understanding our changing attitude and practice toward discipline and social control in general.

By implying that surveillance is becoming more universal and thus oddly   32
more democratic, I am *not* suggesting that we are all necessarily subject to the same quantity or quality of social control or that it does not have differential effects. Historically and cross-culturally, the amount and character of monitoring, discipline, and punishment that individuals are afforded have varied considerably by such defining characteristics as age, racial and ethnic categories, class, and sex. We see, therefore, teenagers more likely to be subjected to police scrutiny, the poorly dressed to reap more inspection by store security, and women to experience more informal and formal social control of their bodies.[13] Without question, this continues today. My point is that there are more impersonal, more methodical, and more technology-driven forms of surveillance and social control in our society than ever before, and today's forms and their sheer volume are enveloping even those who might have been previously immune.[14] For example, the surveillance camera positioned in the bookstore I discussed earlier where I

sat with my friend does not differentiate or discriminate whose image it captures; breathalyzers are administered to all the students attending the prom, and no employee is exempt from a health "screening" program.

For those who have traditionally been the target of more monitoring and control than others, these developments serve only to intensify and increase the amount of ritualized regulation and monitoring already in their daily lives. Moreover, as David Lyon points out, surveillance often supports a process of "social sorting."[15] That is, some surveillance practices should be considered not only as potential threats to individual privacy and liberties but, from a sociological perspective, they may operate as a powerful means of creating and reinforcing social differences and enhancing the life chances of some while diminishing those of others. For instance, "data mining" techniques can tell a bank that certain "high-value" customers should be offered low-interest loans and personal services and advice while other "low-value" ones are charged higher interest rates and fees or are even discouraged from becoming a customer at all.

Reflecting on the simultaneous modem and postmodern world we live in today, I should also point out that my analysis is centered on a "sociology of the postmodern" period rather than "postmodern sociology." The former approach applies a blend of both classical and contemporary social theory and methods— for example, the ideas of Max Weber (1864–1920) on the functioning of bureaucracy along with the insights of Jean Bauldriard (1929–2007) regarding our inability in a mediated culture to distinguish reality from fantasy, or David Harvey (1935–) who views postmodernity as a new stage of global capitalism. By contrast, the latter tactic—postmodern sociology—tends to be associated with more avant-garde ways of writing and thinking about the social world that are more artistic than traditionally analytical in style.

This book was written as an essay-argument rather than as a typical academic monograph. Fitting this style, it is filled with anecdotal evidence, journalistic accounts, and my own and others' research of contemporary surveillance practices. I use this pastiche of material as my primary data for several reasons. First, like many sociologists, I see culture as inconsistent, contradictory, and complex; it simply defies the more linear, "cause and effect" models associated with "scientific" inquiry. Does this mean that I do not need empirical evidence to support my claims? Hardly. It simply means that my objective is, as Diana Crane states, "to interpret a wide range of materials in order to identify what might be described as an underlying 'gestalt.'"[16] Therefore, I take recorded culture to be both a window into society as well as a legitimate source for the interpretation of social meaning.

Second, my goal is to offer an account of how ordinary people experience, live with, and actually contribute to the new surveillance practices. Sociology is

33

34

35

36

sometimes referred to as "slow journalism" since it often takes quite some time to conduct formal studies, collect data, and publish findings. By bringing in and referencing the work of professional journalists, I hope to weave together accounts of the current, lived experiences of average citizens and the power of sociological theory and analysis.[17] And third, while I recount the stories of particular individuals in my narrative, I also try to support my arguments by referencing, where available, broader trends as indicated by government reports and data, pertinent legal cases, changes to federal and state laws, the results of national opinion polls, industry-wide trends and assessments, and relevant scholarship and debate.

Finally, readers will notice my frequent use of quotation marks on words and   37
phrases without necessarily citing sources (when I am indeed quoting someone in particular, I do indicate the source). The use of these marks in this way is both stylistic and substantive. Some of this punctuation simply references everyday colloquialisms. Yet others are intended to alert the reader to the socially constructed nature of language and to suggest that meanings are inherently unstable and potentially contested. Expressions such as "substance abuse," "dysfunctional family," "at risk," and "learning disability" are labels created by those who claim professional expertise or are used by those in positions of authority. Readers should decide if they agree with the meanings evoked by this language or if they wish to contest their legitimacy.

NOTES

1. Since I began working in the area of surveillance about twenty years ago, there are now dozens of books, hundreds of articles, and even an academic journal devoted to the topic. Today, surveillance studies is a vital, interdisciplinary field, and I will cite work from this area throughout the book. For a comprehensive overview of the field, see Kirstie Ball, et al., *Routledge Handbook of Surveillance Studies* (New York: Routledge, 2012). Also John Gilliom and Torin Monahan, *SuperVision: An Introduction to the Surveillance Society* (Chicago: University of Chicago Press, 2013); David Lyon, *Surveillance Studies: An Overview* (Malden, MA: Polity, 2007); Sean Hier and Joshua Greenberg, eds., *The Surveillance Studies Reader* (Maidenhead, UK: Open University Press, 2007); and the online, open-access journal, *Surveillance and Society*.

2. The term social control has a long history in sociology. See E. A. Ross, *Social Control: A Survey of the Foundations of Order* (New Brunswick, NJ: Transaction Publishers, 2009 [1901]); Jack Gibbs, *Norms, Deviance, and Social Control: Conceptual Matters* (New York: Elsevier, 1981); Stanley Cohen, and Andrew Scull, *Social Control and the State* (New York: St. Martin's Press, 1983).

3. This kind of informal social control may still be operating in small, rural communities throughout the United States, although through the process of urban and

suburbanization, the percentage of the total population living is such communities is relatively small. Moreover, the market penetration of corporate convenience stores, Wal-Mart, and others means that not only do we see fewer and fewer small shop owners but we see the importation of the kind of technological store surveillance regimes I am characterizing here.

4. In fact, our "virtual" doppelgängers may be "better" representations of our "real" selves. Can you remember all the videos you watched last year? Netflix, HuLu, or Amazon can tell you. Mark Poster, "Databases as Discourse; or, Electronic Interpellations," in *Computers, Surveillance, and Privacy*, eds. David Lyon and Elia Zureik (Minneapolis: University of Minnesota Press, 1996), 175–192.

5. Donald Lowe, *The Body in Late Capitalism USA* (Durham, NC: Duke University Press, 1995).

6. See Bruce Western, *Punishment and Inequality in America* (New York: Russell Sage, 2007), and Becky Pettit, *Invisible Men: Mass Incarceration and the Myth of Black Progress* (New York: Russell Sage, 2010).

7. This perspective is rooted in recent "neoliberal" models of managing the "risk society" where "risk" becomes the concept for the understanding of how dangers are both identified and responded to technologically. See Ericson V. Richard, *Policing the Risk Society* (Toronto: University of Toronto Press, 1997). This phenomenon has been referred to as "actuarial justice" where the criminal justice system serves a kind of "waste management function." Malcolm Feeley and Jonathan Simon, "Actuarial Justice: The Emerging New Criminal Law," in *The Futures of Criminology*, ed. David Nelken (London: Sage, 1994), 173–201.

8. The idea of the "postmodern" has gone out of fashion in many academic circles. However, I find many of the ideas and concepts developed around this notion to still be highly relevant to understanding contemporary culture. This position is articulated well by Steven Best and Douglas Kellner in *The Postmodern Adventure: Science, Technology and Cultural Studies at the Third Millennium* (New York: Guilford Press, 2001).

9. In the field of crime and punishment studies, some, like myself, have argued that a new, postmodern penology has taken hold in contemporary justice practice (See Malcolm Feeley and Jonathan Simon, "The New Penology: Notes on the Emerging Strategy of Corrections and Its Implications," *Criminology* 30, no. 4 (1992): 449–474; Jonathan Simon, "From Confinement to Waste Management: The Post-Modernization of Social Control," *Focus on Legal Studies* 8, no. 2 (1993): 6–7, while others such as David Garland contend that no such transition has taken place and have defended the "persistence of penal modernism." David Garland, "Penal Modernism and Postmodernism," in *Punishment and Social Control*, eds. Thomas Blomberg and Stanley Cohen (New York: Aldine de Gruyter, 1995), 45–74.

I contend, rather than representing a historical rupture, postmodern developments as I describe them here should be seen as extensions of disciplinary power that invest, colonize, and link up preexisting institutional forms.

10. Best and Kellner, *Postmodern Adventure*, 6.

11. Michel Foucault, *Discipline and Punish: The Birth of the Prison*, trans. A. M. Sheridan (New York: Pantheon, 1977). Foucault was one of the most influential thinkers of the late twentieth century and his ideas have appeared in the work of scholars across the social sciences, humanities, law, architecture, and medicine. Bibliographies of his writing, lectures, and interviews can be found on websites such as http://foucaultsociety.wordpress.com.

12. There is an enormous literature on the development and influence of technology on social life. For some recent titles see Wenda K. Bauchspies, Jennifer Croissant, and Sal Restivo, *Science, Technology, and Society: A Sociological Approach* (Malden, MA: Wiley-Blackwell, 2005); Wenceslao J. Gonzalez, *Science, Technology and Society: A Philosophical Perspective* (A Coruña, Spain Netbiblo, 2005); and Barry M. Dumas, *Diving into the Bitstream: Information Technology Meets Society in a Digital World* (New York: Routledge, 2012).

13. On these examples, see Rob Tillyer, Charles F. Klahm, and Robin S. Engel, "The Discretion to Search: A Multilevel Examination of Driver Demographics and Officer Characteristics," *Journal of Contemporary Criminal Justice* 28, no. 2 (2012): 184–205; Shaun L. Gabbidon, "Profiling by Store Clerks and Security Personnel in Retail Establishments. An Exploration of 'Shopping While Black,'" *Journal of Contemporary Criminal Justice* 19, no. 3 (2003): 345–364; Christine I. Williams, "Racism in Toyland," *Contexts* 4 (2005): 28–32; Torin Monahan, "Dreams of Control at a Distance: Gender, Surveillance, and Social Control," *Cultural Studies=Critical Methodologies* 9, no. 2 (2009): 286–305; Heather McLaughlin, Christopher Uggen, Amy Blackstone, "Sexual Harassment, Workplace Authority, and the Paradox of Power," *American Sociological Review* 77, no. 4 (2012): 625–647; Elisa Puvia and Jeroen Vaes, "Being a Body: Women's Appearance Related Self-Views and Their Dehumanization of Sexually Objectified Female Targets," *Sex Roles* 68, no. 7–8 (2013): 484–495.

14. As Haggerty and Ericson put it, "we are witnessing a rhizomatic leveling of the hierarchy of surveillance, such that groups which were previously exempt from routine surveillance are now increasingly being monitored." See Kevin D. Haggerty and Richard V. Ericson, "The Surveillant Assemblage," *British Journal of Sociology* 51, no. 4 (2000): 606.

15. David Lyon, ed., *Surveillance as Social Sorting: Privacy, Risk and Digital Discrimination* (New York: Routledge, 2003). See also Oscar Gandy Jr., *The Panoptic Sort: A Political Economy of Personal Information* (Boulder, CO: Westview, 1993).

16. Diana Crane, *The Sociology of Culture* (Cambridge: Blackwell, 1994). See also Clifford Geertz, *The Interpretations of Cultures* (New York: Basic, 1973).

17. In fact, I treat the content of a good number of news stories as my "data" and I often quote and paraphrase journalists and the people that they have interviewed in my text and cite the sources. While this quasi-content analysis of news sources has its obvious limitations, historians and cultural analysts have been using newspapers as legitimate sources for years. See Vernon Dibble, "Four Types of Inference from Documents to Events," *History and Theory* 3, no. 2 (1963): 203–221; Elizabeth Ann Danto, *Historical Research* (Oxford: Oxford University Press, 2008); Bridget Somekh and Cathy Lewin, *Theory and Methods in Social Research* (London: Sage, 2011).

Sherry Turkle   Sherry Turkle studies the relationship between people and technology - how does technology change our ways of seeing ourselves and the world. There is all that technology does for us, but there is all that technology does to us as people. How does it affect how our children grow up? How we relate to each other?

Her most recent work, Alone Together, argues that we are at a point of decision and opportunity. Technology now invites us to lose ourselves in always-in mobile connections and even in relationships with inanimate creatures that offer to "stand in" for the real. In the face of all this, technology offers us the occasion to reconsider our human values, and reaffirm what they are.

Alone Together

Always on

Pia Lindman walked the halls of MIT with cyborg dreams. She was not the   1
first. In the summer of 1996, I met with seven young researchers at the MIT Media Lab who carried computers and radio transmitters in their back-packs and keyboards in their pockets. Digital displays were clipped onto eyeglass frames.[1] Thus provisioned, they called themselves "cyborgs" and were always wirelessly connected to the Internet, always online, free from desks and cables. The group was about to release three new 'borgs into the world, three more who would live simultaneously in the physical and virtual. I felt moved by the cyborgs as I had been by Lindman: I saw a bravery, a willingness to sacrifice for a vision of being one with technology. When their burdensome technology cut into their skin, causing lesions and then scars, the cyborgs learned to be indifferent. When their encumbrances caused them to be taken as physically disabled, they learned to be patient and provide explanations.

At MIT, there was much talk about what the cyborgs were trying to   2
accomplish. Faculty supporters stressed how continual connectivity could increase productivity and memory. The cyborgs, it was said, might seem exotic, but this technology should inspire no fear. It was "just a tool" for being better prepared and organized in an increasingly complex information environment. The brain needed help.

From the cyborgs, however, I heard another story. They felt like new selves.   3
One, in his mid-twenties, said he had "become" his device. Shy, with a memory that seemed limited by anxiety, he felt better able to function when he could literally be "looking up" previous encounters with someone as he began a new conversation. "With it," he said, referring to his collection of connectivity devices,

"it's not just that I remember people or know more. I feel invincible, sociable, better prepared. I am naked without it. With it, I'm a better person." But with a sense of enhancement came feelings of diffusion. The cyborgs were a new kind of nomad, wandering in and out of the physical real. For the physical real was only one of the many things in their field of vision. Even in the mid-1990s, as they walked around Kendall Square in Cambridge, the cyborgs could not only search the Web but had mobile e-mail, instant messaging, and remote access to desktop computing. The multiplicity of worlds before them set them apart: they could be with you, but they were always somewhere else as well.

Within a decade, what had seemed alien was close to becoming everyone's   4
way of life, as compact smartphones replaced the cyborgs' more elaborate accoutrements. This is the experience of living full-time on the Net, newly free in some ways, newly yoked in others. We are all cyborgs now.

People love their new technologies of connection. They have made par-   5
ents and children feel more secure and have revolutionized business, education, scholarship, and medicine. It is no accident that corporate America has chosen to name cell phones after candies and ice cream flavors: chocolate, strawberry, vanilla. There is a sweetness to them. They have changed how we date and how we travel. The global reach of connectivity can make the most isolated outpost into a center of learning and economic activity. The word "apps" summons the pleasure of tasks accomplished on mobile devices, some of which, only recently, we would not have dreamed possible (for me, personally, it is an iPhone app that can "listen" to a song, identify it, and cue it up for purchase).

Beyond all of this, connectivity offers new possibilities for experimenting   6
with identity and, particularly in adolescence, the sense of a free space, what Erik Erikson called the *moratorium*. This is a time, relatively consequence free, for doing what adolescents need to do: fall in and out of love with people and ideas. Real life does not always provide this kind of space, but the Internet does.

No handle cranks, no gear turns to move us from one stage of life to another.   7
We don't get all developmental tasks done at age-appropriate times—or even necessarily get them done at all. We move on and use the materials we have to do the best we can at each point in our lives. We rework unresolved issues and seek out missed experiences. The Internet provides new spaces in which we can do this, no matter how imperfectly, throughout our lives. So, adults as well as adolescents use it to explore identity.

When part of your life is lived in virtual places—it can be Second Life, a   8
computer game, a social networking site—a vexed relationship develops between what is true and what is "true here," true in simulation. In games where we expect to play an avatar, we end up being ourselves in the most revealing ways;

on social-networking sites such as Facebook, we think we will be presenting ourselves, but our profile ends up as somebody else—often the fantasy of who we want to be. Distinctions blur. Virtual places offer connection with uncertain claims to commitment. We don't count on cyberfriends to come by if we are ill, to celebrate our children's successes, or help us mourn the death of our parents.[2] People know this, and yet the emotional charge on cyberspace is high. People talk about digital life as the "place for hope," the place where something new will come to them. In the past, one waited for the sound of the post—by carriage, by foot, by truck. Now, when there is a lull, we check our e-mail, texts, and messages.

The story of my own hesitant steps toward a cyborg life is banal, an example   9
of the near universality of what was so recently exotic. I carry a mobile device with me at all times. I held out for years. I don't like attempting to speak to people who are moving in and out of contact as they pass through tunnels, come to dangerous intersections, or otherwise approach dead zones. I worry about them. The clarity and fidelity of sound on my landline telephone seems to me a technical advance over what I can hear on my mobile. And I don't like the feeling of always being on call. But now, with a daughter studying abroad who expects to reach me when she wants to reach me, I am grateful to be tethered to her through the Net. In deference to a generation that sees my phone calls as constraining because they take place in real time and are not suitable for multitasking, I text. Awkwardly.

But even these small things allow me to identify with the cyborgs' claims   10
of an enhanced experience. Tethered to the Internet, the cyborgs felt like more than they could be without it. Like most people, I experience a pint-sized version of such pleasures. I like to look at the list of "favorites" on my iPhone contact list and see everyone I cherish. Each is just a tap away. If someone doesn't have time to talk to me, I can text a greeting, and they will know I am thinking of them, caring about them. Looking over recent text exchanges with my friends and family reliably puts me in a good mood. I keep all the texts my daughter sent me during her last year of high school. They always warm me: "Forgot my green sweater, bring please." "Can you pick me up at boathouse, 6?" "Please tell nurse I'm sick. Class boring. Want to come home." And of course, there are the photos, so many photos on my phone, more photos than I would ever take with a camera, always with me.

Yet, even such simple pleasures bring compulsions that take me by surprise.   11
I check my e-mail first thing in the morning and before going to bed at night. I have come to learn that informing myself about new professional problems and demands is not a good way to start or end my day, but my practice unhappily continues. I admitted my ongoing irritation with myself to a friend, a woman in

her seventies who has meditated on a biblical reading every morning since she was in her teens. She confessed that it is ever more difficult to begin her spiritual exercises before she checks her e-mail; the discipline to defer opening her inbox is now part of her devotional gesture. And she, too, invites insomnia by checking her e-mail every night before turning in.

Nurturance was the killer app for robotics. Tending the robots incited our engagement. There is a parallel for the networked life. Always on and (now) always with us, we tend the Net, and the Net teaches us to need it.   12

Online, like MIT's cyborgs, we feel enhanced; there is a parallel with the robotic moment of more. But in both cases, moments of more may leave us with lives of less. Robotics and connectivity call each other up in tentative symbiosis, parallel pathways to relational retreat. With sociable robots we are alone but receive the signals that tell us we are together. Networked, we are together, but so lessened are our expectations of each other that we can feel utterly alone. And there is the risk that we come to see others as objects to be accessed—and only for the parts we find useful, comforting, or amusing.   13

Once we remove ourselves from the flow of physical, messy, untidy life—and both robotics and networked life do that—we become less willing to get out there and take a chance. A song that became popular on You Tube in 2010, "Do You Want to Date My Avatar?" ends with the lyrics "And if you think I'm not the one, log off, log off and we'll be done."[3]   14

Our attraction to even the prospect of sociable robots affords a new view of our networked life. In Part One we saw that when children grow up with fond feelings for sociable robots, they are prepared for the "relationships with less" that the network provides. Now I turn to how the network prepares us for the "relationships with less" that robots provide. These are the unsettling isolations of the tethered self. I have said that tethered to the network through our mobile devices, we approach a new state of the self, itself. For a start, it presumes certain entitlements: It can absent itself from its physical surround—including the people in it. It can experience the physical and virtual in near simultaneity. And it is able to make more time by multitasking, our twenty-first-century alchemy.   15

THE NEW STATE OF THE SELF: TETHERED AND MARKED ABSENT

These days, being connected depends not on our distance from each other but from available communications technology. Most of the time, we carry that technology with us. In fact, being alone can start to seem like a precondition for being together because it is easier to communicate if you can focus, without interruption, on your screen. In this new regime, a train station (like an airport, a café, or a park) is no longer a communal space but a place of social collection: people   16 come together but do not speak to each other. Each is tethered to a mobile device and to the people and places to which that device serves as a portal. I grew up in Brooklyn where sidewalks had a special look. In every season—even in winter, when snow was scraped away—there were chalk-drawn hopscotch boxes. I speak with a colleague who lives in my old neighborhood. The hopscotch boxes are gone. The kids are out, but they are on their phones.

When people have phone conversations in public spaces, their sense of pri-   17
vacy is sustained by the presumption that those around them will treat them not only as anonymous but as if absent. On a recent train trip from Boston to New York, I sat next to a man talking to his girlfriend about his problems. Here is what I learned by trying not to listen: He's had a recent bout of heavy drinking, and his father is no longer willing to supplement his income. He thinks his girlfriend spends too much money and he dislikes her teenage daughter. Embarrassed, I walked up and down the aisles to find another seat, but the train was full. Resigned, I returned to my seat next to the complainer. There was some comfort in the fact that he was not complaining to me, but I did wish I could disappear. Perhaps there was no need. I was already being treated as though I were not there.

Or perhaps it makes more sense to think of things the other way around: it   18
is those on the phone who mark themselves as absent. Sometimes people signal their departure by putting a phone to their ear, but it often happens in more subtle ways—there may be a glance down at a mobile device during dinner or a meeting. A "place" used to comprise a physical space and the people within it. What is a place if those who are physically present have their attention on the absent? At a café a block from my home, almost everyone is on a computer or smartphone as they drink their coffee. These people are not my friends, yet somehow I miss their presence.

Our new experience of place is apparent as we travel. Leaving home has   19
always been a way to see one's own culture anew. But what if, tethered, we bring our homes with us? The director of a program that places American students in Spanish universities once complained to me that her students were not "experiencing Spain." They spent their free time on Facebook, chatting with their friends from home. I was sympathetic, thinking of the hours I had spent walking with my teenage daughter on a visit to Paris the summer after she first got her mobile phone. As we sat in a café, waiting for a friend to join us for dinner, Rebecca received a call from a schoolmate who asked her to lunch in Boston, six hours behind us in time. My daughter said simply, "Not possible, but how about Friday?" Her friend didn't even know she was out of town. When I grew up, the idea of the "global village" was an abstraction. My daughter lives something concrete. Emotionally, socially, wherever she goes, she never leaves home.

I asked her if she wouldn't rather experience Paris without continual reminders of Boston. (I left aside the matter that I was a reminder of Boston and she, mercifully, did not raise it.) She told me she was happy; she liked being in touch with her friends. She seemed to barely understand my question. I was wistful, worried that Rebecca was missing an experience I cherished in my youth: an undiluted Paris. My Paris came with the thrill of disconnection from everything I knew. My daughter's Paris did not include this displacement.

When Rebecca and I returned home from France, I talked about the trip   20
with a close friend, a psychoanalyst. Our discussion led her to reminisce about her first visit to Paris. She was sixteen, travelling with her parents. But while they went sightseeing with her younger brother, she insisted on staying in her hotel room, writing long letters to her boyfriend. Adolescents have always balanced connection and disconnection; we need to acknowledge the familiarity of our needs and the novelty of our circumstances. The Internet is more than old wine in new bottles; now we can always be elsewhere.

In the month after Rebecca and I returned from Paris, I noted how often I   21
was with colleagues who were elsewhere as well: a board meeting where members rebelled when asked to turn off their mobile devices; a faculty meeting where attendees did their e-mail until it was their turn to speak; a conference at which audience members set up Internet back channels in order to chat about speakers' presentations during the presentations themselves.[4]

Since I teach in a university, I find examples of distracted academics of par-   22
ticular interest. But it is the more mundane examples of attention sharing that change the fabric of daily life. Parents check e-mail as they push strollers. Children and parents text during family dinners. As I watched the annual marathon in Florence, Italy, in November 2009, a runner passed me, texting. Of course, I tried to take her picture on my cell phone. After five years, my level of connectivity had finally caught up with my daughter's. Now when I travel, my access to the Net stays constant. There is security and pleasure in a good hotel on the other side of the world, but it cannot compare to the constancy of online connections.

Research portrays Americans as increasingly insecure, isolated, and lonely.[5]   23
We work more hours than ever before, often at several jobs. Even high school and college students, during seasons of life when time should be most abundant, say that they don't date but "hook up" because "who has the time?" We have moved away, often far away, from the communities of our birth. We struggle to raise children without the support of extended families. Many have left behind the religious and civic associations that once bound us together.[6] To those who have lost a sense of physical connection, connectivity suggests that you make your own page, your own place. When you are there, you are by definition where you

belong, among officially friended friends. To those who feel they have no time, connectivity, like robotics, tempts by proposing substitutions through which you can have companionship with convenience. A robot will always be there, amusing and compliant. On the Net, you can always find someone. "I never want to be far from my BlackBerry," a colleague told me. "That is where my games are. That is where my sites are. Without it, I'm too anxious."

Today, our machine dream is to be never alone but always in control. This   24 can't happen when one is face-to-face with a person. But it can be accomplished with a robot or, as we shall see, by slipping through the portals of a digital life.

THE NEW STATE OF THE SELF: FROM LIFE TO THE LIFE MIX

From the very beginning, networked technologies designed to share practical   25 information were taken up as technologies of relationship. So, for example, the Arpanet, grandfather of the Internet, was developed so that scientists could collaborate on research papers, but it soon became a place to gossip, flirt, and talk about one's kids. By the mid-1990s, the Internet throbbed with new social worlds. There were chat rooms and bulletin boards and social environments known as multiuser domains, or MUDs. Soon after came massively multiplayer online role-playing games such as Ultima 2 and EverQuest, the precursors of game worlds such as World of Warcraft. In all of these, people created avatars—more or less richly rendered virtual selves—and lived out parallel lives. People sat at their computers and moved from windows that featured the spreadsheets and business documents of the real world to those in which they inhabited online personae. Although the games most often took the form of quests, medieval and otherwise, the virtual environments were most compelling because they offered opportunities for a social life, for performing as the self you wanted to be. As one player on an adventure-style MUD told me in the early 1990s, "I began with an interest in 'hack and slay,' but then I stayed to chat."[7]

In the course of a life, we never "graduate" from working on identity; we   26 simply rework it with the materials at hand. From the start, online social worlds provided new materials. Online, the plain represented themselves as glamorous, the old as young, the young as older. Those of modest means wore elaborate virtual jewelry. In virtual space, the crippled walked without crutches, and the shy improved their chances as seducers. These days, online games and worlds are increasingly elaborate. The most popular "pay-to-play" game, World of Warcraft, puts you, along with 11.5 million other players, in the world of Azeroth. There, you control a character, an avatar, whose personality, natural gifts, and acquired skills are under continual development as it takes on a trade, explores the landscape, fights monsters, and goes on quests. In some games, you can play alone—in which case you mostly have artificial intelligences for company, "bots" that play the role of human characters. Or you can band together with other players on the network to conquer new worlds. This can be a highly collaborative endeavor, a social life unto itself: you routinely e-mail, talk to, and message the people you game with.

In a different genre, Second Life is a virtual "place" rather than a game. Here, there is no winning, only living. You begin by naming and building an avatar. You work from a menu with a vast array of choices for its looks and clothes. If these are not sufficient, you can design a customized avatar from scratch. Now, pleased with *your* looks, you have the potential, as Second Life puts it, to live a life that will enable you to "love your life."[8] You can, among other things, get an education, launch a business, buy land, build and furnish a home, and, of course, have a social life that may include love, sex, and marriage. You can even earn money—Second Life currency is convertible into dollars.

As all this unfolds, you hang out in virtual bars, restaurants, and cafés. You relax on virtual beaches and have business meetings in virtual conference rooms. It is not uncommon for people who spend a lot of time on Second Life and role-playing games to say that their online identities make them feel more like themselves than they do in the physical real. This is play, certainly, but it is serious play.[9]

Historically, there is nothing new in "playing at" being other. But in the past, such play was dependent on physical displacement. As a teenager I devoured novels about young men and women sent abroad on a Grand Tour to get over unhappy love affairs. In Europe, they "played at" being unscathed by heartbreak. Now, in Weston, Massachusetts, Pete, forty-six, is trying find a life beyond his disappointing marriage. He has only to turn on his iPhone.

I meet Pete on an unseasonably warm Sunday in late autumn. He attends to his two children, four and six, and to his phone, which gives him access to Second Life.[10] There, Pete has created an avatar, a buff and handsome young man named Rolo. As Rolo, Pete has courted a female avatar named Jade, a slip of a girl, a pixie with short, spiky blonde hair. As Rolo, he "married" Jade in an elaborate Second Life ceremony more than a year before, surrounded by their virtual best friends. Pete has never met the woman behind the avatar Jade and does not wish to. (It is possible, of course, that the human being behind Jade is a man. Pete understands this but says, "I don't want to go there.") Pete describes Jade as intelligent, passionate, and easy to talk to.

On most days, Pete logs onto Second Life before leaving for work. Pete and Jade talk (by typing) and then erotically engage their avatars, something

27

28

29

30

31

that Second Life software makes possible with special animations.[11] Boundaries between life and game are not easy to maintain. Online, Pete and Jade talk about sex and Second Life gossip, but they also talk about money, the recession, work, and matters of health. Pete is on cholesterol-lowering medication that is only partially successful. Pete says that it is hard to talk to his "real" wife Alison about his anxieties; she gets "too worried that I might die and leave her alone." But he can talk to Jade. Pete says, "Second Life gives me a better relationship than I have in real life. This is where I feel most myself. Jade accepts who I am. My relationship with Jade makes it possible for me to stay in my marriage, with my family." The ironies are apparent: an avatar who has never seen or spoken to him in person and to whom he appears in a body nothing like his own seems, to him, most accepting of his truest self.

Pete enjoys this Sunday in the playground; he is with his children and with Jade. He says, "My children seem content. . . . I feel like I'm with them. . . . I'm here for them but in the background." I glance around the playground. Many adults are dividing their attention between children and mobile devices. Are they scrolling through e-mails and texts from family, friends, and colleagues? Are they looking at photographs? Are they in parallel worlds with virtual lovers? 32

When people make the point that we have always found ways to escape from ourselves, that neither the desire nor the possibility is new with the Internet, I always tell them they are right. Pete's online life bears a family resemblance to how some people use more traditional extramarital affairs. It also resembles how people can play at being "other" on business trips and vacations. When Pete pushes a swing with one hand and types notes to Jade with the other, something is familiar: a man finding that a relationship outside his marriage gives him something he wants. But something is unfamiliar: the simultaneity of lives, the interleaving of romance with a shout-out to a six-year-old. Pete says that his online marriage is an essential part of his "life mix." I ask him about this expression. I have never heard it before. Pete explains that the life mix is the mash-up of what you have on- and offline. Now, we ask not of our satisfactions in life but in our life mix. We have moved from multitasking to multi-lifing. 33

You need mobile communication to get to the notion of the life mix. Until recently, one had to sit in front of a computer screen to enter virtual space. This meant that the passage through the looking glass was deliberate and bounded by the time you could spend in front of a computer. Now, with a mobile device as portal, one moves into the virtual with fluidity and on the go. This makes it easier to use our lives as avatars to manage the tensions of everyday existence. We use social networking to be "ourselves," but our online performances take on lives of their own. Our online selves develop distinct personalities. Sometimes 34 we see them as our "better selves." As we invest in them, we want to take credit for them. Recently—although, admittedly, at MIT I live in the land of the technosophisticated—I have been given business cards that include people's real-life names, their Facebook handles, and the name of their avatar on Second Life.

In talking about sociable robots, I described an arc that went from seeing simulation as better than nothing to simply better, as offering companions that could meet one's exact emotional requirements. Something similar is happening online. We may begin by thinking that e-mails, texts, and Facebook messaging are thin gruel but useful if the alternative is sparse communication with the people we care about. Then, we become accustomed to their special pleasures—we can have connection when and where we want or need it, and we can easily make it go away. In only a few more steps, you have people describing life on Facebook as better than anything they have ever known. They use the site to share their thoughts, their music, and their photos. They expand their reach in a continually growing community of acquaintance. No matter how esoteric their interests, they are surrounded by enthusiasts, potentially drawn from all over the world. No matter how parochial the culture around them, they are cosmopolitan. In this spirit, when Pete talks about Second Life, he extols its international flavor and his "in-world" educational opportunities. He makes it clear that he spends time "in physical life" with friends and family. But he says that Second Life "is my preferred way of being with people."[12]

In addition to the time he spends on Second Life, Pete has an avatar on World of Warcraft, and he is a regular on the social-networking sites Facebook, LinkedIn, and Plaxo. Every day he checks one professional and three personal e-mail accounts. I once described this kind of movement among identities with the metaphor of "cycling through."[13] But now, with mobile technology, cycling through has accelerated into the mash-up of a life mix. Rapid cycling stabilizes into a sense of continual copresence. Even a simple cell phone brings us into the world of continual partial attention.[14]

Not that many years ago, one of my graduate students talked to me about the first time he found himself walking across the MIT campus with a friend who took an incoming call on his mobile phone. My student was irritated, almost incredulous. "He put me on 'pause.' Am I supposed to remember where we were and pick up the conversation after he is done with his call?" At the time, his friend's behavior seemed rude and confusing. Only a few years later, it registers as banal. Mobile technology has made each of us "pauseable." Our face-to-face conversations are routinely interrupted by incoming calls and text messages. In the world of paper mail, it was unacceptable for a colleague to read his or her correspondence during a meeting. In the new etiquette, turning away from those in front of you to answer a mobile phone or respond to a text has become close to the norm. When someone holds a phone, it can be hard to know if you have that person's attention. A parent, partner, or child glances down and is lost to another place, often without realizing that they have taken leave. In restaurants, customers are asked to turn their phones to vibrate. But many don't need sound or vibration to know that something has happened on their phones. "When there is an event on my phone, the screen changes," says a twenty-six-year-old lawyer. "There is a brightening of the screen. Even if my phone is in my purse . . . I see it, I sense it. . . . I always know what is happening on my phone."

People are skilled at creating rituals for demarcating the boundaries between the world of work and the world of family, play, and relaxation. There are special times (the Sabbath), special meals (the family dinner), special clothes (the "armor" for a day's labor comes off at home, whether it is the businessman's suit or the laborer's overalls), and special places (the dining room, the parlor, the kitchen, and the bedroom). Now demarcations blur as technology accompanies us everywhere, all the time. We are too quick to celebrate the continual presence of a technology that knows no respect for traditional and helpful lines in the sand.[15] 38

Sal, sixty-two, a widower, describes one erased line as a "Rip van Winkle experience." When his wife became ill five years before, he dropped out of one world. Now, a year after her death, he wakes up in another. Recently, Sal began to entertain at his home again. At his first small dinner party, he tells me, "I invited a woman, about fifty, who works in Washington. In the middle of a conversation about the Middle East, she takes out her BlackBerry. She wasn't speaking on it. I wondered if she was checking her e-mail. I thought she was being rude, so I asked her what she was doing. She said that she was blogging the conversation. She was *blogging* the conversation." Several months after the event, Sal remains incredulous. He thinks of an evening with friends as private, as if surrounded by an invisible wall. His guest, living the life mix, sees her evening as an occasion to appear on a larger virtual stage. 39

THE NEW STATE OF THE SELF: MULTITASKING AND THE ALCHEMY OF TIME

In the 1980s, the children I interviewed about their lives with technology often did their homework with television and music in the background and a hand-held video game for distraction. Algebra and Super Mario were part of the same package. Today, such recollections sound almost pastoral. A child doing homework is usually—among other things—attending to Facebook, shopping, music, online games, texts, videos, calls, and instant messages. Absent only is e-mail, considered by most people under twenty-five a technology of the past, or perhaps required to apply to college or to submit a job application. 40

Subtly, over time, multitasking, once seen as something of a blight, was   41
recast as a virtue. And over time, the conversation about its virtues became
extravagant, with young people close to lionized for their ability to do many
things at once. Experts went so far as to declare multitasking not just a skill but
the crucial skill for successful work and learning in digital culture. There was
even concern that old-fashioned teachers who could only do one thing at a time
would hamper student learning.[16] Now we must wonder at how easily we were
smitten. When psychologists study multitasking, they do not find a story of new
efficiencies. Rather, multitaskers don't perform as well on any of the tasks they
are attempting.[17] But multitasking feels good because the body rewards it with
neurochemicals that induce a multitasking "high." The high deceives multitaskers into thinking they are being especially productive. In search of the high, they
want to do even more. In the years ahead, there will be a lot to sort out. We fell
in love with what technology made easy. Our bodies colluded.

These days, even as some educators try to integrate smartphones into class-   42
rooms, others experiment with media fasts to get students down to business. At
my university, professors are divided about whether they should meddle at all. Our
students, some say, are grown-ups. It is not for us to dictate how they take notes or
to get involved if they let their attention wander from class-related materials. But
when I stand in back of our Wi-Fi enabled lecture halls, students are on Facebook
and YouTube, and they are shopping, mostly for music. I want to engage my students in conversation. I don't think they should use class time for any other purpose. One year, I raised the topic for general discussion and suggested using note-
books (the paper kind) for note taking. Some of my students claimed to be relieved.
"Now I won't be tempted by Facebook messages," said one sophomore. Others were
annoyed, almost surly. They were not in a position to defend their right to shop
and download music in class, so they insisted that they liked taking notes on their
computers. I was forcing them to take notes by hand and then type them into computer documents later. While they were complaining about this two-step process, I
was secretly thinking what a good learning strategy this might be. I maintained my
resolve, but the following year, I bowed to common practice and allowed students
to do what they wished. But I notice, along with several of my colleagues, that the
students whose laptops are open in class do not do as well as the others.[18]

When media are always there, waiting to be wanted, people lose a sense of   43
choosing to communicate. Those who use BlackBerry smartphones talk about
the fascination of watching their lives "scroll by." They watch their lives as
though watching a movie. One says, "I glance at my watch to sense the time;
I glance at my BlackBerry to get a sense of my life."[19] Adults admit that inter-
rupting their work for e-mail and messages is distracting but say they would

never give it up. When I ask teenagers specifically about being interrupted during homework time, for example, by Facebook messages or new texts, many seem not to understand the question. They say things like, "That's just how it is. That's just my life." When the BlackBerry movie of one's life becomes one's life, there is a problem: the BlackBerry version is the unedited version of one's life. It contains more than one has time to live. Although we can't keep up with it, we feel responsible for it. It is, after all, our life. We strive to be a self that can keep up with its e-mail.

Our networked devices encourage a new notion of time because they prom-   44
ise that one can layer more activities onto it. Because you can text while doing something else, texting does not seem to take time but to give you time. This is more than welcome; it is magical. We have managed to squeeze in that extra little bit, but the fastest living among us encourage us to read books with titles such as *In Praise of Slowness*.[20] And we have found ways of spending more time with friends and family in which we hardly give them any attention at all.

We are overwhelmed across the generations. Teenagers complain that par-   45
ents don't look up from their phones at dinner and that they bring their phones to school sporting events. Hannah, sixteen, is a solemn, quiet high school junior. She tells me that for years she has tried to get her mother's attention when her mother comes to fetch her after school or after dance lessons. Hannah says, "The car will start; she'll be driving still looking down, looking at her messages, but still no hello." We will hear others tell similar stories.

Parents say they are ashamed of such behavior but quickly get around to   46
explaining, if not justifying, it. They say they are more stressed than ever as they try to keep up with e-mail and messages. They always feel behind. They cannot take a vacation without bringing the office with them; their office is on their cell phone.[21] They complain that their employers require them to be continually online but then admit that their devotion to their communications devices exceeds all professional expectations.

Teenagers, when pressed for time (a homework assignment is due), may try   47
to escape the demands of the always-on culture. Some will use their parents' accounts so that their friends won't know that they are online. Adults hide out as well. On weekends, mobile devices are left at the office or in locked desk drawers. When employers demand connection, people practice evasive maneuvers. They go on adventure vacations and pursue extreme sports. As I write this, it is still possible to take long plane rides with no cell phone or Internet access. But even this is changing. Wi-Fi has made it to the skies.

In a tethered world, too much is possible, yet few can resist measuring success   48
against a metric of what they could accomplish if they were always available.

Diane, thirty-six, a curator at a large Midwestern museum, cannot keep up with the pace set by her technology.

I can hardly remember when there was such a thing as a weekend, or when   49
I had a Filofax and I thought about whose name I would add to my address book. My e-mail program lets me click on the name of the person who wrote me and poof, they are in my address book. Now everyone who writes me gets put in my address book; everybody is a potential contact, a buyer, donor, and fund-raiser. What used to be an address book is more like a database.

I suppose I do my job better, but my job is my whole life. Or my whole life is   50
my job. When I move from calendar, to address book, to e-mail, to text messages, I feel like a master of the universe; everything is so efficient. I am a maximizing machine. I am on my BlackBerry until two in the morning. I don't sleep well, but I still can't keep up with what is sent to me.

Now for work, I'm expected to have a Twitter feed and a Facebook presence   51
about the museum. And do a blog on museum happenings. That means me in all these places. I have a voice condition. I keep losing my voice. It's not from talking too much. All I do is type, but it has hit me at my voice. The doctor says it's a nervous thing.

Diane, in the company of programs, feels herself "a master of the universe." Yet,   52
she is only powerful enough to see herself as a "maximizing machine" that responds to what the network throws at her. She and her husband have decided they should take a vacation. She plans to tell her colleagues that she is going to be "off the grid" for two weeks, but Diane keeps putting off her announcement. She doesn't know how it will be taken. The norm in the museum is that it is fine to take time off for vacations but not to go offline during them. So, a vacation usually means working from someplace picturesque. Indeed, advertisements for wireless networks routinely feature a handsome man or beautiful woman sitting on a beach. Tethered, we are not to deny the body and its pleasures but to put our bodies somewhere beautiful while we work. Once, mobile devices needed to be shown in such advertisements. Now, they are often implied. We know that the successful are always connected. On vacation, one vacates a place, not a set of responsibilities. In a world of constant communication, Diane's symptom seems fitting: she has become a machine for communicating, but she has no voice left for herself.

As Diane plans her "offline vacation," she admits that she really wants to   53
go to Paris, "but I would have no excuse not to be online in Paris. Helping to build houses in the Amazon, well, who would know if they have Wi-Fi? My new nonnegotiable for a vacation: I have to be able to at least pretend that there is no reason to bring my computer." But after her vacation in remote Brazil finally takes place, she tells me, "Everybody had their BlackBerries with them. Sitting

there in the tent. BlackBerries on. It was as though there was some giant satellite parked in the sky."

Diane says she receives about five hundred e-mails, several hundred texts, and around forty calls a day. She notes that many business messages come in multiples. People send her a text and an e-mail, then place a call and leave a message on her voicemail. "Client anxiety," she explains. "They feel better if they communicate." In her world, Diane is accustomed to receiving a hasty message to which she is expected to give a rapid response. She worries that she does not have the time to take her time on the things that matter. And it is hard to maintain a sense of what matters in the din of constant communication.   54

The self shaped in a world of rapid response measures success by calls made, e-mails answered, texts replied to, contacts reached. This self is calibrated on the basis of what technology proposes, by what it makes easy. But in the technology-induced pressure for volume and velocity, we confront a paradox. We insist that our world is increasingly complex, yet we have created a communications culture that has decreased the time available for us to sit and think uninterrupted. As we communicate in ways that ask for almost instantaneous responses, we don't allow sufficient space to consider complicated problems.   55

Trey, a forty-six-year-old lawyer with a large Boston firm, raises this issue explicitly. On e-mail, he says, "I answer questions I can answer right away. And people want me to answer them right away. But it's not only the speed. . . . The questions have changed to ones that I *can* answer right away." Trey describes legal matters that call for time and nuance and says that "people don't have patience for these now. They send an e-mail, and they expect something back fast. They are willing to forgo the nuance; really, the client wants to hear something now, and so I give the answers that can be sent back by return e-mail . . . or maybe answers that will take me a day, max. . . . I feel pressured to think in terms of bright lines." He corrects himself. "It's not the technology that does this, of course, but the technology sets expectations about speed." We are back to a conversation about affordances and vulnerabilities. The technology primes us for speed, and overwhelmed, we are happy to have it help us speed up. Trey reminds me that "we speak in terms of 'shooting off' an e-mail. Nobody 'shoots something off' because they want things to proceed apace."   56

Trey, like Diane, points out that clients frequently send him a text, an e-mail, and a voicemail. "They are saying, 'Feed me.' They feel they have the right." He sums up his experience of the past decade. Electronic communication has been liberating, but in the end, "it has put me on a speed-up, on a treadmill, but that isn't the same as being productive."   57

I talk with a group of lawyers who all insist that their work would be impossible without their "cells"—that nearly universal shorthand for the smartphones   58 of today that have pretty much the functionality of desktop computers and more. The lawyers insist that they are more productive and that their mobile devices "liberate" them to work from home and to travel with their families. The women, in particular, stress that the networked life makes it possible for them to keep their jobs and spend time with their children. Yet, they also say that their mobile devices eat away at their time to think. One says, "I don't have enough time alone with my mind." Others say, "I have to struggle to make time to think." "I artificially make time to think." "I block out time to think." These formulations all depend on an "I" imagined as separate from the technology, a self that is able to put the technology aside so that it can function independently of its demands. This formulation contrasts with a growing reality of lives lived in the continuous presence of screens. This reality has us, like the MIT cyborgs, learning to see ourselves as one with our devices. To make more time to think would mean turning off our phones. But this is not a simple proposition since our devices are ever more closely coupled to our sense of our bodies and minds.[22] They provide a social and psychological GPS, a navigation system for tethered selves.

As for Diane, she tries to keep up by communicating during what used to be "downtime"—the time when she might have daydreamed during a cab ride or while waiting in line or walking to work. This may be time that we need (physiologically and emotionally) to maintain our ability to focus.[23] But Diane does not permit it to herself. And, of course, she uses our new kind of time: the time of attention sharing.   59

Diane shies away from the telephone because its real-time demands make too much of a claim on her attention. But like the face-to-face interactions for which it substitutes, the telephone can deliver in ways that texts and e-mails cannot. All parties are present. If there are questions, they can be answered. People can express mixed feelings. In contrast, e-mail tends to go back and forth without resolution. Misunderstandings are frequent. Feelings get hurt. And the greater the misunderstanding, the greater the number of e-mails, far more than necessary. We come to experience the column of unopened messages in our inboxes as a burden. Then, we project our feelings and worry that our messages are a burden to others.   60

We have reason to worry. One of my friends posted on Facebook, "The problem with handling your e-mail backlog is that when you answer mail, people answer back! So for each 10 you handle, you get 5 more! Heading down towards my goal of 300 left tonight, and 100 tomorrow." This is becoming a common sentiment. Yet it is sad to hear ourselves refer to letters from friends as "to be handled" or "gotten rid of," the language we use when talking about garbage. But this is the language in use.   61

An e-mail or text seems to have been always on its way to the trash. These days, as a continuous stream of texts becomes a way of life, we may say less to each   62 other because we imagine that what we say is almost already a throwaway. Texts, by nature telegraphic, can certainly be emotional, insightful, and sexy. They can lift us up. They can make us feel understood, desired, and supported. But they are not a place to deeply understand a problem or to explain a complicated situation. They are momentum. They fill a moment.

FEARFUL SYMMETRIES

When I speak of a new state of the self, itself, I use the word "itself" with pur-   63
pose. It captures, although with some hyperbole, my concern that the connected life encourages us to treat those we meet online in something of the same way we treat objects—with dispatch. It happens naturally: when you are besieged by thousands of e-mails, texts, and messages—more than you can respond to—demands become depersonalized. Similarly, when we Tweet or write to hundreds or thousands of Facebook friends as a group, we treat individuals as a unit. Friends become fans. A college junior contemplating the multitudes he can contact on the Net says, "I feel that I am part of a larger thing, the Net, the Web. The world. It becomes a thing to me, a thing I am part of. And the people, too, I stop seeing them as individuals, really. They are part of this larger thing."

With sociable robots, we imagine objects as people. Online, we invent ways   64
of being with people that turn them into something close to objects. The self that treats a person as a thing is vulnerable to seeing itself as one. It is important to remember that when we see robots as "alive enough" for us, we give them a promotion. If when on the net, people feel just "alive enough" to be "maximizing machines" for e-mails and messages, they have been demoted. These are fearful symmetries.

In Part One, we saw new connections with the robotic turn into a desire   65
for communion that is no communion at all. Part Two also traces an arc that ends in broken communion. In online intimacies, we hope for compassion but often get the cruelty of strangers. As I explore the networked life and its effects on intimacy and solitude, on identity and privacy, I will describe the experience of many adults. Certain chapters focus on them almost exclusively. But I return again and again to the world of adolescents. Today's teenagers grew up with socia-ble robots as playroom toys. And they grew up networked, sometimes receiving a first cell phone as early as eight. Their stories offer a clear view of how technology reshapes identity because identity is at the center of adolescent life. Through their eyes, we see a new sensibility unfolding.

These days, cultural norms are rapidly shifting. We used to equate growing   66
up with the ability to function independently. These days always-on connection leads us to reconsider the virtues of a more collaborative self. All questions about

autonomy look different if, on a daily basis, we are together even when we are alone.

The network's effects on today's young people are paradoxical. Networking   67
makes it easier to play with identity (for example, by experimenting with an avatar that is interestingly different from you) but harder to leave the past behind,
because the Internet is forever. The network facilitates separation (a cell phone
allows children greater freedoms) but also inhibits it (a parent is always on tap).
Teenagers turn away from the "real-time" demands of the telephone and disappear into role-playing games they describe as "communities" and worlds." And
yet, even as they are committed to a new life in the ether, many exhibit an unexpected nostalgia. They start to resent the devices that force them into performing
their profiles; they long for a world in which personal information is not taken
from them automatically, just as the cost of doing business. Often it is children
who tell their parents to put away the cell phone at dinner. It is the young who
begin to speak about problems that, to their eyes, their elders have given up on.

I interview Sanjay, sixteen. We will talk for an hour between two of his class   68
periods. At the beginning of our conversation, he takes his mobile phone out of
his pocket and turns it off.[24] At the end of our conversation, he turns the phone
back on. He looks at me ruefully, almost embarrassed. He has received over a
hundred text messages as we were speaking. Some are from his girlfriend who,
he says, "is having a meltdown." Some are from a group of close friends trying to
organize a small concert. He feels a lot of pressure to reply and begins to pick up
his books and laptop so he can find a quiet place to set himself to the task. As
he says good-bye, he adds, not speaking particularly to me but more to himself
as an afterthought to the conversation we have just had, "I can't imagine doing
this when I get older." And then, more quietly, "How long do I have to continue
doing this?"

ENDNOTES

1. This chapter expands on themes explored in Sherry Turkle, "Tethering," in *Senso-
   rium: Embodied Experience, Technology, and Contemporary Art*, ed. Caroline Jones
   (Cambridge, MA: Zone, 2006), 220–226, and "Always-On/Always-on-You: The
   Tethered Self," in *Handbook of Mobile Communication Studies*, ed. James E. Katz
   (Cambridge, MA: MIT Press, 2008), 121–138.
2. These statements put me on a contested terrain of what constitutes support and
   shared celebration. I have interviewed people who say that flurries of virtual con-
   dolence and congratulations are sustaining; others say it just reminds them of how
   alone they are. And this in fact is my thesis: we are confused about when we are
   alone and when we are together.

3. See "The Guild—Do You Want to Date My Avatar," YouTube, August 17, 2009, www.youtube.com/watch?v=urNyg1ftMIU (accessed January 15, 2010).

4. Internet Relay Chat is a form of real-time Internet text messaging (chat) or synchronous conferencing. It is mainly designed for group communication in discussion forums, called channels, but also allows one-to-one communication via private message as well as chat and data transfers. It is much used during academic conferences, now in addition to Twitter. See, for example, this note on a conference invitation for a conference on media literacy: "Conference attendees are encouraged to bring their laptops, PDAs, netbooks or Twitter enabled phones, so they can participate in on-line social networking that will be part of this year's conference. Directions on how to obtain Internet connectivity and where people will be talking, will be provided in your attendee packet. For those who can not attend, tell them they can backchannel with us on Twitter at #homeinc." See "Conference Program," 2009 Media Literacy Conference, http://ezregister.com/events/536 (accessed October 20, 2009).

5. Hugh Gusterson and Catherine Besteman, eds., *The Insecure American: How We Got Here and What We Should Do About It* (Los Angeles: University of California Press, 2009).

6. See, for example, Robert D. Putnam, *Bowling Alone: The Collapse and Revival of American Community* (New York: Simon and Schuster, 2001); Gusterson and Besteman, eds., *The Insecure American*; Theda Skocpol, *Diminished Democracy: From Membership to Management in American Civic Life* (Norman: University of Oklahoma Press, 2003).

7. Sherry Turkle, *Life on the Screen: Identity in the Age of the Internet* (New York: Simon and Schuster, 1995), 182.

8. See "What Is Second Life," Second Life, http://secondlife.com/whatis (accessed June 13, 2010).

9. There is evidence that people experience what they do online as though it happened in the physical real. See, for example, Nick Yee, Jeremy Bailenson, and Nicolas Ducheneaut, "The Proteus Effect: Implications of Transformed Digital Self-representation on Online and Offline Behavior," *Communication Research* 36, no. 2: 285–312. For a video introduction to work in this area by Stanford University's Virtual Human Interaction Laboratory, directed by Jeremy Bailenson, see, "The Avatar Effect," PBS.org, www.pbs.org/wgbh/pages/frontline/digitalnation/virtual-worlds/second-lives/the-avatar-effect.html?play (accessed September 2, 2009).

10. Pete accesses Second Life through an iPhone application known as Spark. It does not bring the entire world to him, but it does enable conversation.

11. Pete insists that Alison does not know of his double life. Over the past twenty years I have had many conversations about virtual infidelity. In the case of women whose husbands are virtually unfaithful, there are sharp differences of opinion. Some think it is preferable to any physical infidelity. Others think it is the worst kind of infidelity, an infidelity that involves not simply sex but talking, considering another, making plans, and building a life.

12. In online life, weak ties—the ties of acquaintanceship—are often celebrated as the best ties of all. For the seminal work on weak ties, see Mark Granovetter, "The Strength of Weak Ties," *American Journal of Sociology* 78, no. 6 (1973): 1360–1380, and "The Strength of Weak Ties: A Network Theory Revisited," *Sociological Theory* 1 (1983): 201–233.

13. Turkle, *Life on the Screen.*

14. This is sometimes referred to as "continuous partial attention," a phrase widely credited to media researcher Linda Stone. See Stone's blog at www.lindastone.net (accessed August 24, 2009).

15. Those who study the boundaries between work and the rest of life suggest that it is helpful to demarcate our changing roles. Sue Campbell Clark, "Work/Family Border Theory: A New Theory of Work/Family Balance," *Human Relations* 53, no. 6 (2000): 747–770; Stephan Desrochers and Leisa D. Sargent, "Work-Family Boundary Ambiguity, Gender and Stress in Dual-Earner Couples" (paper presented at the conference "From 9-to-5 to 24/7: How Workplace Changes Impact Families, Work, and Communities," 2003 BPW/Brandeis University Conference, Orlando, Florida, March 2003); and Michelle Shumate and Janet Fulk, "Boundaries and Role Conflict When Work and Family Are Colocated: A Communication Network and Symbolic Interaction Approach," *Human Relations* 57, no. 1 (2004): 55–74.

16. Media theorist Henry Jenkins is an eloquent spokesperson for the significance of multitasking. See "The Skill of the Future: In a Word 'Multitasking,'" PBS.org, www.pbs.org/wgbh/pages/frontline/digitalnation/living-faster/split-focus/the-skill-of-the-future.html? (accessed November 16, 2009). His other online interviews on the Digital Nation website beautifully capture a vision of schools bending to new media sensibilities. See "The Tech Fix," PBS.org, www.pbs.org/wgbh/pages/frontline/digital-nation/learning/schools/the-tech-fix.html?play (accessed November 14, 2009), and "Defenders of the Book," PBS.org, www.pbs.org/wgbh/pages/frontline/digital-nation/learning/literacy/defenders-of-the-book.html?play (accessed November 14, 2009).

17. The literature on the downside of multitasking is growing. An influential and much-reported study is Eyal Ophir, Clifford Nass, and Anthony Wagner, "Cognitive Control in Media Multitaskers," *Proceedings of the National Academy of Sciences* 106 (2009): 15583–15587, www.pnas.org/content/106/37/15583 (accessed August

10, 2010). This study found that when people multitask, everything they do is degraded in quality. An excellent work on the general topic is Maggie Jackson, *Distracted: The Erosion of Attention and the Coming Dark Age* (New York: Prometheus, 2008). On the practical downside of thinking that we can do more than one thing at once, see, for example, the nine-part series on the *New York Times* website titled "Driven to Distraction," covering such topics as doing office work while driving at 60 mph, drivers and legislators dismissing cell phone risks, and New York taxi drivers ignoring the ban on cell phone use while driving. "Driven to Distraction," *New York Times*, http://topics.nytimes.com/topics/news/technology/series/driven_to_distraction/index.html (accessed November 14, 2009).

Teenagers routinely drive and text; we know this because their automobile accidents are traced back to texting and cell phone use. A 2009 study of twenty-one teenagers showed them changing speed and weaving in and out of lanes while texting. Eastern Virginia Medical School, "Texting While Driving Can Be Deadly, Study Shows," *ScienceDaily*, May 5, 2009, www.sciencedaily.com/releases/2009/05/090504 094434.htm (accessed January 4, 2010). A larger study of nine hundred teenagers in 2007 showed 50 percent of them texted while driving despite the fact that 36 percent of them thought this was dangerous. See Steve Vogel, "Teen Driver Menace: Text-Messaging," Suite101, October 22, 2007, http://parentingteens.suite101. com/article.cfm/ teen_driver_menace_textmessaging (accessed January 4, 2009).

Adults also text while driving. Trains collide while conductors text. A plane flies past its destination airport because its pilots are absorbed in a new computer program. In October 2009, pilots attending to their laptop computers—behavior in defiance of safety regulations—were the cause of an aircraft overshooting its Minneapolis destination by 150 miles. "The pilots told the National Transportation Safety Board that they missed their destination because they had taken out their personal laptops in the cockpit, a violation of airline policy, so the first officer, Richard I. Cole, could tutor the captain, Timothy B. Cheney, in a new scheduling system put in place by Delta Air Lines, which acquired Northwest last fall." See Micheline Maynard and Matthew L. Wald, "Off-Course Pilots Cite Computer Distraction," *New York Times*, October 26, 2009, www.nytimes.com/2009/10/27/ us/27plane.html?_r=1 (accessed November 16, 2009).

18. In practical terms, what works best is to remind students that media literacy is about knowing when not to use technology as well as how to use it. I am optimistic that over time, we will make better use of technology in the classroom and we will be less afraid to turn it off when that is what makes sense pedagogically.

19. Melissa Mazmanian, "Some Thoughts on BlackBerries" (unpublished memo, Massachusetts Institute of Technology, 2005). See also Melissa Mazmanian, Wanda Orlikowski, and Joanne Yates, "Ubiquitous E-mail: Individual Experiences and

Organizational Consequences of BlackBerry Use," *Proceedings of the 65th Annual Meeting of the Academy of Management*, Atlanta, Georgia, August 2006, http://seeit. mit.edu/ Publications/BlackBerry_AoM.pdf (accessed August 24, 2009).

20. The first book club selection by Arianna Huffington for the *Huffington Post's* book club was Carl Honoré's *In Praise of Slowness: How a Worldwide Movement Is Challenging the Cult of Speed* (New York: HarperCollins, 2004).

21. Diana B. Gant and Sara Kiesler, "Blurring the Boundaries: Cell Phones, Mobility and the Line Between Work and Personal Life," in *Wireless World: Social and Interactional Aspects of the Mobile Age*, ed. N. G. R. H. Brown (New York: Springer, 2001).

22. Donna Haraway, "A Cyborg Manifesto," in *Simians, Cyborgs and Women: The Reinvention of Nature* (New York; Routledge, 1991), 149–181.

23. Thomas R. Herzog et al., "Reflection and Attentional Recovery As Distinctive Benefits of Restorative Environments," *Journal of Environmental Psychology* 17 (1997): 165–170. See also Stephen Kaplan, "The Restorative Benefits of Nature: Toward an Integrative Framework," *Journal of Environmental Psychology* 15 (1995): 169–182.

24. I studied teenagers from a wide range of economic, social, and ethnic backgrounds. They attended seven different schools: two private boys preparatory schools, one in an urban center (Fillmore) and one in a rural setting (Hadley), one urban private girls school (Richelieu), an urban Catholic coeducational high school (Silver Academy), a private urban coeducational high school (Cranston), and two public high schools, one suburban (Roosevelt) and one urban (Branscomb). All students, from wealthy to disadvantaged, had cell phones with texting capability. Class distinctions showed themselves not in whether students possessed a phone but in what kind of contract they had with their providers. Teenagers with fewer resources, such as Julia in the following chapter, tended to have plans that constrained who they could text for free. Free texts are most usually for people on the same network. Ever resourceful, students with restricted plans try to get their friends to sign up with their cell providers. We shall see that teenagers don't care much about who they can call. I often hear, "I never use my calling minutes." On teenagers and digital culture, see Mizuko Ito et. al., *Hanging Out, Messing Around, and Geeking Out: Kids Learning and Living with New Media* (Cambridge, MA: MIT Press, 2010) and Danah Boyd, "Why Youth (Heart) Social Network Sites: The Role of Networked Publics in Teenage Social Life," MacArthur Foundation Series on Digital Learning—Youth, Identity, and Digital Media, ed. Davind Buckingham (Cambridge, MA: Mit Press 2007), 119–142.

James Paul Gee James Paul Gee was born in San Jose, California. He received his B.A. in philosophy from the University of California at Santa Barbara and both his M.A. and Ph.D in linguistics from Stanford University. He started his career in theoretical linguistics, working in syntactic and semantic theory, and taught initially at Stanford University and later in the School of Language and Communication at Hampshire College in Amherst Massachusetts. After doing some research in psycholinguistics at Northeastern University in Boston and at the Max Planck Institute for Psycholinguistics in Holland, Prof. Gee's research focus switched to studies on discourse analysis, sociolinguistics, and applications of linguistics to literacy and education. He went on to teach in the School of Education at Boston University, where he was the chair of the Department of Developmental Studies and Counseling, and later in the Linguistics Department at the University of Southern California. At Boston University he established new graduate programs centered around an integrated approach to language and literacy, combining programs in reading, writing, bilingual education, ESL, and applied linguistics. From 1993 to 1997 he held the Jacob Haiti Chair in Education in the Haiti Center for Urban Education at Clark University in, Massachusetts. In January of 1997, Prof. Gee accepted the Tashia Morgridge Chair in Reading in the Department of Curriculum and Instruction at the University of Wisconsin at Madison. Prof. Gee's work over the last decade has centered on the development of an integrated theory of language, literacy, and schooling, a theory that draws on work in socially situated cognition, sociocultural approaches to language and literacy, language development, discourse studies, critical theory, and applied linguistics. This work has served as a theoretical base for a number of school-based projects run by the Hiatt center at Clark University in elementary, middle, and high schools, as well as in an after-school science project funded by the Spencer Foundation. Prof. Gee's recent work has extended his ideas on language, literacy, and society to deal with the so-called "new capitalism" and its cognitive, social, and political implications for literacy and schooling. He has published widely in journals in linguistics, psychology, the social sciences, and education. His books include Sociolinguistics and Literacies (1990, Second Edition 1996); The Social Mind (1992); Introduction to Human Language (1993); and, with Glynda Hull and Colin Lankshear, The New Work Order: Behind the Language of the New Capitalism (1996).

WHAT VIDEO GAMES HAVE TO TEACH US ABOUT LEARNING AND LITERACY

Good computer and video games like System Shock 2, Deus Ex, Pikmin, Rise of   1
Nations, Neverwinter Nights, and Xenosaga: Episode 1 are learning machines. They get themselves learned and learned well, so that they get played long and hard by a great many people. This is how they and their designers survive and perpetuate themselves. If a game cannot be learned and even mastered at a certain level, it won't get played by enough people, and the company that makes it will go broke. Good learning in games is a capitalist-driven Darwinian process of selection of the fittest. Of course, game designers could have solved their learning problems by making games shorter and easier, by dumbing them down, so to speak. But

most gamers don't want short and easy games. Thus, designers face and largely solve an intriguing educational dilemma, one also faced by schools and workplaces: how to get people, often young people, to learn and master something that is long and challenging—and enjoy it, to boot.

In my book, *What Video Games Have to Teach Us About Learning and Literacy*   2 (New York: Palgrave/Macmillan,2003); http://www.amazon.com/exec/obidos/ASIN/1403961697/qid=1062706188/sr=21/ref=sr_2_1/002-5282466-9651248, I argue that schools, workplaces, families, and academic researchers have a lot to learn about learning from good computer and video games. Such games incorporate a whole set of fundamentally sound learning principles, principles that can be used in other settings, for example in teaching science in schools. In fact, the learning principles that good games incorporate are all strongly supported by contemporary research in cognitive science—the science that studies human thinking and learning through laboratory research, studies of the brain, and research at actual learning sites like classrooms and workplaces [e.g., see Bruer 1993; Clark 1997; Cognition and Technology Group at Vanderbilt 1997; Lave 1996; New London Group 1996; Lave and Wenger 1991].

Beyond using the learning principles that good games incorporate, I also   3 argue that schools, workplaces, and families can use games and game technologies to enhance learning. Further, I believe that use of games and game technologies for learning content in schools and skills in workplaces will become pervasive. Many parents, by getting their sometimes quite young children to play games while actively thinking about the game's connections to other games, media, texts, and the world are already doing so. In field studies we are conducting at the University of Wisconsin, we have watched seven-year-olds play *Age of Mythology*, read about mythology inside and outside the game on web sites, borrow books on mythology from the library, and draw pictures and write stories connected to the game and other mythological themes. They think about the connections between *Age of Mythology* and *Age of Empires*, between mythological figures and popular culture superheroes, and the connections of all of them to history and society. This is education at its best, and it is happening at home, outside of school.

Let me give a few examples of the good learning principles that are incorpo-   4 rated in good games (36 principles are discussed in my book). Good games give information "on demand" and "just in time," not out of the contexts of actual use or apart from people's purposes and goals, something that happens too often in schools. *System Shock 2*, for instance, spreads, throughout the game, the sort of information typically found in a manual. As they move through the initial levels of the game, players can request just the right information (by pressing on a little green kiosk) and make use of it or see it applied soon after having read it. People are quite poor at understanding and remembering information they have received out of context or too long before they can make use of it [Barsalou 1999; Brown et al. 1989; Glenberg and Robertson 1999]. Good games never do this to players, but find ways to put information inside the worlds the players move through, and make clear the meaning of such information and how it applies to that world.

Good games operate at the outer and growing edge of a player's competence, 5 remaining challenging, but do-able, while schools often operate at the lowest common denominator [diSessa 2000]. Since games are often challenging, but do-able, they are often also pleasantly frustrating, which is a very motivating state for human beings. To achieve this, good games allow players to customize the game to their own levels of ability and styles of learning. For instance, Rise of Nations lets players tweak almost every element in the game, and offers skills tests as well, to ensure that nearly everyone can find the outer edge of their competence. Furthermore, players can continually adjust the game as their competence grows.

Games allow players to be producers and not just consumers. Along with the 6 designer, the player's actions co-create the game world. As players make choices about what to build in *Rise of Nations*, what skills and missions to choose in *The Elder Scrolls: Morrowind*, or what moral decisions to make in *Star Wars: Knights of the Old Republic* players are as much designers of the game as the original innovators. Furthermore, players can use software that comes with the game to build new scenarios, maps, or episodes (for example, a scenario in *Age of Mythology* or a skateboard park in *Tony Hawk*). Too often, students in schools consume, but do not produce, knowledge, and rarely get to help design the curriculum [Brown 1994].

Good games confront players in the initial game levels with problems that 7 are specifically designed to allow players to form good generalizations about what will work well later when they face more complex problems. Often, in fact, the initial levels of a game are in actuality hidden tutorials. Work in cognitive science has shown that people need to be presented with problems in a fruitful order, getting initial problems that set up good generalizations for later problems. If they are confronted too early with problems that are too complex, they often come up with creative solutions, but ones that turn out, in the end, not to be very helpful for working on other problems later on [Elman 1993]. Good games don't do this, but order problems in helpful ways.

At the same time, games create "a cycle of expertise" [Bereiter and Scar- 8 damalia 1989].

At the outset, the game repeatedly confronts players with a similar type 9 of problem, for example, enemies like the head crabs in *Half-Life*, until players achieve a routinized, taken-for-granted mastery of certain skills. Then the game confronts players with a new problem, for instance, a new type of enemy or a boss, which forces the players to rethink their now taken-for-granted mastery and to integrate their old skills with new ones. Then these new sorts of problems are practiced until a new higher-order routinized, taken-for-granted mastery occurs. This cycle is repeated throughout the game. In many a game, the last boss requires a last re-opening of one's taken-for-granted tool kit. This cycle is the basis for producing expertise in any area. Good games are models for the production of expertise.

Motivation is the most important factor that drives learning. When motiva-   10
tion dies, learning dies and playing stops. Cognitive science has had a hard time defining motivation, though one definition is a learner's willingness to make an extended commitment to engage in a new area of learning [diSessa 2000]. Since good games are highly motivating to a great many people, we can learn from them how motivation is created and sustained.

In computer and video games, players engage in "action at a distance," much   11
like remotely manipulating a robot, but in a far more fine-grained fashion. Cognitive research suggests that such fine-grained action at a distance actually causes humans to feel as if their bodies and minds have stretched into a new space [Clark 2003], a highly motivating state. Books and movies, for all their virtues, cannot do this. The more a player can manipulate a game character and make decisions that impact on the character, the more the player invests in the character and the game at a deep level. This investment appears to be the deepest foundation of a player's motivation in sticking with and eventually mastering a game.

In a sense, all learning involves "playing a character." In a science classroom,   12
learning works best if students think, act, and value like scientists. Games can show us how to get people to invest in new identities or roles, which can, in turn, become powerful motivators for new and deep learning in classrooms and workplaces.

Finally, we can state that when players play in massive multiplayer games,   13
they often collaborate in teams, each using a different, but overlapping, set of skills, and share knowledge, skills, and values with others both inside the game and on various Internet sites. In the process, they create distributed and dispersed knowledge within a community in ways that would please any contemporary high-tech, cross-functional-team-centered workplace [Wenger et al. 2002]. In this respect, games may be better sites for preparing workers for modern workplaces than traditional schools. However, in the end, the real importance of good computer and video games is that they allow people to re-create themselves in new worlds and achieve recreation and deep learning at one and the same time.

REFERENCES

BARSALOU, L. W. 1999. Language comprehension: Archival memory or preparation for situated action. *Discourse Process.* 28 (1999), 61–80.

BEREITER, C. AND SCARDAMALIA, M. 1993. *Surpassing Ourselves: An Inquiry into the Nature and Implications of Expertise.* Open Court, Chicago:

BROWN, A.L. 1994. The advancement of learning. *Eduational Res.* 23 (1994), 4–12.

BROWN, A. L., COLLINS, A., AND DUGUID 1989. Situated cognition and the culture of learning. *Educational Res.* 18 (1989), 32–42.

BRUER, J. T. 1993. *Schools for Rhought: A Science of Learning in the Classroom.* MIT Press, Cambridge, MA.

CLARK, A. 1997. *Being There: Putting Brain, Body, and World Together Again.* MIT Press, Cambridge, MA.

CLARK, A. 2003. *Natural-Born Cyborgs: Why Minds and Technologies Are Made to Merge.* Oxford University Press, Oxford, UK.

COGNITION AND TECHNOLOGY GROUP AT VANDERBILT. 1997. *The Jasper Project: Lessons in Curriculum, Instruction, Assessment, and Professional Development.* Erlbaum, Mahwah, NJ.

DISESSA, A. A. 2000. *Changing Minds.* MIT Press, Cambridge, MA.

ELMAN, J. 1991. Incremental learning, or the importance of starting small. Tech. Rep. 9101, Center for Research in Language, Univ. of California at San Diego.

GLENBERG, A. M. AND ROBERTSON, D. A. 1999. Indexical understanding of instructions. *Discourse Process.* 28 (1999), 1–26.

LAVE, J. 1996. Teaching, as learning, in practice. *Mind, Culture, and Activity* 3 (1996), 149-164.

LAVE, J. AND WENGER, E. 1991. *Situated Learning: Legitimate Peripheral Participation.* Cambridge University Press, Cambridge, UK.

NEW LONDON GROUP. 1996. A pedagogy of multiliteracies: Designing social futures. *Harvard Educational Rev.* 66 (1996), 60-92.

PELLIGRINO, J. W., CHUDOWSKY, N., AND GLASER, R. 2001. *Knowing What Students Know: The Science and Design of Educational Assessment.* National Academy Press, Washington, DC.

WENGER, E., MCDERMOTT, R., AND SNYDER, W. M. 2002. *Cultivating Communities of Practice.* Harvard Business School Press, Cambridge, MA.